Hypocrisy Trap

Hypocrisy Trap

THE WORLD BANK AND
THE POVERTY OF REFORM

Catherine Weaver

PRINCETON UNIVERSITY PRESS

PRINCETON AND OXFORD

HG
3881.5
.W57
W427
2008

Published by Princeton University Press, 41 William Street,
Princeton, New Jersey 08540
In the United Kingdom: Princeton University Press, 6 Oxford Street,
Woodstock, Oxfordshire OX20 1TW

Library of Congress Cataloging-in-Publication Data

Weaver, Catherine, 1971–
Hypocrisy trap : the World Bank and the poverty of reform / Catherine Weaver.
p.   cm.
Includes bibliographical references and index.
ISBN 978-0-691-13434-5 (hardcover : alk. paper) —
ISBN 978-0-691-13819-0 (pbk. : alk. paper)
1. World Bank. 2. Economic development—Political aspects. 3. Poverty—
Government policy. 4. Economic assistance—Political aspects.
5. International organization. I. Title.
HG3881.5.W57W427   2008
332.1′532—dc22   2008014931

British Library Cataloging-in-Publication Data is available

This book has been composed in Palatino

Printed on acid-free paper. ∞

press.princeton.edu

Printed in the United States of America

10   9   8   7   6   5   4   3   2   1

For Michael and Annika

Contents

Figures and Tables

Preface

ON THE MORNING OF 11 September 2001, I was walking up Eighteenth Street from my office in the Brookings Institution to the World Bank headquarters in Washington, D.C. It was midmorning, and traffic was still in its usual state of barely controlled chaos. I was looking forward to an exciting day of interviews with staff members that I was conducting as part of my research on the Bank's organizational culture. The massive World Bank building, which occupies an entire city block of H Street, was in its final preparations for the annual meetings with its sister institution next door, the International Monetary Fund. Dignitaries from all over the world were soon to arrive, and along with them an anticipated 150,000 antiglobalization protestors. The city was preparing to shut down a six-block radius around the World Bank and IMF headquarters. In anticipation of likely riots, several New York City police units would soon arrive to reinforce the D.C. police department. The weeks leading up to the annual meetings had been replete with editorials and articles by critics from both sides of the political spectrum, most of them questioning the World Bank's legitimacy, effectiveness, and relevance in the new millennium. In turn these observers offered their conflicting opinions on how to reinvent, reform, or demolish the World Bank. The World Bank was in crisis.

The tragedies that struck New York City and Washington, D.C., later that morning quickly overshadowed the hype surrounding the World Bank and IMF meetings. For several months after 9/11, the World Bank by and large disappeared from the headlines of major newspapers. Yet the fundamental questions regarding its future did not disappear from public discourse. Instead, the Bank continued to attract criticism, particularly from those who believed that the institution's actions did not correspond to its espoused dream of achieving a "world free of poverty."

This book is concerned with a critical problem facing the World Bank today: its perceived hypocrisy. A label often affixed to the World Bank and other international organizations (IOs), hypocrisy refers to the gap between what an IO says and what it does, or in Nils Brunsson's definition, the contradictions between "organizational talk, decision, and action."[1] Hypocrisy is evident in the Bank's well-documented incom-

---

[1] Brunsson 1989.

pliance with its own mandates and policies, and in the gaps between its espoused developmental goals and its daily operational practices. Hypocrisy is a powerful rallying cry for critics who believe that the Bank's support for development and globalization results in political and economic inequities, social injustices, and environmental ruin. Such accusations of hypocrisy can be devastating because they undermine the Bank's authority, influence, and effectiveness.

As a concept hypocrisy packs a polemical punch without giving much analytical leverage. It has been widely recognized as a common feature of the behavior of international organizations, but it has not been well explained in conventional theories on IOs. Thus the objective of this book is to unpack the puzzle of organized hypocrisy, both theoretically and empirically. What *is* organized hypocrisy, as opposed to personal hypocrisy, and what causes it? Why are IOs so easily ensnared by hypocrisy and, once caught, so unable to escape? What is it about the determinants of bureaucratic behavior and the nature of organizational change that causes hypocrisy to persist even when it threatens the resources and legitimacy an IO needs to survive? Why is hypocrisy so difficult to uproot and eliminate?

My quest to understand the sources and dynamics of organized hypocrisy has led me beyond the disciplinary bounds of political science to the field of organizational theory within sociology. In this sense, the concepts and methods represented in this book fall in line with the sociological constructivist turn in international organizational theory, best represented by the pathbreaking work of Michael Barnett and Martha Finnemore.[2] In practical terms, to investigate hypocrisy and change, I had to tackle both the external and the internal politics and culture of the World Bank. This required learning how to navigate the Bank's complex bureaucratic history, hierarchy, and language (not to mention its mazelike building). The result is a foray deep into the proverbial "black box" to explain what makes the World Bank tick. Consequently, the empirical work in this book does not focus on states, but instead treats IOs as actors in their own right, investigating their internal workings through methodologies appropriate to their power and pathologies.

Acknowledgments

This book would not have been possible without the support of many people. First and foremost, I want to express my profound gratitude

---

[2] Barnett and Finnemore 1999, 2004.

to Michael Barnett, my former dissertation advisor, mentor, and good friend. Well past the dissertation, Michael continued to give me invaluable advice and encouragement. I owe a huge debt as well to Paul D'Anieri, Ralf Leiteritz, Michael Lipson, Michael Mosser, and Michael Tierney, all of whom were critical in helping me craft my central argument and who kindly acquiesced to my persistent requests for feedback. For comments on the original proposal, individual chapters, and the overarching argument of the book, I would also like to thank Rawi Abdelal, Jacqueline Best, Mark Blyth, Jeffrey Chwieroth, Bruce Cronin, Martha Finnemore, Orfeo Fioretos, Erica Gould, Tamar Gutner, Larry Hamlet, Thomas Heilke, Kathryn Hendley, Peter Katzenstein, Juliet Kaarbo, Rick Messick, Steven Ndegwa, Dan Nielson, Susan Park, Craig Parsons, Mark Pollack, Bruce Rich, Leonard Seabrooke, Phil Schrodt, Mark Suchman, Duncan Snidal, Brent Steele, and Antje Vetterlein. For sheer emotional support at the most difficult stage of the primary research, I extend my thanks and lasting friendship to my two "pod buddies" at the Brookings Institution, Steven Cook and Hilary Driscoll-Price. In addition, I owe an intellectual debt to Robert Wade and Devesh Kapur, whose work on the World Bank has inspired me from the start. I would also like to thank Chuck Myers, my editor at Princeton University Press, Richard Isomaki, my copy editor, and two anonymous reviewers who provided amazing feedback on the entire draft manuscript. And finally, I would like to express my deep appreciation to all the World Bank and NGO staff members who granted me interviews and offered important information. I respect their requests for confidentiality.

Funding and institutional support for the early stages of this research were provided by the University of Wisconsin, the Institute for the Study of World Politics, and the Brookings Institution. Later research and writing support were provided by the University of Kansas General Research Fund, College of Liberal Arts and Sciences, Institute for Policy and Social Research, and the Department of Political Science. Research assistance was provided by Darrah McCracken, Adam Shanko, Leslie Eldridge, Selena Self, and Cristina Fernandez. Parts of chapter 3 appeared in "The World's Bank and the Bank's World," *Global Governance* 13, no. 4 (2007): 493-512. Parts of chapter 5 appeared in an article I coauthored with Ralf Leiteritz, "'Our Poverty Is a World Full of Dreams': Reforming the World Bank," *Global Governance* 11, no. 3 (2005): 369-88. These parts have been reprinted with the permission of Lynne Rienner Publishers.

Finally, I am profoundly grateful to my entire family for their enduring patience and support. A special note of thanks to my father, political science professor David Weaver, for instilling in me a passion for politics and for learning at a very young age. At last, I am most indebted to my husband and my daughter, who spent many weekends at home alone while I buried myself in the office to write this book. This book is dedicated, with love, to Michael and Annika.

Abbreviations

ARPP	*Annual Review of Portfolio Performance*
CAS	Country Assistance Strategy
CD	Country Director
CSO	civil society organization
DEC	Development Economics Department
EIA	environmental impact assessment
ESSD	Environmental and Socially Sustainable Development Network
GAC	Governance and Anticorruption
GAP	Government Accountability Project
GDP	gross domestic product
HIPC	Heavily Indebted Poor Countries Initiative
IBRD	International Bank for Reconstruction and Development
ICSID	International Centre for the Settlement of Investment Disputes
IDA	International Development Association
IEG	Independent Evaluation Group
IFC	International Finance Corporation
IMF	International Monetary Fund
INT	Department of Institutional Integrity
M&E	monitoring and evaluation
MCA	Millennium Challenge Account
MDB	multilateral development bank
MDG	Millennium Development Goal
MIGA	Multilateral Investment Guarantee Agency
NEAP	national environmental action plan
NGO	nongovernmental organization
ODA	official development assistance
OED	Operations Evaluation Department
PREM	Poverty Reduction and Economic Management
PRSP	Poverty Reduction Strategy Paper
QAG	Quality Assurance Group
UNDP	United Nations Development Program

USAID   United States Agency for International Development
USGAO   United States General Accounting Office
WDR   *World Development Report*
WTO   World Trade Organization

CHAPTER ONE

Introduction: Hypocrisy and Change in the World Bank

IN HIS BRIEF TENURE AS World Bank president between May 2005 and June 2007, Paul Wolfowitz made fighting corruption his top priority. He aggressively pushed the governance agenda on the Bank's reluctant borrowing states. He openly criticized the Bank's management and staff for tolerating corruption in lending. He went so far as to unilaterally cancel big loans and projects, over the objections of Bank staff and client governments, where he suspected corruption was present. Wolfowitz declared that under his watch the World Bank would have "zero tolerance" for corruption.[1]

Then in late March 2007 news broke of the generous secondment, salary, and promotion deal Wolfowitz had arranged for his romantic partner, staff member Shaha Riza. Opponents of Wolfowitz—including his own management and staff—accused the leader of contradicting his own standard of good governance. Events quickly snowballed. Many European donor states threatened to pull the plug on the World Bank's financial support and their passive support of the U.S. privilege of selecting the Bank's president.[2] Major developing country borrowers, especially in Latin America, used the crisis to ramp up anti-U.S. sentiment and called for a clean break from dependence on the World Bank and its sister institution, the International Monetary Fund.[3] Inside the normally staid institution, staff members openly booed the president, wrote open letters of protest, and donned blue ribbons to symbolize support for good governance in the World Bank itself. In an editorial published on 15 April 2007, the *Financial Times* bluntly stated: "if the president stays, [the Bank] risks becoming an object not of respect, but of scorn, and its campaign in favor of good governance not a believable struggle, but blatant hypocrisy."

[1] See, e.g., World Bank 2005.
[2] Weisman 2007a.
[3] Lapper 2007; Cavallo et al. 2007.

While many reacted with indignation at Wolfowitz's transgression, longtime observers of the World Bank were not shocked to find that behavior did not match declared standards. In the past few decades, strange bedfellows from the political left and right have pointed with outrage to the gaps between the rhetoric and the reality of the international organization. In critics' eyes, hypocrisy is not monopolized by the Bank's president, but is in fact endemic to the institution. Hypocrisy is apparent in the Bank's incompliance with its own policies. It is evident in the "mainstreaming gaps" between what the Bank *says* are its priorities in alleviation of poverty and in socioeconomic development and what it actually *does* to pursue these goals. Hypocrisy is in essence the persistent failure of the Bank, as a collective entity, to act in accordance with its ideals.[4]

Accusations of hypocrisy, once considered inflammatory, are now quite commonplace. Consider for a moment the recent scandal over the Bank's financing of the Bujagali Hydropower Power project in Uganda.[5] The $225 million loan approved for the dam in 2001 provoked a massive NGO protest campaign, triggering an investigation by the Bank's own Independent Inspection Panel. At heart were charges that the proposed project violated the World Bank's policies and espoused goals on numerous fronts: safeguards against the involuntary resettlement of indigenous peoples, adequate assessment of the potential environmental impact, disclosure of information, a proactive consultation with local "stakeholders" (i.e., the affected population), and an objective evaluation to ensure a positive economic return on the investment. Further allegations of corruption in the contract procurement process eventually led to a temporary suspension of the loan. In April 2007, despite continued concerns about the project's viability, the political instability in Uganda, and the pending inspections panel investigation, the Bank renewed and even increased the size of the loan.[6] For activists, the Bujagali project is an example of the hypocrisy of a self-depicted "green" Bank. Indeed, from their perspective, the Bu-

---

[4] Lipson (2007, 6) claims that such failures give rise to accusations of hypocrisy directed at the United Nations.

[5] For an overview of this project and its problems, see the report of the World Bank Independent Inspection Panel 2002 and Bretton Woods Project 2002. For a critique of the NGOs' depiction of the Bujagali project, see Mallaby 2004, chapter 8.

[6] Bank Information Center 2007. The loan included $130 million in funds from the International Finance Corporation (IFC) and $230 million in guarantees from the International Development Agency (IDA) and (Multilateral Investment Guarantee Agency (MIGA). The total cost of the project was estimated in May 2007 to be $750 million ($200 million more than when the dam was first approved in 2001).

jagali case continues a long record of environmental and social neglect and tolerance of corruption in the Bank's work. To the most unforgiving critics, the Bujagali case exemplifies the Jekyll and Hyde character of the Bank, which preaches sustainable, participatory, and accountable development while, in practice, doing whatever is necessary to get big loans approved and out the door as quickly as possible.

Charges of hypocrisy exert a heavy toll on the Bank. Since the mid-1990s, malaise and open dissent have grown within the organization, already beleaguered by demands for reform, reinvention, or even demolition.[7] Increasingly, its highly trained and well-intentioned staff works under politically charged conditions as the Bank takes on goals and tasks that challenge its mandates, modus operandi, and raison d'être. The result is an institution under persistent pressure to change, yet increasingly uncertain about its identity and path to reform.

For these reasons, the phenomenon of the Bank's hypocrisy merits a close examination that gets beyond polemics to an analytically satisfying explanation. Indeed, the goal of this book is not to prove the Bank guilty of hypocrisy. My intent is to explain the nature of, and reasons for, the hypocrisy, a behavioral characteristic I find to be embedded in the Bank's political environment, its internal bureaucratic culture, and the complex process of organizational change. Paradoxically, in investigating the causes and dynamics of hypocrisy, I also argue that hypocrisy may be a natural, enduring, and even *necessary* feature of Bank life.[8]

While I do not seek to generalize my explanation of hypocrisy beyond the critical case of the Bank, I do see its hypocrisy as an exemplar of the bureaucratic "pathologies," dysfunctions, and legitimacy crises that we observe in international organizations today.[9] Others have invoked the concept of organized hypocrisy[10] and in some cases have explicitly theorized on the types of organized hypocrisies found in other IOs.[11] Organized hypocrisy constitutes a salient puzzle for IO the-

---

[7] See, e.g., Pincus and Winters 2002.

[8] Wade 2005; Hobbs 2005.

[9] Barnett and Finnemore 1999, 2004; Dijkzeul and Beigbeder 2003; Lipson 2007.

[10] E.g., Steinberg (2002) on the WTO; Schimmelfennig (2002) on NATO; and Iankova and Katzenstein (2003) on the European Union.

[11] E.g., Kiersey et al. 2006 on the European Union and Turkish accession; Bukovansky 2006 on the WTO and agricultural subsidies; and Lipson 2007 on United Nations peacekeeping. These works are a different take on Krasner's (1999) understanding of sovereignty as organized hypocrisy. See Lipson 2007 for a discussion of the distinction between "Brunssonian" and "Krasnerian" organized hypocrisy, and Bukovansky (2005) for a discussion of realist (e.g., Krasner 1999) versus liberal (e.g., Walzer 1977) versus constructivist (e.g., Shklar 1984) approaches to hypocrisy.

ory. Increasingly, scholars (particularly those in the constructivist tradition) recognize IOs to be relatively autonomous and powerful actors who help both to regulate and to constitute the world by "defining meanings, norms of good behavior . . . and categories of legitimate social action."[12] Hypocrisy impedes these functions, undermining the authority, and potentially limiting the normative and material influence, of IOs. Hypocrisy may be linked to the ineffectiveness or overt failure of an IO.[13] For these reasons, the phenomenon of organized hypocrisy is directly relevant to those considering how to rationally design and delegate authority and tasks to IOs in ways that avoid errant behavior by agents.[14] At first glance, therefore, it seems counterintuitive to view hypocrisy as predictable, even essential for organizational survival. Yet this is exactly what an empirical investigation of the World Bank leads us to believe.

The Sociology of Organized Hypocrisy and Change

This book is driven by two sets of questions. First, why does the Bank exhibit hypocrisy? What does this hypocrisy look like in the manifested behavior of the Bank? What factors, external or internal to the Bank, drive the divergence of bureaucratic talk and action? Second, why is hypocrisy so difficult to resolve, especially when it is exposed as a critical threat to legitimacy and authority? Stated differently, what is it about the nature of change, and specifically strategic reform efforts within international organizations, that enables or even requires hypocrisy?

I tackle these questions theoretically in chapter 2. I draw extensively from organizational sociology, in particular work on sociological institutionalism, resource dependency, and organizational culture. Here I owe a large intellectual debt to the work of Nils Brunsson (1989, 2003), who first theorized the concept of hypocrisy and later, in collaboration with Johan P. Olsen (1993), linked it to the study of organizational reform. Collectively these sociological theories share the assumption that organizations depend upon their external environments for critical resources, including both material (financial) support and conferred legitimacy.[15] An organization must appear responsive to environmental

---

[12] Barnett and Finnemore 2004, 7.

[13] Lipson 2007.

[14] Koremenos, Lipson, and Snidal 2002; Hawkins et al. 2006.

[15] Pfeffer and Salancik 1978.

demands in order to survive. Hypocrisy arises when these demands clash and the organization is compelled to separate talk from action so as to reconcile conflicting societal norms or placate multiple political masters with heterogeneous preferences.

These sociological theories also recognize that organizations develop informal structures and cultures—internal systems of ideologies, values, norms, and ways of interpreting the world—that over time create organizational preferences and behaviors that are quite distinct from those in the external environment.[16] Bureaucratic culture provides stability and meaning to organizational identity and action, enabling the organization to respond predictably and efficiently to environmental uncertainty. Culture is not immutable. But by its nature, culture changes slowly and incrementally, in a path-dependent fashion often at odds with the direction and pace of change in the organization's environment.[17]

Hypocrisy is thus most likely to surface and endure when conflicts arise between institutional pressures and bureaucratic goals. In other words, when the demands imposed by the external material and normative environment conflict with internal structures and culture, organizations will decouple, building gaps between, on one hand, formal structures and "espoused theories" erected for symbolic purposes to obtain external resources and, on the other hand, the informal structures and "theories in use" that drive actual work.[18] To cope with irreconcilable pressures, organizations in fact develop distinct "political" and "action" roles.[19]

With these theories in mind, there is good reason to believe that international organizations, and the Bank specifically, are especially susceptible to hypocrisy.[20] As multilateral governmental agencies, IOs are

[16] Barnett and Finnemore 2004, 19, citing Alvesson 1993.

[17] Brunsson 2003, 212.

[18] Meyer and Rowan 1977; Argyris and Schön 1978.

[19] Brunsson 1989; Lipson 2007.

[20] One key distinction of my approach is the focus on *bureaucratic* hypocrisy. In other accounts, such as the hypocrisy in United Nations peacekeeping (Lipson 2007) and the WTO agricultural trade regime (Bukovansky 2006), hypocrisy is largely behavior exhibited by the member states and institutionalized in the rules of the regime, not the bureaucracies per se. I argue that bureaucratic hypocrisy is more characteristic of large IOs that have sizable bureaucracies with permanent (as opposed to seconded) staff and service-oriented missions. Cox and Jacobson (1973) make this key distinction between service and forum organizations, arguing that service IOs (like the World Bank, other multilateral development banks, and the International Monetary Fund) are more likely to attain higher degrees of autonomy and develop over time distinct organizational cultures that lead the IOs to develop preferences and actions that cannot be directly explained by reference to the interests of their most powerful member states. Therefore, when dis-

particularly dependent upon externally conferred legitimacy, public funding, and demand for services.[21] Their authorizing and task environments are highly politicized, as legitimacy and material resources come from multiple member states as well as other actors (see chapter 3). This environmental complexity increases the likelihood of contradictory expectations and marching orders.[22] Moreover, many large service IOs like the World Bank have developed distinct bureaucratic cultures over their lifetimes. While these cultures reflect in part the IO's dependent relationship with its environment (particularly in the formative years), over time the professionalization and socialization of staff engender organizational preferences and worldviews that are often not easily deduced from the interests of dominant member states.[23] In turn, bureaucratic cultures and the internal battles over ideas and practices play a large part in shaping how the IO behaves and changes over time. Understanding the dichotomy between the external environment and the internal culture of an IO can reveal the tensions that drive hypocrisy.

Underpinning these issues is the argument foreshadowed above: hypocrisy plays a paradoxical role in the life of an IO like the Bank. On the one hand, hypocrisy serves a critical function, shielding the Bank from the inconsistent demands of its political and task environments. It is lip service employed as a strategic tool. On the other hand, hypocrisy can become a liability. As evident in the NGO "whistle-blower" campaigns against the Bank over the past two decades, hypocrisy rarely stays hidden. Instances where the Bank is caught in an act of hypocrisy can become sources of dysfunction, undermining the organization's legitimacy and moral authority, its political and financial support, and ultimately its ability to pursue its mission and to survive.

At such critical junctures, the Bank is called to task and compelled to try to rid itself of hypocrisy through strategic reform, as seen in the

---

cussing organized hypocrisy, I make the explicit nonrealist assumption that IOs are actors, rather than merely structures or arenas, whose dynamic preferences and behavior merits explanation.

[21] Barnett 1997 and 2002; Hurd 2002; Bukovansky 2005; Lipson 2007.

[22] This is akin to the principal-agent model argument regarding the problem of multiple and collective principal (member state) preference heterogeneity in the delegation of authority and tasks from member states to IOs. See, e.g., Pollack 1997, 2003; Nielson and Tierney 2003; Lyne and Tierney 2003; Lyne, Nielson, and Tierney 2006; and Hawkins et al. 2006.

[23] On the professionalization and socialization of the staff in the International Monetary Fund, see Babb 2003; Momani 2005, 2007; and Chwieroth 2007. On the general scope conditions and mechanisms of socialization, see Checkel 2005.

Strategic Compact reorganization in 1997 (see chapter 5). Yet reform programs may become a part of hypocrisy.[24] Reform goals and formal structural changes may be enacted to signal conformity to environmental expectations, to mold public opinion and fend off external criticism, to secure needed resources and get on with the work. "Such an interpretation," Brunsson and Olsen argue, "helps to explain why so many reforms are attempted, even though they have little effect on structures and processes, let alone results."[25] In the case of the Bank, Toye and Toye conclude, "the rhetoric of change [has moved] faster than the reality."[26]

At the same time, reform programs are not simply acts of smoke and mirrors. Quite often changes are initiated as the result of learning and the advocacy of new ideas and practices within the organization. In these instances, the intent to uproot hypocrisy and incite change is genuine, at least on the part of the champions of reform. Reform goals are pronounced and plans are enacted to align formal and informal structures and behavior with espoused goals. Yet change remains elusive. Why?

Aligning talk with action across an entire organization, especially one the size and age of the Bank, is not a straightforward task. Talk is cheap, but putting the Bank's money where its mouth is can be very expensive. Reducing hypocrisy necessitates reorienting the staff's expectations and behavior to comply with new agendas. Accomplishing such a change is not merely a matter of political will or of creating effective incentives and sanctions. Rather, uprooting hypocrisy requires arduous changes in structures, policies, mind-sets, and behavior. Such systemic cultural change is notoriously difficult to engineer. Moreover, reforms can be hindered by the very incongruence in environmental and bureaucratic goals that compels hypocrisy in the first place. When reform goals are inconsistent, and when they clash with existing ideologies, norms, incentive structures, and routines, reform is unlikely to succeed. Quite often such attempts produce unintended and undesired consequences, including continued hypocrisy. In the

---

[24] Brunsson and Olsen 1993, 10. Lipson (2007) calls this "reform as meta-hypocrisy," and argues that reforms that are successful in terms of creating consistency between organizational talk, decisions, and actions may actually render the organization incapable of decoupling in a manner that allows it to continue to cope with inconsistent environmental demands. In this sense, "rhetorical reform"—symbolic change enacted to signal intent to change without actual implementation—is necessary for organizational survival.

[25] Brunsson and Olsen 1993, 10.

[26] Toye and Toye 2005, iii.

end, hypocrisy can become a trap: easy to fall into and hard to get out of. For these reasons, this book examines both the contentious process of change in the Bank and the sources and manifestations of organized hypocrisy.

Hypocrisy and Change in the World Bank

> The road to hell is paved with good intentions. We have a lot of good intentions.
> —*John Alvey, outgoing president, World Bank Staff Association, December 2004*

Why the World Bank?

The Bank is a critical case for the study of organized hypocrisy and change if only because its "talk" and "action" have a profound influence on the theory and practice of global development. Since its rather humble beginnings sixty years ago, the World Bank Group[27] has grown from an original staff of seventy-two people, all located in Washington, D.C., to a current staff of over ten thousand located at the Washington headquarters and in over one hundred country offices. In its first six years of lending (1947–52), the Bank issued loans totaling less than $1.4 billion (approximately $12.6 billion in 2006 dollars),[28] whereas in the last fifteen years the Bank has averaged nearly $22 billion *per year.*[29] Furthermore, in the first ten years of its existence, the Bank issued loans almost exclusively for reconstruction in Europe and other infrastructure projects, including sector lending in electrical power, transportation, industry, and agricultural and forestry.

By the 1990s, the scope of the Bank's lending had expanded tremendously. It now tackles development projects ranging from sweeping adjustment lending for macroeconomic restructuring to social, environmental, and political areas of development, including social protec-

---

[27] The World Bank Group officially is composed of five organizations: the International Bank for Reconstruction and Development (IBRD), the International Development Agency (IDA), the International Finance Corporation (IFC), the Multilateral Guarantee Investment Agency (MIGA), and the International Centre for Settlement of Investment Disputes (ICSID). The main focus of this study will be the activities of the IBRD and IDA, which together account for the bulk of World Bank concessional and nonconcessional lending operations. Unless otherwise indicated, references to the "World Bank" (or simply the "Bank") will be synonymous with the IBRD and IDA.

[28] Mason and Asher 1973, 178–79.

[29] World Bank Annual Reports 1990–2006.

tion and pensions, designated environmental protection programs, and public sector management. The Bank's loan and grant commitments in 2005 approximately equaled the combined commitments of the four major regional development banks, nearing $22.5 billion in the same year that official development assistance totaled around $100 billion.[30] Annual World Bank lending in fact represents an amount greater than the annual gross domestic product of most of the world's countries.[31] Insofar as its lending policies are mimicked by other development agencies and national governments, the real effect of its material power is immeasurable.

The financial leverage of the Bank, however, is perhaps surpassed by the normative power of its development theories. In the past sixty years, the Bank has accrued a reputation as the premier global development institution with the greatest in-house expertise. The budgetary resources and staff allocation for research alone far exceeds that of any academic institution. More importantly, the Bank publishes each year the highly influential *World Development Report*, the most widely read publication in the area of international development, with fifty to one hundred thousand printed copies in English and additional copies in seven other languages.[32] The Bank puts out an enormous volume of other publications, including conference proceedings, working papers, and economic reports on specific countries. The capacity of the Bank to gather and disseminate data is a tremendous source of influence. The *World Development Indicators* aggregated yearly by the Bank are used extensively to gauge progress in socioeconomic development and aid, and are the primary source of statistics for the major publications of other international organizations, including the United Nations Development Program's annual *Human Development Report*. The data generated not only reflect the Bank's stance on what issues should be weighed in assessing development, but also set the stage for the scope and content of aid policies and programs.

Through these various sources of influence the Bank holds a unique position of authority in the world of ideas on development. Joseph

---

[30] Annual Reports for 2005 of the World Bank, Inter-American Development Bank, Asian Development Bank, African Development Bank, and the European Bank for Reconstruction and Development; ODA statistics represent the total new ODA (Official Development Assistance) and OA (Official Assistance to post-Communist transition economies) by Part I Developed Countries to Development Countries, available from the OECD 2006 Aid Statistics (www.oecd.stat).

[31] According to the gross domestic product (GDP) statistics of the United Nations Development Program's 2005 *Human Development Report*, over one hundred countries reported a GDP in 2003 less than the average amount of Bank lending over the decade, including most of the developing countries that borrow from the Bank.

[32] Wade 2001a, 1436.

Stiglitz, Nobel Prize winner in economics and former chief economist at the Bank, commented that its "predominant role in development research is so strong that, were it involved in the production of an ordinary commodity, it might be accused of anti-trust violation, dominating an industry."[33] As a result, not only the Bank's financial lending, but also what it *says* about development, shapes other multilateral, bilateral, and national development strategies and defines the conventional wisdom on global development.

Because what the Bank says and does is so influential, particularly in the developing world, contradictions between its words and deeds are grist for the mills of those who challenge its discourses and practices. Critics are quick to see hypocrisy and use it as justification for calls for reform or even dismantlement of the Bank. Its management and staff are incredibly sensitive to the effects that perceived hypocrisy has on the organization's credibility and thus their ability to carry out their operations. As Alison Cave, head of the World Bank Staff Association commented in 2007: "We have to be an example. We can't go and preach one thing and do another."[34]

Road Map to the Empirical Chapters

Before we can empirically examine the sources of organizational hypocrisy and processes of change, we need a detailed understanding of both the outside and the inside of the Bank—both the contentious politics that surround the Bank and the way things work within the belly of the beast. This is the objective of chapter 3, entitled "The World's Bank and the Bank's World." In the first half of the chapter, I describe the historical and contemporary relationships between the Bank and its member states (both donors and recipients), international nongovernmental organizations, epistemic communities, and the other actors relevant to the international development regime. The objective here is to establish the dependent relationship between the Bank and the entities that constitute its authorizing and task environments. This outline helps us sort out the cacophony of external demands upon the Bank, and the scope of the autonomy that enables it to evade these pressures, with greater or lesser success, through organized hypocrisy.

In the second half of chapter 3, I explore the social life within the Bank. I investigate the sources and evolution of its distinct intellectual and operational features and the political dynamics of its bureaucratic hierarchy. I examine the effect of bureaucratic politics and an econo-

---

[33] Stiglitz 2007, 1.
[34] Interview on CNN, 22 April 2007.

mistic, apolitical, and technocratic culture on the organization's ideas, policies, and practices. This description enables us to understand the dominant bureaucratic preferences and goals of the Bank and how they conflict with the preferences and goals of actors in the external environment as well as internal advocates of change. The chapter paints a rich portrait of the social and political environments within and without the World Bank, providing a basis for understanding the incongruence of goals that contributes to hypocrisy, and in turn the opportunities for, and constraints on, organizational change.

Chapter 4 is a case study of the how "talk" and "action" evolve within the Bank, and how and why the two diverge. The specific subject of the case study is the Bank's most prominent development agenda today: the promotion of "good governance" and the fight against corruption. From the start of this effort in the early 1990s, even talking about governance and corruption was difficult in the Bank. Donors and borrowers alike considered overt attention to weak or failed states and to corruption-busting "too political" for the Bank's mandate, particularly during the Cold War. Internally, friction with the Bank's intellectual and operational cultures led to the marginalization of early efforts to mobilize staff resources for governance reform work in borrowing countries.

Easing political tensions after the Cold War shifted donors' attitudes regarding the political scope of the Bank's work. At the same time, there was growing awareness outside and inside the organization that inattention to the politics of reform, and particularly to pervasive corruption in development projects, reduced the effectiveness of aid. Nonetheless, even with shifting environmental pressures, "talking" about politics in the context of the Bank's work was still considered taboo and incompatible with the Bank's conventional (i.e., economic) theories and models. The discourse and theories on governance and corruption in the early to mid-1990s thus emerged through a hard-fought cultural battle of ideas within the organization. The path-dependent effect of neoliberalism in the Bank's theory, reinforced by the dominance of economists in key intellectual positions, led to a peculiar articulation and justification of "good governance" work that to many (including some operational staff) avoided the kind of blunt political language and analytical tools necessary to put the new ideas into practice.

Not surprisingly, mainstreaming good governance in the Bank's lending operations was handicapped by its ways of talking about governance and corruption, even after James Wolfensohn's famous "cancer of corruption" speech. Moreover, persistent features of the operational culture, most critically the pressure to keeping lending, deterred operational staff from pushing the good governance and anticorruption agenda on reluctant borrowers, despite growing pressures from donor states and NGOs. Mainstreaming progressed, but with gaps that were well documented by the Bank's own internal evaluations units.

When Paul Wolfowitz took over from Wolfensohn in 2005, he made it clear that he planned to turn the anticorruption rhetoric into reality. However, his heavy-handed methods, unilaterally freezing or canceling high-profile loans, clashed predictably with the institution's culture and the interests of client countries. Moreover, Wolfowitz stirred resistance from European donor states and NGOs, who found his approach arbitrary (and aligned with the unpopular U.S. neoconservative geopolitical agenda) and dangerously resembling "neoconditionality." The result was a pushback from multiple sides, manifested in the contentious drafting and consultation process surrounding the new governance and anticorruption strategy paper passed in March 2007. There exists a strong consensus within the Bank on the importance of good governance for development, but an equally strong disagreement on how to pursue these ideals in practice.

Chapter 5 turns back to the question of resolving organized hypocrisy, and more specifically the promises and pitfalls of strategic reform. I examine the most recent large-scale reorganization of the Bank, entitled the Strategic Compact. The three-year initiative, launched in 1997 by James Wolfensohn, entailed a dramatic reorganization of the formal hierarchy as well as an effort to introduce incentive structures and norms that would disrupt the organizational culture and bureaucratic politics of the "old Bank." The stated objective of the Compact was to realign staff behavior with the envisioned "new Bank," particular in areas where organized hypocrisy was most evident.

However, navigating the conflicting demands of the Bank's external environments while simultaneously transforming bureaucratic culture proved to be anything but straightforward. The Compact itself, reflecting inconsistent environmental pressures, adopted contradictory goals that undermined the potential for success in key areas. For example, efforts to revamp the Bank's formal structures and to institutionalize compliance with environmental and social safeguards (a demand of watchdog NGOs and donor states) were countered by efforts to streamline the approval of projects (a demand of borrower states). Not surprisingly, success was most apparent where the reforms were consistent with the existing bureaucratic culture. In some cases, this success reinforced structural and cultural features that impeded mainstreaming in other targeted areas. Thus strategic reform inadvertently perpetuated organized hypocrisy. At a minimum, the architects of the

Compact learned the difficulty of engineering cultural change in such a complex organization.

The concluding chapter reflects on the theoretical and empirical lessons learned in this study. I comment on the endurance of hypocrisy in the Bank and on the connection between legitimacy, hypocrisy, and organizational survival. Most critically, I speculate on whether we will see more or less hypocrisy in the Bank in the near future. Mounting calls to reform the content and delivery of international aid challenge the core mandates, capacity, and culture of the Bank. We observe today the continued incongruence of environmental and bureaucratic goals. Paul Wolfowitz's own hypocrisy exacerbated these tensions, creating stronger divisions between the Bank's member countries and between its leader and his staff. Even under the new leadership of Robert Zoellick, the World Bank is today in crisis and is seeking to restore its legitimacy to justify its continued existence. Yet to the extent that legitimacy is sought through organized hypocrisy, the path to survival is precarious.

METHODOLOGY OF STUDYING ORGANIZED HYPOCRISY AND CHANGE

This book may best be labeled a sociological study or ethnography of the Bank. Here, the focus is not the "objects" or recipients of developmental finance, but the aid industry itself—a focus that already has a rich tradition.[35] As Michael Watts describes, the ethnographic approach asks how ideas and practices are institutionalized, in particular by examining the internal dynamics of IOs. This in turn "takes the *social construction* of knowledge (by whom, with what materials, with what authority, with what effects), and the relations between knowledge and practice very seriously, and in so doing can identify struggles and spaces in which important changes can be and are made."[36]

The research for this book was carried out between September 1999 and January 2007. During this time I conducted over one hundred formal and informal interviews inside and outside the Bank, both in Washington, D.C., and (for three months in late 1999) in Moscow. Under the auspices of a Brookings Institution Research Fellowship, I had the good fortune of working in Washington for one full year

---

[35] See, for example, Tendler 1975, 1997; Hancock 1989; Ferguson 1994; Cooper and Packard 1997; Escobar 1995; Dichter 2003; Lewis et al. 2003; Bebbington et al. 2004, 2006; Guess 2005; Goldman 2005. For an excellent summary critique of the development aid industry, see Easterly 2002 and Birdsall 2004.

[36] Watts 2001, 286.

(September 2001–August 2002), only a twenty-minute walk from the Bank's headquarters. The Brookings affiliation enabled me to develop valuable connections to staff within the Bank, which led to snow-balling interviews and the privilege of being blind-copied on emails and sent internal documents. The time in Washington also allowed me to indulge in the "scientific" activity of simply hanging out at 1818 H Street to see how life worked within the Bank. This included nonpartic-ipant observation of meetings, brown-bag discussions, and casual con-versations in the cafeteria and atrium coffee bar. Since 2002, I have re-turned to Washington at least once a year to conduct follow-up interviews in the Bank and surrounding NGOs.

Ethnographic research also entails reading the immense amount of material (both official and unofficial) produced by the Bank. A great deal of my time was spent combing through the latest reports, from the flagship *World Development Reports* to operational documents (in-cluding Country Assistance Strategy papers), to departmental notes and Bank Staff Association newsletters. Perhaps the most valuable publications were the evaluation reports published by the Operations Evaluation Department (OED, now named the Independent Evalua-tion Group, or IEG) and the Quality Assurance Group (QAG). In par-ticular, starting in the late 1990s, the OED began to evaluate the pro-cesses of mainstreaming in several areas of the Bank's work (including the environment, gender, and governance). In addition, there is a wealth of information about the Bank's mainstreaming gaps and in-compliance with policy in reports written by NGOs and government agencies, such as the United States General Accounting Office.

Conducting ethnographies of international organizations is not easy. The researcher has to gain access to them, which can be quite difficult. As Lewis et al. argue, ethnographic studies of this sort are few "not least because of the logistical and methodological difficulties of being able to 'get inside' such organizations in order to study them—espe-cially if the researcher has traditionally had a critical stance towards development. Organizations do not easily and willingly open doors to such researchers."[37]

There is indeed a considerable start-up cost in such research. Gain-ing initial access and learning how things work at the Bank takes pa-tience and persistence. Nonetheless, most management and staff were receptive and even eager to talk once I became familiar with the exter-nal and internal politics of the Bank and fluent enough in "Bankese" to ask trenchant questions. At the same time, staff members experience

---

[37] Lewis et al. 2003, 545 n. 6. See also Ghosh 1994 on conducting ethnographies of IOs.

a pervasive sense of insecurity, stemming in part from the intolerance of open dissent, which compels most people to prefer anonymity or to speak off the record. Thus, a large portion (approximately 75 percent) of the information I collected in interviews is used as background only or is attributed simply to a "Bank official." Those who requested such anonymity are not named in the list of interviewees at the end of this book, but I am grateful for their candor.

Conducting ethnographic research on the Bank may in fact be easier today than in the past, for three key reasons. First, over the past decade there has been tremendous pressure from member states and NGOs for increased openness and transparency.[38] This has greatly eased access to information, particularly official project documents, evaluation reports, and research papers. Many materials once marked not for public release are now accessible on the Bank's immense website or available for purchase (at an oddly high fixed cost) through the Bank's Public Information Center. Other documents may be requested through a country's executive director.[39]

Second, a significant amount of "leaked" information is readily accessible to the public. Beyond the stories that appear regularly in the *Washington Post* and *Financial Times*, watchdog organizations, such the Washington-based Bank Information Center and the London-based Bretton Woods Project, are dedicated to gathering sensitive data on the Bank, including internal documents and information about the conduct and impact of the Bank's programs in borrowing countries. One needs to be aware that many NGO reports are intended to reveal problems rather than successes, but they are a fantastic source of current information and a good counterweight to the Bank's own publications (which, understandably, emphasize the positive impact of its work). These NGOs are quite willing to share their information, and their staff members are well versed in the internal affairs of the Bank as well as other multilateral development banks. I am extremely appreciative of the many NGO activists, particularly Bruce Rich at Environmental Defense, who helped me to gain access to key individuals and documents and generally pointed me in the right directions.

[38] See, e.g., Nelson 2001.

[39] Ironically, one area of research that remains difficult is archival research, which I attempted in 2005–7 in order to see internal documents regarding past reorganization programs. Due to rather arcane and very cumbersome information disclosure policies, which require the Bank's legal counsel to review and approve most access requests from researchers, much of the Bank's wealth of internal documents is still untapped. The information disclosure policies are under review, as of spring 2007, and may be reformed to facilitate access for external researchers.

Finally, as I have hinted above, the current malaise within the Bank has peculiar implications for access to the organization. It is not difficult to find disillusioned staff members who are ready to dissent from the Bank's official stance. They are often quite willing to share stories, draft reports, and internal correspondence that reveal the gap between official rhetoric and the "way things actually happen." One staff member joked that if a document is marked "for internal use only," you can bet the NGOs and newspapers will have it within twenty-four hours.[40] Moreover, the sheer size of the World Bank and the rate of staff turnover mean that former employees and consultants populate Washington think tanks, NGOs, and other aid organizations, and many feel free to speak bluntly about their former employer.

CONCLUSION: ON THE MEASUREMENT AND NORMATIVE IMPLICATIONS OF ORGANIZED HYPOCRISY

Two key lessons I learned in conducting this research merit final comment. First, it is difficult to create objective, universally accepted standards for observing and measuring hypocrisy. Inevitably, hypocrisy is a matter of perception. There are also gradations of organized hypocrisy (e.g., the number of instances of incompliance with policy, and size of the mainstreaming gaps) that make it more or less damaging to institutional legitimacy. Hypocrisy is also uneven across an organization: it may be quite prevalent in some units or areas of the Bank's work, and not in others.

Ardent critics are quick to decry individual acts of incompliance with policy as hard evidence of systemic hypocrisy. Other observers are less likely to jump to such conclusions. There is a natural tendency to apply Justice Stewart's pornography standard to hypocrisy: we know it when we see it. One way to avoid this arbitrary subjectivity is to refrain from identifying hypocrisy without substantial evidence and agreement from multiple sources. In this book, I have sought verification of my evaluations from a balance of sources, including NGOs, official Bank reports, and interviews with staff. I also directed due attention to discerning where hypocrisy was expanding or disappearing, by looking for evidence of changes in behavior.

Second, there is an inherent danger of conflating individual and organized hypocrisy. The dictionary does not distinguish them, but rather leads us to believe that all hypocrisy is conscious "pretense" and "false claims." Implicit is the assumption that the hypocrite is a coher-

---

[40] Interview with Bank staff member, April 2005, Lawrence, Kansas.

ent, unitary actor who consciously decides whether to deceive or to be true to her word. Yet organizations are not unitary actors, but, as Lipson argues, "collectivities constituted and endowed with social agency by their social environments. . . . Just as it makes little sense to speak of an individual afflicted with schizophrenia or dissociative identity disorder (i.e. multiple personalities) as hypocritical, the censure associated with the term is inappropriate to consideration of organized hypocrisy in open systems organizations."[41] Bukovansky likewise argues that "'institutional hypocrisy' may . . . be very different from the hypocrisy of an individual, and the former may not deserve the moral condemnation we might level at the latter."[42]

In the case of the Bank, it is easy to identify specific acts of hypocrisy and to pinpoint individual responsibility, especially if you happen to name the president of the Bank. Determining responsibility for systemic hypocrisy, on the other hand, is much more difficult. In sociological terms, the Bank is a loosely coupled organization. Those who "talk" for the Bank are not always those who "act." In fact, we tend to observe the talk through presidential speeches, high-profile publications such as the *World Development Report*, and major strategy and research papers. The individuals and units that produce these public messages are not usually those in the front line of operations.[43]

The distance between those who produce the discourse on development and those who carry out the Bank's practice thus reflects the structural separations between its research and operational branches. Despite attempts in recent years to bridge these parts, for example through new networks and by assigning research staff to field operations, many staff members still feel that research and operations inhabit separate planets. Moreover, the incentive structures and cultures of these branches diverge, particularly in terms of *whose* expectations staff members must respond to in their daily work. For operations staff, the buck quite literally stops with client governments (or more proximally, the country directors), whereas researchers feel more pressure from donors and the broader intellectual community.[44] This source of goal incongruence multiplies the external sources of incongruence that drive organized hypocrisy.

[41] Lipson 2007, 9.

[42] Bukovansky 2005, 6.

[43] The six regional operational units are Middle East and North Africa, South Asia, East Asia and Pacific, Europe and Central Asia, Africa, and Latin America and the Caribbean.

[44] A recent external evaluation of the Development Economics Department made this essential point. See Deaton et al. 2006.

These two key lessons have normative implications for efforts to determine *who* is the hypocrite and where to lay blame. To the extent that organized hypocrisy is rooted in structural and cultural constraints (inconsistent environmental and bureaucratic pressures) that are impossible to resolve, hypocrisy may be an unavoidable feature of Bank life. Organized hypocrisy may also be necessary to ensure the Bank's survival. And that leaves a dilemma, best articulated by renowned Bank scholar Robert Wade: "Anyone concerned to protect and expand the scope of international organizations and international public goods has to be concerned with how either to improve the ability of IOs to be hypocritical and get away with it, or to reduce the need for organized hypocrisy. Or both."[45]

[45] Wade 2005, 3.

CHAPTER TWO

The World Bank Hypocrisy Trap

> In modern society, there are many popular ideas of what is
> generally rational, just, or good. Such ideas tend to be gen-
> eral, vague, and simple, making them attractive as ideas,
> but more difficult to translate into concrete, specific actions
> in a way that is as attractive and uncontroversial as the
> ideas. Organizations are systems that are supposed to act,
> so for them the tension between attractive ideas and the
> limits and specificities of practice becomes acute. They are
> easy victims for the criticism of having perverted our ide-
> als. Modern organizations are squeezed between ideology
> and practice.
>
> —*Brunsson 2003, 204*

> Our Dream is a World Free of Poverty.
> —*Motto of the World Bank*
> *under James Wolfensohn, 1995–2005*

The hypocrisy of an organization is, at heart, the gaps between its talk,
decisions, and actions.[1] In the case of the World Bank, hypocrisy reflects the conflicts between what the Bank as a collective actor says—
its espoused goals, ideals, and policies—and what the Bank does. Organizational hypocrisy is a "disjuncture between word and deed, or
between publicly-accepted norms and behavior,"[2] a disparity that reflects the inconsistencies between what the Bank expected to say and
do in an idealistic world, and what it is able to accomplish within its
political, financial and cultural environments. Such hypocrisies can be
observed in the Bank's selective pursuit of mandates, its weak compliance with rules, and its half-hearted or thwarted efforts to carry out
new agendas.[3]

[1] Brunsson 2003.

[2] Bukovansky 2005, 5.

[3] Critically, I do not equate organizational hypocrisy with an IO's failure to achieve
desired results. Performance failures are often shaped by factors outside of the organization's control (such as corruption in borrowing countries, external shocks in global price
systems, or natural disasters). More importantly, my concept of organizational hypocrisy
is subtly distinct from Gutner's (2005a) understanding of the "gap between mandate
and performance." In Gutner's account, the primary focus is on the unwillingness or

I identify two distinct types of organizational hypocrisy. The first is the most blatant: outright violation of organizational mandates and policies. Evidence of this sort of hypocrisy can be found, for example, in the Bank's violation of its own environmental and social policies in its infrastructure projects. This blatant hypocrisy is in fact the target of most NGO watchdog campaigns exposing the Bank's failure to comply with its own rules in lending operations and project management.

A second form of hypocrisy is much more subtle and difficult to measure, yet far more pervasive. Here hypocrisy emerges in the form of "mainstreaming gaps." It occurs, for example, when the Bank proclaims its commitment to sustainable development, gender equality, and good governance, but does not commit the human and financial resources or enforce the rules necessary to integrate these values into organizational practices. The result is a separation or even an overt contradiction between proclaimed priorities and goals and the reality of the Bank's activity.

Mainstreaming is not merely a matter of reallocating resources or rewriting formal rules to align organizational practice with newly espoused goals. It is often a matter of changing mind-sets, shifting expectations, and disrupting the habits of staff and management. Robert Picciotto, former director general of the Operations Evaluation Department of the World Bank (now called the Independent Evaluations Group), provides this definition of mainstreaming in the context of the Bank's ongoing efforts to enhance evaluation and feedback:

> [Mainstreaming] suggests a deliberate perturbation in the natural order of things. It creates winners and losers, challenges vested interests and triggers changes in alliances. It subverts the status quo and yet it does not evoke chaotic change or painful disruption. It effect, mainstreaming connotes gradual reform rather than frantic revolution. In policy terms, it is typically achieved through incremental changes in program goals, protocols of operations and organizational cultures.[4]

---

inability of the Bank's staff (as the principals in the lending relationship) to reign in the errant behavior of client governments (the agents). (See Killick 1997 for a similar approach. See also Nielson and Tierney 2005 for a critical assessment of Gutner's application of principal-agent models to Bank-client government relations). My focus is less on the results of the Bank's projects on the ground and more on the institutional processes *within* the bureaucracy that produce contradictions between the way development ideas are theorized and publicly articulated, on the one hand, and the way they are translated into operational routines and lending priorities, on the other. Thus, an instance when the Bank says a development program will work, and it does not, is not hypocrisy.

[4] Picciotto 2002, 323.

In instances of either incompliance with policy or mainstreaming gaps, organizational hypocrisy is not a binomial variable, present or not. Rather, as described at the end of chapter 1, hypocrisy is matter of perception and degree: a critical amount of observable incompliance or failure to mainstream contributes to an overall belief that the Bank is behaving hypocritically. Hypocrisy decreases when instances of incompliance with policies and mandates become rare rather than expected behavior. Likewise, "something is said to be mainstreamed when it is so routine that it provokes neither conflict or comment."[5]

Green or Greenwashed? A Brief Illustration of Hypocrisy

In the past three decades, the Bank has espoused a commitment to the environment in its development theories, adopted sophisticated means to assess the environmental impact of loans, and dramatically increased lending for stand-alone environmental projects. Why do critics then still conclude that the Bank is hypocritical when it comes to its agenda of sustainable development? What does this hypocrisy look like, and what explains the persistent policy incompliance and mainstreaming gaps that undermine the perceived legitimacy of the Bank's work in sustainable development? In other words, what has shaped the uneven "greening" of the Bank?[6]

The devil here lies in the details of the evolution of the Bank's environmental agenda—a story that captures the complex external and internal political environments in which the agenda emerged. Environmental issues surfaced quite early in the Bank's history. In 1970, in reaction to shifts in thinking about economic development and growing concerns about the ecological impact of infrastructure projects, Robert McNamara (then the Bank's president) created the position of environmental advisor. This gesture quickly proved to be no more than symbolic. At that time, there were no strong external and internal advocates able to monitor and push for the integration of environmental standards in the Bank's research and operations. More importantly, the environmental agenda faced resistance from senior management and client governments who viewed environmental concerns as "luxuries of the rich countries" too costly for developing nations still struggling

---

[5] World Bank Operations Evaluation Department 2000, 1.

[6] There has been a plethora of recent studies on the evolution and problematic mainstreaming of the Bank's sustainable development agenda, from both external and internal approaches. For excellent in-depth accounts, see especially Wade 1997; Fox and Brown 1998; Miller-Adams 1999; and Gutner 2002.

to industrialize their economies.[7] As a result, management provided the tiny environmental unit with few staff and budget resources. It lacked decision-making authority that would have allowed it to affect policy and operations. In the following twenty years, the Bank fell far behind other aid organizations in adopting such practices as environmental assessments.[8]

In the early 1980s, however, several high-profile projects drew critical public attention, resulting in external pressure to reform the Bank's environmental policies. Among them was the disastrous Northwest Region Development Program in Polonoroeste, Brazil.[9] The $443.4 million road-building and agricultural colonization scheme across a fifteen-hundred-kilometer section of the Amazon forest was intended to attract settlers who would raise trees and grow cocoa and coffee for export. However, the Bank-financed project failed to anticipate the scale of migration to the regions and the massive ecological damage it caused. The project resulted in unprecedented deforestation in the Brazilian Amazon, as well as the spread of malaria and tuberculosis to the indigenous populations. Environmental activists and NGOs started a global public campaign, bringing political attention to their concerns by appealing to the U.S. Congress during the 1983 negotiations over the replenishment of funds to the International Development Association.[10] Engaging the "power of the purse" belonging to the Bank's principal member state proved decisive in linking external critics and a small group of advocates within the Bank, who joined to push for reform of the Bank's environmental agenda when Barber Conable become president in 1987.

Conable's massive reorganization of the Bank in 1987–88 brought sweeping changes, including the creation of a new Environment Department and four regional environmental units to watch over the projects in the four regional operation departments.[11] The number of envi-

---

[7] Caufield 1996, 178.

[8] Wade 1997, 635; and World Bank Operations Evaluation Department 2001a.

[9] For details accounts of this and similar projects, such as the Arun III dam project in Nepal, the Chixoy Hydroelectric Project in Guatemala, and the Chad-Cameroon petroleum development project, see especially Rich 1994; Wade 1997; Fox and Brown 1998; Rich 2002; and Gutner 2002.

[10] The International Development Association (IDA) is the "soft-loan" or concessional lending arm of the World Bank. It lends only to the poorest countries at near 0 percent interest rates. It depends upon the triannual contributions of the Part I (donor) member states. See chapter 3 for more details.

[11] These regional departments in 1987 included Asia, Africa, Latin America and the Caribbean, and Europe and the Middle East. Current Bank structure divides the regional classifications into six units: Latin America and Caribbean, East Asia and Pacific, South Asia, sub-Saharan Africa, Middle East and North Africa, and Europe and Central Asia. Under the new matrix management system launched in 1996 during yet another reorga-

ronmental staff increased from 70 to over 300 by 1990 (dropping to 250 by the year 2000). The Bank launched a series of environmental papers, increased stand-alone environmental projects, and allocated greater budget resources to environmental research.[12] In theory, the new environmental units possessed the authority, autonomy, and resources to supervise projects. In reality their authority was limited, and real decision-making power continued to rest in the hands of country directors, who remained attuned to the interests of borrowing governments.

Only two years later, in 1989, however, concern over another project, the Sardar Sarovar dam in the Narmada region of India, created more heat for the World Bank. The project triggered a protest by five thousand villagers threatened with forced displacement, resulting in a "long march" over three weeks during which, under intense international media attention, many people were beaten and 140 arrested.[13] The Bank responded by appointing an independent commission to look into claims that it was violating its own policies. The final report of the Morse Commission, named for its team leader and former UNDP head Bradford Morse, endorsed critics' claims about the Bank's action. The report recommended greater accountability and informational disclosure in the Bank. Picked up by NGOs and Congress during the next IDA replenishment negotiation, the report led to the creation of the Independent Inspection Panel in 1993. Just two years prior, in 1991, the Bank had adopted Operational Directive 4.01, requiring environmental impact assessments for all projects having potential environmental effects. IDA later called for the preparation of national environmental action plans (NEAPs) as a means of including environmental issues in the Country Assistance Strategy papers.[14] A series of high-profile Bank conferences and publications, including the *World Development Report 1992: Development and the Environment*, appeared to signal that the World Bank had finally "greened." Indeed, lending levels for environmental projects since 1993 have risen, giving the appear-

---

nization effort, the Environmental Department was integrated into the thematic network of Environment and Socially Sustainable Development (ESSD).

[12] World Bank Operations Evaluation Department 2001a, 6.

[13] Rich 1994, 150–53, 249–54; and Fox and Brown 1998, 8.

[14] The Country Assistance Strategy paper is the primary operational "five-year plan of action" for any borrower. It includes a brief overview of the country's development progress and problems, and then highlights priorities for the next several years that include the use of development aid. Because the documents are meant to be clear and succinct, they often are very selective in their attention. Traditionally, macroeconomic stability and growth progress and strategies form the core of the report, while all other development issues—such as environmental and social concerns, gender, human development, as so forth—fight over the remaining space.

ance that the Bank has finally made good on its espoused commitment to sustainable development.[15]

Despite these significant rhetorical and structural shifts, environmental scholars and activists within and without the organization continue to argue that the Bank has not fully internalized the environmental agenda, primarily because of obstacles within its entrenched organizational culture and the continued opposition of many borrower governments.[16] Gutner suggests, for example, that increased lending for environmental projects does not by itself indicate a significant shift in the Bank's thinking and action, and may in fact hide the Bank's failure to mainstream the agenda.[17] Critically, these evaluations consistently point to the incongruence of sustainable development goals with the intellectual and operational cultures of the Bank.

On an ideological level, environmental advocates inside and outside the Bank have waged a constant war with its conservative macroeconomists on the very meaning of sustainable development. In the reaction to Conable's 1987 reform, Lisa Jordan writes, "what was at stake ... was not simply the Bank's approach to sustainable development but the entire range of policy advice and project lending which the Bank forwards to developing countries. By 1992 the macroeconomists had won the battle squarely, relegating the emerging sustainable development paradigm to the confines of the standard development paradigm championed by the Bank for the past fifty years."[18] Fox and Brown add that "according to the World Bank's director of environmental economics, at a basic conceptual level changes have been mainly limited to 'grafting environmental concerns onto business as usual.'"[19]

On an operational level, attempts to green the Bank ran counter to incentive structures, norms, and routines that are still strongly embedded within its other agendas. Despite the high profile of the environment in the Bank's publications, the OED in 2001 noted the absence of environment issues within the Bank's main action plans, the Country Assistance Strategy (CAS) papers. CAS papers still privilege traditional development based on macroeconomic indicators.[20] Moreover,

---

[15] Nielson and Tierney 2003.

[16] See for example, Fox and Brown 1998; and Miller-Adams 1999.

[17] Gutner 2005a, 2005b.

[18] Jordan 1997, 2.

[19] Fox and Brown 1998, 9.

[20] World Bank Operations Evaluation Department 2002a, 3. The report cites a 2000 review by the Bank's Quality Assurance Group (QAG) finding that for projects with significant safeguard aspects, the mitigation actions and arrangement were inadequate in 20 percent of the cases. See also International Development Association 2001.

the formal requirements of environmental assessments are marginalized in the management of projects. Fearing exposure by diligent environmental activists, project managers dutifully carry out EIAs, but often with too few resources and time, little public consultation, and too late to affect the project's design.[21] Staff members are often instructed in training seminars, "Don't get zapped by the Narmada Effect, do your EIAs!"[22] Yet in practice, formal compliance with EIAs and NEAPs (national environmental action plans) are not always matched by an internalization of their intent, in part because environmental specialists have to "sell" their services to country departments within the operational division.[23] A reputation for being a stickler for environmental assessment rules can reduce a person's marketability, and project managers will not seek out the services of anyone who might hold up the approval process.[24]

A 2001 review by the Bank's own Operations Evaluation Department of efforts to mainstream the environmental agenda implicates the structure of incentives and the lines of accountability that have resisted the inclusion of environmental issues, hindered effective monitoring and evaluation, and failed to reward compliance or sanction noncompliance with EIAs and supervision requirements. Like a number of other external studies, the OED report notes consistent resistance on the part of both borrowing governments and project task managers, who see the EIAs and other environmental measures as barriers to the appraisal and execution of projects, and thus counter to the Bank's imperative to disburse money.[25] In a sobering conclusion, the same OED report summarizes the persistent gap between rhetoric and reality:

> the translation of this wide ranging agenda into concrete action has proved elusive. . . . Having identified the pervasive aspects of environmental issues, recorded their importance to poverty alleviation, and confirmed that mainstreaming is essential to achieving its environmental objectives and commitment, in practice, the Bank has done little institutionally to promote, monitor, and otherwise make mainstreaming happen.[26]

---

[21] Wade 1997; United States General Accounting Office 1998; Goldman 2000; World Bank Operations Evaluation Department 2001a; and Rich 2002.

[22] Goldman 2000, 200. See also Goldman 2005.

[23] This is the result of the reforms conducted in 1997–2001 as part of the "matrix management" reorganization. Nielson, Tierney, and Weaver 2006. See also chapter 5.

[24] Wade 1997, 717.

[25] See Wade 1997; Fox and Brown 1998; and Goldman 2000 for excellent discussions on how EIAs are carried out and the various organizational factors that impede their influence upon project management.

[26] World Bank Operations Evaluation Department 2001a, 2, 18.

This brief overview of the Bank's environmental agenda illustrates the difficulty of aligning the Bank's action with its green talk. Critically, the evidence reveals that both external and internal pressures contributed to policy incompliance and mainstreaming shortfalls. At some points, that hypocrisy appears intentional, particularly in the period when management made little effort to allocate needed resources and authority to environmental staff. But from 1987 onward, increasing resources and staff were committed to environmental research and lending, and strict policies were enacted. Yet by the end of the 1990s the agenda was not fully internalized, and policies were not evenly enforced by the Bank as a whole. Hypocrisy was apparent, and yet attempts to uproot it proved elusive. To this day, the Bank's rhetoric on sustainable development is a persuasive example of the Bank's organized hypocrisy.[27]

The Roots of Organized Hypocrisy

The hypocrisy evident in the Bank's sustainable development agenda is not an anomaly, but rather a predictable feature of organizational behavior. In fact, sociological theory clearly states that organized hypocrisy is actually quite common. Form does not always follow function. Structures, codified rules, and advertised corporate philosophies often conflict with the informal norms and routines that govern daily operations. As a result, organizations often take on a public persona in official speeches and texts that is not mirrored by organizational output.

According to both resource dependency theory and sociological institutionalism, hypocrisy is rooted in the organization's dependency on its external (institutional) environment. Environmental pressures and constraints are material in nature (including factors shaping the financial autonomy, competitiveness, and viability of the organization), as well as social (factors shaping the legitimacy and authority of the organization). Resource dependency theory has tended to focus on the technical task and the competitive environment, which compels organizations to adopt certain structures and behavior to manage their dependency through tactics that seek to enhance organizational security by maximizing autonomy.[28] Sociological institutionalism emphasizes the authorizing environment, arguing that organizations must signal conformity with societal norms and rules in order to obtain the

[27] Bosshard 2004.
[28] Pfeffer and Salancik 1978.

legitimacy necessary to demonstrate social worthiness and mobilize resources.[29] Taken together, both theories highlight organizations' search for both material resources and legitimacy to survive. These are mutually reinforcing goals unified by a strategic logic: organizations, as rational actors, adopt symbols, structures, and rules that conform to normative expectations in order to generate legitimacy and enhance authority; such legitimacy and authority attract material resources and "market share" in a competitive environment; and in turn these resources ensure organizational security and survival.[30]

Although the two theories differ somewhat on the degree to which organizational responses to environmental pressures are driven by the logic of appropriateness (legitimacy imperatives) or consequence (material resources imperatives), they agree that dependency creates a dilemma, insofar as an organization's environment is often constituted by *inconsistent* expectations. Confronting conflicting demands is difficult if the actions needed to satisfy one principal or constituent require the organization to ignore or defy the demands of another.[31] If the nature of dependency is such that organizations must placate multiple masters to attain needed material resources and conferred legitimacy, neither acquiescence nor defiance is a viable option. Likewise, if environmental demands strongly diverge, compromise is not a likely strategy. Rather, as Christine Oliver argues, the most likely response is *avoidance*, which conceals organizational nonconformity with environmental pressures. The concealment tactics employed may involve "elaborate rational plans and procedures . . . in order to disguise the fact that [the organization] does not intend to implement them. Organizations may, additionally, engage in window dressing, ritualism, ceremonial pretense, or symbolic acceptance of institutional norms, rules or requirements."[32]

[29] Oliver 1999; DiMaggio and Powell 1983; Meyer and Rowan 1977; Meyer and Scott 1983; Covaleski and Dirsmith 1988. See also Finnemore 1996a for an overview of sociological institutionalism; and Barnett and Coleman 2005 for a discussion of resource dependency and sociological institutionalism as applied to an analysis of change in Interpol.

[30] Barnett and Coleman 2005, 596.

[31] Oliver 1999, 162. For example, a prototypical retail company (e.g. Nike) must appear responsive to both stockholders and customers. It is easy to see where the expectations of stockholders and customers may diverge, for example over the desirability of costly corporate codes of conduct. As Barnett and Coleman (2005) note, in this instance the sociological theory is consistent with the insights of rationalist principal-agent models found in economic theory.

[32] Oliver 1999, 154–55 (citing Meyer and Rowan 1977). Using Oliver's typology, Barnett and Coleman (2005) describe six possible strategic responses by organizations to environmental demands, which they hypothesize to be contingent upon the degree of organizational insecurity (dependence upon external resources and conferred legiti-

At the same time, resource dependency and institutional theories also recognize that organizations seek to maintain *internal* consistency and stability. The objective is to provide staff with a certainty about missions that allows them to pursue tasks with sustained efficiency in the face of environmental uncertainty. At key stages of organizational life (particularly in the formative years) internal organizational skills, technologies, routines, and cultures evolve to provide predictable norms and standard operating procedures flexible enough to deal with a variety with external demands. Yet to the extent that these internal formal and informal structures reinforce continuity and stability in organizational work-life, they tend to change slowly and in an incremental, path-dependent manner. Over time, the demands of the authorizing and task environments may clash with the way of life within an organization, producing incongruity between the goals belonging to the external and the internal worlds and compounding the problem of conflicting pressures within the external environment.

Thus, when the demands imposed by the external material and normative environment conflict with internal structures and culture, sociological theory predicts that organizations will "decouple" or "disconnect," "building gaps between their formal structures and actual work activities" to buffer themselves against the irreconcilable pressures of their external authorizing and task environments.[33] In fact, Oliver argues, such avoidance strategies are most common when there is "only moderate consistency between organizational goals and institutional pressures."[34]

Such conditions leading to decoupling are the jumping-off point for Nils Brunsson's theory of organized hypocrisy. Brunsson argues

---

macy) and culture congruence (degree to which internal bureaucratic culture is consistent or not with external pressures). These responses include acquiescence, compromise, avoidance, defiance, manipulation, and strategic social construction. The argument presented here seeks to articulate the conditions under which we are most likely to observe avoidance, the strategic response that is most often perceived as organized hypocrisy. In Barnett and Coleman's case of Interpol, avoidance became the key strategy between 1946 and 1958 when organizational insecurity was high (Interpol needed material resources from member states), but cultural congruence was low (Interpol's professional culture zealously sought to protect its autonomy and thus resisted efforts by states to politicize its mandates). Interpol chose a tactic of "ceremonial conformity" through symbolic structural change that would increase its legitimacy and hence funding, but did little to change operational procedures and organizational behavior.

[33] Meyer and Rowan 1977, 340–41. See also earlier notions of "loosely coupled" formal organization in Dalton 1959; Downs 1967; Homans 1950; March and Olsen 1976; and Weick 1976.

[34] Oliver 1999, 165. This is similar to the "cultural incongruity" hypothesis put forth by Barnett and Coleman (2005).

that such tensions between internal goals and institutional pressures compel organizations to develop dual roles as "political" and "action" organizations:

> two organizational structures evolve. One is the formal organization, which obeys the institutional norms and which can easily be adapted to new fashions or law, literally by a few strokes of a pen on an organizational chart. A quite different organizational structure can be used in "reality," i.e. in order to coordinate action. This second type is generally referred to as an "informal" organization. . . . Organizations can also produce double standards or double talk; i.e. keep different ideologies for external and internal use. The way management presents the organization and its goals to the outside world need not agree with the signal conveyed to the workforce.[35]

Brunsson's distinction between the "political" and "action" organization follows from Chris Argyris and Donald Schön's description of organizations' "espoused theories" versus "theories-in-use."[36] Espoused theories employed by the political organization first include the official ideology announcing organizational goals, strategic rationale, and justification for the organization's continued existence. Likewise, the espoused theories construct and portray external norms that signal conformity with external expectations about the appropriate behavior of organizational staff. These ideologies and norms are supported by carefully crafted and maintained rhetorical language that attempts to hide internal contradictions or dissent that may blur or undermine the organization's public image and message.[37] Finally, the espoused theories also attempt to exhibit conformity with external demands by formally adopting rules, guidelines, and procedures, such as new assessment requirements or evaluation techniques.

Theories-in-use, on the other hand, reflect the informal ideology (or shared beliefs), internal norms, nonrhetorical language, and informal and noninstitutionalized routines or habits of the action organization. These theories-in-use comprise the "implicit assumptions that govern actual behavior, that tell group members how to perceive, think, and feel about things."[38] Theories-in-use are by nature designed to provide stability and are thus resistant to swift change. Espoused theories, in contrast, may change very quickly to external shocks on the organization's market environment or the demands of its political masters.

---

[35] Brunsson 1989.

[36] Argyris and Schön 1974. See also Meyer and Rowan 1977; Perrow 1991; Dobbin 1994.

[37] Wade (1996) refers to this as "paradigm maintenance."

[38] Schein 1992, 22. See also Argyris and Schön 1974, 1978.

Edgar Schein, Nils Brunsson, and other sociological scholars thus imply that this "decoupling" or hypocrisy is an endemic and even acceptable facet of organizational life in the common scenario of contradictory pressures coming from the authorizing and task environments. Brunsson argues:

> Hypocrisy . . . makes it easier to maintain the legitimacy of organizations, even when they are subjected to conflicting demands. . . . Without hypocrisy, one party or interest would be completely satisfied and all others completely dissatisfied. With hypocrisy, several parties and interests can be somewhat satisfied. . . . . An organization that could not deal in hypocrisy would have a more difficult time working in a world of conflict than will one that can.[39]

The sociological work on organizational hypocrisy primarily focuses on private organizations, with the occasional foray in the public bureaucracies. But the utility of the sociological concept of organizational hypocrisy seems equally appropriate in the case of international organizations and specifically the World Bank.[40] As a multilateral bureaucracy, the Bank is expected to talk in a way that reflects not only the interests of those that provide critical material resources (foremost the member states it serves, both donors and borrowers, as well as private capital markets) but also prevailing international ideals and norms in the broader global development regime (including a highly activist NGO network and critical epistemic community of development scholars). Yet this in turn makes the Bank particularly prone to the problem of conflicting demands from its multiple member states and the complex material and normative environment in which it works. Not all of these demands and norms can be reconciled or translated into feasible operational goals consistent with preexisting operational norms and routines.

In this sense, "in view of the legitimacy requirement, it is acceptable [for the Bank] to demonstrate to the outside world conflicts and ideologies which do not actually typify the internal operations."[41] Moreover, talk and action may often be intentionally decoupled to placate multiple masters: espoused theories and policies to appease one set of demands and theories in action to satisfy others. And as long as the hy-

---

[39] Brunsson 2003, 206–7.

[40] There is a substantial body of prior work on the World Bank that employs sociological organizational theory. See, e.g., Tendler 1975; Crane and Finkle 1981; Ness and Brechin 1988; Nelson 1995; Brechin 1997; and Miller-Adams 1999.

[41] Brunsson 1989, 21.

pocrisy stays hidden (a rather utopian assumption for a high-profile IO like the Bank), external legitimacy and resources are sustained while internal efficiency needs are met. Hypocrisy is rational, strategic, and necessary for organizational survival.

THE WORLD BANK'S "ART OF HYPOCRISY"

The recent work of Robert Wade, a former Bank employee and a world- renowned Bank scholar, colorfully summarizes the inconsistent environmental pressures that drive its organized hypocrisy. Wade likens the Bank to an elephant in a Hindi proverb: "The elephant has two sets of teeth, one to eat, the other to show."[42] Using Brunsson's theory of organized hypocrisy, Wade describes the Bank's dual role as an "action" and "political" organization. As an action organization, it must fulfill its function as a highly specialized and neutral service organization providing expertise in development aid, technical assistance, project proposals, and loans. However, as a political organization, it must appear subservient to the demands of its shareholders and clientele. They include donor and borrowing country governments, private capital markets, and an increasing number of international nongovernmental organizations acting as watchdog agencies on behalf of civil society and indigenous populations in developing countries. As an international governmental organization whose members are political entities, the Bank must talk "in a way that reflects back and affirms many of the beliefs and demands of those whose support it needs, even though the beliefs and demands may be inconsistent."[43]

The current hypocrisies of the Bank, according to Wade's hypothesis, are thus the effect of its "necessary unforthrightness." In other words, the contradictory signals coming from its multifarious authorizing environment compel the Bank to be Janus-faced. On the one side, the interests of its dominant Part I (donor) member states (especially the United States through the U.S. Treasury) and the private capital market on which the Bank depends for its continuous flow of funds, pressure the Bank to embrace what Wade terms the "finance ministry" agenda. This prompts the Bank to adopt a development philosophy and lending programs aimed at supporting a decidedly liberal economic viewpoint, conceptualizing the alleviation of poverty as best achieved

---

[42] Wade 2002, 218.

[43] Wade 2002, 218. See also Wade 2005 and the discussion of Wade's thesis of the "Art of Hypocrisy" in World Bank Staff Association 2005.

through market-oriented policies favoring macroeconomic adjustment, privatization, financial liberalization, export-oriented trade, and institutional reform necessary for encouraging foreign and domestic investment.[44] This serves the interests of the aforementioned parties by first stabilizing and then opening the developing country economies to northern trade and financial flows.

On the other side, the Bank must tip its hat to the increasingly vigilant NGOs and national parliaments (particularly the U.S. Congress). These groups are pushing a "civil society" agenda, premised on the idea of empowerment of the poor through greater participation in the formation of development aid projects and loans and the pursuit of more socially oriented policies such as socioeconomic and human security (social safety nets, education, income equality, access to justice, micro lending programs) and environmental protection. Many of the means and goals of the civil society agenda do not merge well with those of the finance ministry agenda. The Bank, faced with the necessity of appearing responsive to both sets of demands, reacts by rhetorically embracing both agendas in its broad policy paradigms,[45] leaving the inconsistencies and contradictions to be worked out in its daily operations.[46]

As a means of coping with this demanding environment, the Bank has separated its role as political organization from its role as action organization. In an effort to placate its various masters, it has adopted many broad development goals (ranging from macroeconomic adjustment to social and environmental projects) and new policy procedures (regarding transparency, openness, and participation) that are intended to exhibit external norms that engender support and legitimacy for its activities. As Wade argues, "the point is to display its positively valued structures, processes, goals, ideologies and intentions to the outside world. . . . Its survival is a function of its ability to reflect and create a symbolic accord with important external entities."[47] This has lead to what many observers describe as "mission creep" or "goal proliferation."[48]

[44] Wade 2002, 218.

[45] The Bank articulates these overarching paradigms through its major publications and policy statements. These include the *World Development Reports*, its annual reports, and major organizational declarations such as the Comprehensive Development Framework and the Long Term Strategic Framework.

[46] This is consistent with Jonathan Pincus's and Tamar Gutner's descriptions of the Bank torn between the identities of a development agency and credit institution. Pincus 2001, 186 and Gutner 2005a, 22.

[47] Wade 2001b, 9.

[48] Fidler 2001; Einhorn 2001; and Pincus and Winters 2002.

Journalist and author Sebastian Mallaby reiterates Wade's essential argument, adding a much stronger critique of NGO campaigns and a forceful statement about the donor states' own hypocrisy. In an article entitled "Saving the World Bank," Mallaby prescribes

> facing down the activists who have forced the Bank to adopt excessive rules on the environment, corruption, and the protection of indigenous peoples. . . The Bank must not be forced to drop projects because of baseless activist campaign, and it must be given political cover in Congress and in European Parliaments so that it can streamline its safeguards. . . . Making this happen will take a fundamental shift in the attitudes of rich countries. The Bank's leading shareholders will have to recognize that they have set the institution up for failure. They have declared grand development objectives, then done little to support the Bank in its efforts to achieve them. They have nobly proclaimed utopian goals, then left the Bank to take the blame for not advancing them. Such hypocrisy has set the world's best development institution on a course of steady but preventable decline.[49]

Wade and Mallaby both see organized hypocrisy as necessary behavior in light of the Bank's dependency on divided authorizing and task environments. More critically, the underlying presumption of the theory and empirical work outlined thus far is that organized hypocrisy is an *intentional* and *strategic* act by management and staff to dupe the Bank's many political masters and external critics. It is a short-term and rational response to the contradictory demands of an exceedingly complex environment. The Bank must maintain the appearance of responsiveness and effectiveness necessary to sustain the political and financial support of its un-like-minded principal members states and to cope with the persistent attacks of "Lilliputian NGOs."[50] The Bank thus strategically commits itself through "ceremonial conformity" to new agendas and policies to appease the diverse preferences of the various masters on which it depends for critical resources or for conferred legitimacy. At the same time, management has little or no intent to follow through on these rhetorical commitments. It purposely disconnects talk from action. The objective is to deceive, and thus "unintentional hypocrisy is an oxymoron."[51]

As parsimonious and powerful as this argument is, it is flawed. It makes an implicit assumption about intentionality in the Bank's hy-

---

[49] Mallaby 2005, 85.
[50] Mallaby 2004.
[51] I thank one external reviewer for this comment.

pocrisy that conflates organized hypocrisy with conventional notions of individual hypocrisy. As discussed at the end of chapter 1, to argue that the hypocrisy is always intentional and strategic is to assume that those who talk for the Bank are the same as those who act for the Bank. If so, we should expect that the "talker" can consciously decide when to disconnect words from action. Yet in reality, the Bank is not a unified actor, but rather a complex social organization in which talk and action (of which there is an immense amount at any given time) are often decoupled for structural reasons or simply lack of coordination. Achieving complete coordination in large and complex organizations with multiple units, such as the Bank, is exceedingly difficult, even under the most optimal hierarchical conditions. Brunsson makes this point:

> hypocrisy is taken as proof that an organization is not actually one actor, but consists of many independent and uncoordinated individuals or departments each being an actor on its owns. . . . Talk, decision and action are being performed by different actors, so we should not have such a high expectation for consistency as when one actor is in charge of all three steps.[52]

Thus, the essential point here is that we may misconstrue the nature of organized hypocrisy if we assume IOs to be unified rational actors. If we instead treat IOs, and specifically the Bank, as complex social organizations, we can discern patterns of unintended (or at least unanticipated) hypocrisy quite distinct from conventional notions of individual hypocrisy. In doing so, we can also uncover persuasive reasons for why hypocrisy, once revealed, is so difficult to resolve.

This is fundamentally linked to a second point. The theoretical and empirical description of organized hypocrisy thus far is too static. While aptly describing the sources or reasons for hypocrisy, it stops short of the deeper problem: organized hypocrisy rarely stays hidden. Particularly for a high-profile international organization like the Bank, sustaining a strategy of avoidance through organized hypocrisy is extremely difficult.

When exposed, organized hypocrisy has significant repercussions for the organization's reputation. This ironically undermines the very reason for hypocrisy, which is to symbolically embrace new policies and agendas to secure legitimacy and resources. Especially for public organizations dependent on political and financial support, revealed hypocrisy can be devastating. Watchdog groups and internal whistle-

---

[52] Brunsson 2003, 214.

blowers will seek to expose contradictions between the rhetoric of the organization's espoused theories and the reality of its theories-in-use. Hypocrisy ceases to be a survival tool and may become a liability. In such situations, organizational leaders may be forced to recognize and compelled to realign the organization's espoused theories and theories-in-use. Yet such realignment often entails organizational relearning and significant shifts in ideologies, norms, and habits that will result in behavioral changes by staff. It is much more than governance reform, which tends to focus on the formal restructuring of top management with the presumption of trickle-down change. Transforming the deeply embedded theories-in-use must cope with bureaucratic politics and pervasive elements of organizational culture that shape the behavior of staff throughout the entire organization. It is this level of change that is most critical for resolving organized hypocrisy.

RESOLVING ORGANIZED HYPOCRISY: THE CULTURE AND POLITICS OF CHANGE

The World Bank certainly fits the above description of a very complex and often uncoordinated bureaucracy. The president and senior management can more easily shift the rhetoric and formal structures of the Bank than they can change the norms, routines, and mind-sets of staff that drive daily operations. After all, it is not easy to compel ten thousand staff members to fall into line with new mandates, internalize new goals, and reorient their behavior. This is all the more difficult if new mandates and goals are inconsistent or if they clash fundamentally with preexisting policies and procedures, cultural norms, or entrenched interests favoring the status quo. In this instance, reform efforts intended to translate new talk into action may be thwarted by old-fashioned bureaucratic politics. New talk or decisions invoked by an individual or group in one part of the organization can provoke resistance from others elsewhere in the organization, preventing "the implementation of action and caus[ing] them to be less anxiously engaged in ensuring that the decision is actually implemented."[53]

This necessitates a sophisticated explanation of the process of organizational change: one that hinges not just on the analysis of external pressures for reform, but more importantly on the investigation of the internal bureaucratic politics and culture. My driving argument here is not that change does not occur in IOs. Quite the contrary,

[53] Brunsson 2003, 210.

change is a constant yet undertheorized aspect of IO life.[54] Rather, the key point from sociological theory once again is that bureaucratic politics and culture are notoriously difficult to manipulate or "reengineer" in a targeted manner, particularly in large and mature organizations.[55] Attempts to connect talk and action—to reorient staff expectations and behavior around new policy mandates and goals—will be very difficult if those new tasks run up against entrenched material interests or entail new ideologies, norms, and routines that clash with the existing culture.

What does it take to shift organizational behavior in a way that resolves the patterns of policy incompliance and mainstreaming gaps that constitute hypocrisy? From a sociological perspective, a central starting point for understanding the process and outcome of organizational change is organizational culture. Culture in turn sets the stage for bureaucratic politics and the battle over the ideas and resources that shape organizational talk and action.

Culture emerges or is created within organizations out of the basic human desire for stability, consistency, and meaning in an uncertain world.[56] The prevalence of uncertainty and "bounded rationality" in decision-making in a complex bureaucratic environment drives actors to construct routines that provide predictable means of responding to daily tasks as well as unforeseen problems.[57] Over time, actors within this bureaucratic environment come to recognize and internalize not only codified rules but also unstated norms, standard operating procedures, and shared understandings about "how things are done." Bureaucratic actors respond to these formal and informal rules from habit or a sense of appropriateness as much as from an individual strategic calculation of consequences.[58] These sets of routines become embodied as organizational culture, which affects staff behavior by setting formal and informal rules and monitoring and sanctioning behavior. Culture further shapes staff behavior by constructing symbolic systems and meanings that clarify how staff views the organization's very identity, goals, and purpose.[59]

[54] Kapur 2000b.
[55] Selznick 1957; Nelson and Winter 1982; Hannan and Freeman 1984; Levitt and March 1988; Hatch 1997; March, Schulz, and Zhou 2000; Burke 2002.
[56] Schein 1992, 11.
[57] Simon 1956; March and Simon 1958.
[58] Simon 1956; March and Simon 1958; and March and Olsen 1998. This view is consistent with what Jeffrey Checkel (2005) would describe as socialization involving "type II internalization."
[59] Scott 1995, 3.

Organizational culture is simply and broadly defined as the set of "basic assumptions" that affect how organizational actors interpret their environment, select and process information, and make decisions so as to maintain a consistent view of the world and the organization's role in it.[60] These basic assumptions encompass the ideologies, norms, language, and routines that comprise the meaning of organizational culture. Organizational *ideology* is defined as the underlying belief system or shared meanings specifying and justifying the primary goals of the organization, as well as the rational strategies for allocating resources and fulfilling core missions. *Norms* include the explicit and implicit principals, values, and underlying incentive structures that shape bureaucratic staff's expectations of what constitutes both instrumental and acceptable behavior and the overall "rules of the game" within the organization. The culture also embodies a distinct vocabulary or bureaucratic *language*, which enables the organization to create a common and efficient means of communicating the shared meanings of ideology and to consistently identify, categorize, and apply standard solutions to tasks. Finally, culture also encompasses the standard operating procedures or *routines* that integrate the ideologies, norms, and linguistic practices of organizations into behavioral regularities that reduce uncertainty and anxiety among staff by triggering stable and predictable responses to environmental stimuli, including external shocks in the market or the changing demands of the organization's political masters.

Much of the inertia or internal resistance to reform of organizational talk and especially action can be explained from the vantage of cultural dynamics. Inciting dramatic behavioral change across an entire organization is very difficult. Past the point of an organization's beginning, its culture becomes deeply embedded and reinforced as new staff members learn the culture through professional training, socialization, and both formal and informal incentive structures that encourage or punish certain behavior. As cultural elements become taken for granted, the assumptions underlying them cease to be questioned or debated and can become cognitive defense mechanisms.[61] As an organization ages, this culture becomes more inert, staff can become slavishly devoted to routines, and those seeking change become more limited in their ability to transform the organization's way of doing things. This culture becomes "solidified," and as a result organizational preferences and behavior are easily predicted from knowledge

---

[60] Schein 1992; Nelson 1995.

[61] Argyris and Schön 1978; Schein 1992. Lorsch (1985) calls this "strategic myopia." See also Levinthal and March 1993.

of these embedded norms and routines. We can thus predict when organized hypocrisy will occur by analyzing the conflicts between new demands and existing culture. Where new talk requires radical change in the underlying ideologies, language, norms, and routines governing action, we can expect hypocrisy to surface and be fairly resilient.

This depiction of an overly socialized staff within a tenacious organizational culture gives little credence to the possibility of rapid organizational change that would enable well-intended reformers from realigning organizational talk and action. Consisting of the taken-for-granted assumptions and internalized modes of thinking and acting, culture is rarely confronted or debated, and hence is extremely difficult to change.[62] An internal document written after the dismal 1987 reorganization of the Bank likened attempts to change the organizational culture to trying to move an iceberg: one can change the visible formal structures and rules that make up the small tip of the iceberg, but little can be done to strategically and quickly transform the hidden assumptions, incentives structures, and habits that inform that majority of decisions and actions that happen "beneath the surface."[63]

Such fatalistic tones may not be warranted. Assuming such cultural tenacity overdetermines the effect the culture has on perpetuating organized hypocrisy by resisting change. Indeed, culture-based accounts run the real danger of depicting organizational actors that are so socialized in their immediate bureaucratic environments that their thoughts and actions are fully dictated by the values, norms, and ideologies that they inevitably internalize as their tenure within the organization lengthens.[64] Actors in this sense are "cultural dupes" who become completely habit-driven and shaped solely by an unmoving "logic of appropriateness" that impels norm- or role-conforming behavior that is "locked in."[65] This is an entirely static notion that leaves little room for

---

[62] Schein 1992, 22. See also a similar argument by North (1990, 91) on "tenacious survival capacity" of culture that impedes change in the underlying informal institutions.

[63] World Bank 1987.

[64] Bourdieu 1990; Powell and DiMaggio 1991. See Checkel 2005 for a discussion of the "socialization" effects of the EU; although here we must make an important distinction between the various EU institutions that are more "forum" organizations or organizations with seconded staff and the Bank, which is a more autonomous service bureaucracy with permanent (nonseconded staff). I would argue that the possibilities for socialization of staff within the Bank are far greater than the potential for state socialization into European institutions.

[65] Swidler 1986; March and Olsen 1989, chap. 2; Barnett 2002. This is similar to what Checkel (2005) and Johnston (2005) describe as role-playing or "mimicking" behavior that may, over time, compel organizational actors to become more deeply socialized into their institutional settings.

strategic agency within the bureaucracy. It limits the possibility that, through open debate and direct engagement with culture, change in organizational talk and action can be engendered and organized hypocrisy reduced.[66]

Yet culture is not immutable, and organizational change does happen. The essential point here is to pay attention to where strategic agency plays into culture-based accounts of organization change, in particular by illuminating the tactics and effects of internal "policy advocacy" and "norm entrepreneurship."[67] One recent example is Bebbington et al.'s analysis of the evolution of the social capital debate within the World Bank.[68] The authors describe in fascinating detail the manner in which key actors and groups (including two of the authors themselves) confronted the dominant economistic and technocratic culture of the Bank to introduce the concept of social capital into its development discourse. The strategies they employed to "get their concepts onto the table" demonstrate the very nature of bureaucratic politics. The first front was a battle over *ideas*: grappling with resistant economists who did not see the value of "squishy" social concepts that did not fit well into their prevailing models or methodologies. For the social development advocates, the strategy became one of convincing these powerful economists of the compatibility and utility of the concept of social capital, framing the concept (including using the language of "capital") in a manner that would resonate and adapt to, rather than directly challenge, existing ideologies—a process that would actually change the way in which social capital and development were articulated in the Bank.

Once embraced more or less on an ideological level, however, the second battle centers on mainstreaming the concept in operations—a process of translating the talk about social capital into action. This is a struggle involving the disruption of previous operational incentives, norms, and routines. It affects the manner in which scarce resources are allocated, including the hiring of new social development staff and integrating social development programs more centrally into lending projects.

In the context of explaining hypocrisy and change, this attention to the interaction between strategic agency and bureaucratic culture is essential. The battles over ideas and resources are often fought on dif-

[66] Hatch 1993.

[67] On policy advocacy within IOs, see Kardam 1993. On "norm entrepreneurs," see Finnemore and Sikkink 1998.

[68] Bebbington et al. 2004, 2006.

ferent fronts with different outcomes, but with real prospects for change. By analyzing how these battles unfold, we are able to better understand *who* and *what* shapes the emergence of new organizational talk, decisions, and action and where disconnects may emerge, persist, or disappear.

Nonetheless, there is an important insight here regarding strategic agency and culture that is relevant to understanding the potential pitfalls of wide-scale organizational reform. A key lesson from both the 1987 Conable reorganization of the Bank and the 1997 Strategic Compact under Wolfensohn (see chapter 5) is the dilemma of replacing deeply rooted bureaucratic ideologies and norms. Changes to formal structures and rules (such as enacting new operational mandates, reorganizing the hierarchical structure, and hiring new staff) are not entirely effective as means of quickly redirecting organizational behavior. These plans presume that reformers can collectively and clearly excise preexisting incentive structures and rely upon staff, as fully rational actors, to respond to new incentive structures. It is simply not easy to disrupt mind-sets about "how things are done at the Bank."

At the same time, the goal incongruence that contributes to organized hypocrisy also exacerbates the challenges of reform. Not all those pushing for reform (from outside or inside the organization) may agree on the desirability and direction of change. In the case of the Bank, the various actors in the external authorizing and task environments have very different ideas of how they would like to see the institution reformed. Internally, the president, his numerous vice presidents, country directors, and managers on down the line are not always on the same page. As a result, senior management as a whole may end up sending mixed signals to lower-level staff about the "real" priorities and rules of the organization. Under persistent conditions of uncertainty and goal incongruity, staff members will likely default to existing expectations and behavior.

This returns us to the insight from chapter 1 about hypocrisy and reform: formal rule change incited by revealed hypocrisy may actually *worsen* the gap between organizational rhetoric and reality if it does not adequately resolve problems of goal incongruence (get the marching orders straight) or bluntly tackle likely areas of cultural resistance and inertia. One of the real dangers is rhetorical reform (an avoidance strategy once again): symbolic efforts to placate multiple demands for change by introducing new formal structures and mandates as well as proclaiming ambitious plans for reorganization and culture reform. "If, as the logic of organized hypocrisy holds, decisions by themselves substitute for action consistent with decisions, then attempts to influence an organization's actions through its formal decision-making processes may be worse than futile: they may be counterproductive."[69]

All these warnings resonate strongly in the case of recent attempts to reform the Bank. Consider for a moment prominent environmentalist and NGO activist Bruce Rich's comments on its hypocrisy:

> The key word for understanding the World Bank in the 1990s is "Disconnect"—the disconnect between its alleged purposes and its record, the disconnect between [President James D.] Wolfensohn's proclamations to change the Bank's culture, and the actual internal reforms needed to address the Bank's systemic failures to implement its most basic policies concerning poverty alleviation and environmental assessment. There is a disconnect between the speeding up of loan approval, weakening Bank policies, and claiming to root out the "culture of [loan] approval."[70]

Rich's comments target Wolfensohn's efforts to reform in the mid-1990s. In an attempt to placate the critics, the architects of the Strategic Compact initiative adopted a plethora of reform goals, many of which were mutually contradictory. As a result, as chapter 5 demonstrates, efforts to meet one goal undermined efforts to achieve goals in other areas. It seems absurdly clear in hindsight, but is worth stating. Reform intended to resolve areas of hypocrisy fell far short of desired results where it failed to address and alleviate the fundamental incongruity in goals that caused the original hypocrisies. This has subsequently led the Bank to openly discuss the need to "be more selective" in its activities, which in more cynical light may be interpreted as "deciding whom we can please, and forgetting about the others." For political organizations that depend upon legitimacy and resources from a wide array of sources, this is more easily said than done.

More critically, the post hoc evaluations of the Strategic Compact spoke volumes about the ability of reformers or "change entrepreneurs" to enact behavioral change through processes of structural reengineering and cultural resocialization: a classic dilemma of trying to balance the "hardware" and "software" of organizational change. Unsurprisingly, rapid change was observed where the goals of the reform program were compatible with the preexisting intellectual and operational culture (a conditional of cultural congruence). Where reform goals clashed with existing ideologies, norms, and routines, change was significantly more modest or nonexistent. This intuitively makes sense. Where newly espoused theories differ greatly from long-stand-

---

[69] Brunsson 2003, 221–22.
[70] Rich 2000, 15.

ing theories-in-use, the sheer complexity of transforming norms, mindsets, and habits will at best produce slow and incremental change. Overall, the internal evaluators of the Compact consistently note gaps between reform goals and actual outcomes, which they attribute to the inability of the reformers to use formal restructuring tools as levers for deeper cultural change. This allows us to speculate a bit further on the prospects for resolving hypocrisy through organizational reform. Where organized hypocrisy is the most blatant, it might be the easiest to expose but simultaneously the hardest to change.

Conclusion

Sociological theories, particularly resource dependency and institutionalism, ultimately provide persuasive means of explaining why we may expect organized hypocrisy to arise and persist in the Bank, notably under conditions of incongruent environmental and bureaucratic (cultural) goals. At the same time, given the nature of complex organizations and the relationship between bureaucratic culture and change, we can question the assumption that hypocrisy is in fact a fully conscious and deliberate act by the Bank to navigate the political waters of its external environment.[71] Indeed, even the most well-intended shifts in organizational "talk" may not be met by a correspondingly swift change in the informal institutions that govern bureaucratic action. The institutionalization of new formal rules and structures can quickly be marginalized if they clash with the existing dominant culture and vested interests, which may continue to be reinforced by interests outside the organization. The new development paradigms, policies, and norms that the Bank presents to the world may not be readily or consistently diffused and internalized throughout the organization in such a way as to truly change the way the collective entity goes about its business.

Organized hypocrisy in this sense may be less a conscious strategy for survival and more a consequence of the difficulty that external and internal reformers face in constantly reengineering the organization's research and operational cultures in line with an ever-changing menu of new development theories and tasks. Thus, the Bank's hypocrisy requires dual levels of explanation. On the one hand, hypocrisy is caused by contradictory environmental pressures, which compel the Bank to adopt competing goals to placate the multiple political and

---

[71] For a blunt discussion of the staff's view of the Bank's political environment, see the World Bank Staff Association 2001a.

financial masters on whom it depends for material resources and conferred legitimacy. On the other hand, organized hypocrisy is rooted in the tensions between new goals and the internal organizational culture, with disconnects emerging and persisting between espoused goals and real action where the new goals overtly challenge preexisting ideologies, norms, languages, and standard operating procedures.

In the end, the mutual constitution and influence of the external and internal environments on resulting talk and action must be sorted out before we can fully understand the dynamics of organized hypocrisy in the Bank. The next chapter is devoted to doing this. In first examining the "world's Bank," I describe the various entities that constitute the Bank's authorizing and task environments, and the nature and extent of its dependency on these actors for critical resources or legitimacy. I then turn to the "Bank's world" to depict the evolution and character of its distinct intellectual and operational culture, to discern where embedded ideologies, norms, language, and routines may create bureaucratic goals that may clash with the changing demands of the Bank's external environment.

CHAPTER THREE

The World's Bank and the Bank's World

AT FIRST GLANCE, the World Bank appears the afterthought of the representatives from the forty-four countries who convened in Bretton Woods, Connecticut, in July 1944. Global leaders, led by distinguished economist John Maynard Keynes from Great Britain and U.S. Assistant Treasury Secretary Harry Dexter White, were primarily preoccupied with establishing a stable international system of exchange rates and preventing the balance-of-payments crises that had caused the Great Depression and contributed to the outbreak of World War II. As a result, they spent a majority of the conference debating the structure and rules of the International Monetary Fund. Only in the last few days did they turn their attention to the proposal for an international bank for reconstruction and development. The driving idea behind such a bank was to supplement weak private financial markets in rebuilding war-torn Europe and, when necessary, lend money for specific development projects in the less economically advantaged countries of the Third World.

It would thus probably come as a great surprise to the Bretton Woods founders that the International Bank for Reconstruction and Development (IBRD), which opened for business on 25 July 1946 with a permanent staff of only seventy-two and a working budget of less than one billion dollars,[1] has now become the premiere international development aid organization. Composed of five institutions constituting the "World Bank Group," the multilateral agency as of 2007 was endowed with 185 member states, a permanent staff of around ten thousand in its Washington, D.C., headquarters and 109 mission offices, and a cumulative committed portfolio of well over $600 billion in outstanding loans, grants, and guarantees to the developing world.[2] Over the past six decades, the World Bank's core mission and strategies have also expanded. It was originally designed to lend primarily for specific projects, such as building roads, dams, and bridges. Today, the Bank's agenda ranges from traditional technical assistance in infra-

[1] Mason and Asher 1973, chap. 3.
[2] World Bank Annual Report 2006.

structure, rural development, education, and health, to sweeping adjustment lending for macroeconomic reform and sustainable development. Most recently, the Bank has moved toward promoting good governance, private sector growth, institutional development, and postconflict reconstruction, all underscored by an espoused commitment to the increased participation and empowerment of the poor.

United by the slogan "Our Dream is a World Free of Poverty," the Bank represents the largest multilateral aid organization in the world today, exercising a profound influence over the lives of billions of people in the developing world. Yet little agreement exists on the sources or the extent of the Bank's autonomy and power. Within the wealth of scholarly work written on the World Bank, one can find descriptions that depict it as a mere creature of its dominant member states (particularly the United States). Alternatively, it is viewed as a highly independent, insular, and self-serving agency whose actions reflect a narrowly defined set of bureaucratic interests and goals unaffected by the external environment. Such extremes, however, are simply unrealistic. The structure and organizational culture of the World Bank did not evolve in isolation from its task and authorizing environment, but rather in response to it. Distinct bureaucratic characteristics such as the ideologies, norms, language, and routines that are collectively defined as the Bank's culture have emerged and become to varying degrees embedded as a result of a dynamic interaction over time between various forces within the external material and normative environment and the interests and actions of the management and staff. Organizational culture creates the context in which internal bureaucratic politics—the struggle over resources and ideas—takes place. Once present, dominant elements of that culture also shape the way the Bank in turn *reacts* to its changing environment, serving as a filter through which it interprets and responds (or fails to respond) to new demands and problems. To truly understand why the Bank talks and act as it does, it is important to unpack both "worlds." But first is it essential to provide a brief background, specifically a description of how the Bank is organized and governed.

ORGANIZATIONAL STRUCTURE OF THE WORLD BANK

The World Bank Group consists of five interrelated agencies: the International Bank for Reconstruction and Development (IBRD), the International Development Agency (IDA), the International Finance Corporation (IFC), the Multilateral Investment Guarantee Agency (MIGA), and the International Centre for Settlement of Investment Disputes

(ICSID) (see figure 3.1). The largest and oldest is the International Bank for Reconstruction and Development. Established in 1945, the IBRD provides loans and technical assistance at near-market interest rates to middle-income and creditworthy poorer countries.[3] It funds these loans in part through the *paid-in capital* subscriptions of its member states, who also pledge *callable capital* (nearly nine times the amount of paid-in capital) that may be tapped if the Bank runs into financial trouble (something that has never happened in its history). However, the IBRD receives the bulk of its funds for development loans by borrowing on the world's private capital markets. Because of its strong backing by government callable capital and the stable rates of return (6–7 percent), the Bank's bonds are highly attractive and have consistently earned triple-A ratings since 1959. Although the IBRD is technically not a profit-making organization, it has earned a substantial net income from the sale of its bonds and the interest rates placed on its loans every year since 1948.

The International Development Association is the second main branch and "soft-loan" window of the World Bank Group and shares the IBRD's staff and management. The IDA was established in 1960 in response to concerns that the poorest of the developing countries could not afford the high interest rates of the IBRD loans. Accordingly, the IDA was designed to provide loans or "credits" at no interest rate, with ten-year grace periods and loan maturities of twenty, thirty-five, or forty years. Only the poorest countries qualify for IDA loans, and are defined within the organizational structure as "Part II" member states, totaling 137 in 2007. "Part I" member states (28 total) are the IDA's donors and sole source of funds beyond loan repayments and allocations from the IBRD's funds. These funds come from triannually negotiated replenishments, which, as discussed below, are a primary means for major donor states to exercise influence over the World Bank. Donor contributions accounted for more than half of the $33 billion replenishment of the IDA in 2005.

The three remaining institutions are less frequently studied, but nonetheless important components of the Bank's overall organization. The International Finance Corporation (IFC) was created in 1956 to further encourage private business and foreign investment in developing countries. Its most important distinction is that it can issue loans and equity financing for private sector projects without a government guarantee—something that is specifically forbidden in the mandates

---

[3] These loans usually have a grace period of three to five years and a maturity period of fifteen to twenty years. Loans may only be directed to governments or agencies with government guarantees.

International Bank for Reconstruction and Development (IBRD) est. 1945	International Development Association (IDA) est. 1960
185 members FY2006 Lending: $14.1 billion for 112 new operations in 33 countries Cumulative Lending: $420.2 billion	165 members FY2006 Lending: $9.5 billion for 167 new operations in 59 countries Cumulative Lending: $170 billion

International Finance Corporation (IFC) est. 1956	International Centre for Settlement of Investment Disputes (ICSID) est. 1966	Multilateral Investment Guarantee Agency (MIGA) est. 1988
178 members FY2006 Commitments: $6.7 billion for 284 projects in 66 countries Committed portfolio: $21.6 billion	143 members FY2006 Cases Registered: 26 Total Cases Registered: 210	167 members FY2006 Guarantees Issued: $1.3 billion Cumulative Guarantees Issued: $16.0 billion

Figure 3.1. The World Bank Group
Source: *2006 World Bank Annual Report*

of the IBRD and IDA. Established in 1988, the Multilateral Investment Guarantee Agency (MIGA) plays a similar role in facilitating the flow of private capital flows to the developing world by offering guarantees to foreign investors against losses caused by noncommercial risks such as expropriation of property, civil war and currency inconvertibility. Finally, the International Centre for Settlement of Investment Disputes, created in 1966, does not offer financial assistance, but rather serves essentially as an international arbitration agency for states and foreign investors.[4]

The World Bank is governed by four boards of executive directors (one each for the IBRD, IDA, IFC, and MIGA). These boards are composed of five appointed directors (representing the major donor states)

[4] Because the ICSID is not a lending arm of the World Bank or central to the organization's identity and activities, it will not be discussed in this book. The IFC and MIGA are more important than the ICSID in the overall composition of the Bank's lending portfolio and range of products. However, since they are structurally and financially independent from the IBRD and IDA (the main project and program "heart" of the World Bank), they should be treated separately and thus are also not central to the discussion presented here. "World Bank" (or simply "the Bank") will refer only to the IBRD and IDA.

Table 3.1
Executive Directors Voting Status, FY2007

IBRD	IDA
1. United States (16.41%)	1. United States (13.01%)
2. Japan (7.87%)	2. Japan (10.11%)
3. Germany (4.49%)	3. Germany (6.49%)
4. France (4.31%)	4. United Kingdom (5.17%)
5. United Kingdom (4.31%)	5. France (4.14%)
6. Belgium (10 countries; 4.81%)	6. Norway (6 countries; 5.16%)
7. Mexico (8 countries; 4.50%)	7. Belgium (9 countries; 4.64%)
8. Netherlands (12 countries; 4.47%)	8. Ethiopia (19 countries; 4.58%)
9. Canada (13 countries; 3.85%)	9. Canada (10 countries; 4.38%)
10. Brazil (8 countries; 3.56%)	10. India (4 countries; 4.19%)
11. Italy (7 countries; 3.51%)	11. Mauritius (24 countries; 3.93%)
12. South Korea (13 countries; 3.45%)	12. Netherlands (10 countries; 3.90%)
13. India (4 countries; 3.40%)	13. Switzerland (7 countries; 3.82%)
14. Ethiopia (21 countries; 3.36%)	14. Italy (5 countries; 3.40%)
15. Norway (8 countries; 3.34%)	15. Saudi Arabia (3.36%)
16. Pakistan (7 countries; 3.19%)	16. South Korea (3.24%)
17. Switzerland (8 countries; 3.04%)	17. Brazil (8 countries; 3.02%)
18. Kuwait (13 countries; 2.91%)	18. Malaysia (10 countries; 2.83%)
19. China (2.79%)	19. Kuwait (11 countries; 2.26%)
20. Saudi Arabia (2.79%)	20. Mexico (7 countries; 2.22%)
21. Russian Federation (2.79%)	21. Pakistan (7 countries; 2.20%)
22. Malaysia (11 countries; 2.54%)	22. China (2.00%)
23. Argentina (6 countries; 2.32%)	23. Argentina (5 countries; 1.61%)
24. Mauritius (24 countries; 2.0%)	24. Russian Federation (0.31%)

Source: Data from www.worldbank.org.

and nineteen elected directors (representing country groups) (see figure 3.2). In practice, the same twenty-four executive directors serve on all four boards, which are responsible for "general operations," including formal approval of all lending decisions and selection of the Bank president. Voting within the boards is not egalitarian as in the United Nations General Assembly. Instead, as negotiated at Bretton Woods, each director has a weighted number of votes, determined roughly by the monetary contributions of his or her country. By tradition, decisions are usually made by consensus. By structure and historical convention, the majority of influence is held by the five major donor states (United States, Japan, Germany, United Kingdom, and France). In fiscal year 2007, these five states collectively held 37.30 percent and 38.92 percent of the voting shares on the IBRD and IDA executive boards.

By tradition, the boards of executive directors always select an American to serve as president of the World Bank group and chairman of the board. The president, thus far always a nominee of the U.S. administration, serves five-year, renewable terms. The president in turn appoints the managing directors, vice presidents, chief financial officer, chief economist, and network heads who run the research and operational units.[5] The bulk of the administrative budget is devoted to operations, governed by a series of vice presidential units covering six regionally defined areas of the world, with thirty-nine country directors directly beneath them. There are also four "sector" or thematic networks on issues of human development, environmental and socially sustainable development, poverty reduction and economic management, and finances. Although research is conducted throughout the Bank, the majority of the high-profile research is conducted through the Development Economics Department (DEC), run by the chief economist.

As previously mentioned, the Bank's headquarters are in Washington, D.C., where approximately 70 percent of the total staff are currently located. The remaining staff resides in 109 mission offices. The Bank prides itself on a highly diverse staff, including 44.7 percent of the headquarters staff who are national citizens of Part II member countries.[6]

THE WORLD'S BANK

The external environment of the World Bank has changed dramatically over the past half century, at different junctures introducing new external actors and forces that have to varying degrees been able to strongly shape the Bank's autonomy and influence. As one might expect, the primary external factors are the interests and power of the organization's most dominant donor and client states. On the one hand, these member states grant considerable authority and independence to the Bank through various delegated functions. On the other hand, they exercise considerable material and normative power through formal and informal oversight and control mechanisms that at times check the autonomous actions of the Bank's bureaucracy. This is especially true of the United States, possessing the strongest leverage, in both financial and ideological terms, over the World Bank throughout its history.

---

[5] The Bank's organizational chart is updated biannually and available on the Bank's official website. The exact number of managing directors, vice presidents, and network heads changes quite often, depending on the initiatives of the president. As of October 2007, there were two managing directors and twenty-one vice presidents.

[6] World Bank 2001a, 63, table A3.2.

However, confining the discussion to member states only leaves out several other critical environmental entities on which the Bank is dependent for materials or conferred legitimacy and who simultaneously represent sources of incongruent goals that are identified here as contributing to organized hypocrisy.[7] These include the private capital markets and epistemic communities of scholars in the international development regime, both of which collectively have had discernible effects upon the development paradigms and practices of the World Bank. More recently, the growth in the number of other multilateral and bilateral development agencies has created an uncertain environment for the Bank, particularly in terms of competition over scarce resources in an era of declining official development assistance and increasing demands for interagency donor coordination that requires elusive bureaucratic cooperation. At the same time, one of the most spectacular features of the Bank's changing external environment is the rise of the "fire alarms" or watchdog groups in the form of international and local nongovernmental organizations and civil society groups, many of which have seriously challenged the World Bank's legitimacy. Finally, it is important not to miss the more immediate checks and balances on the Bank in the form of the independent monitoring and evaluation units as well as the new Inspection Panel, all of which have become more important in recent years as means of holding the Bank accountable for its effectiveness as well as its rhetorical and actual behavior.

The Bank's Donor States

The World Bank has 185 member states, theoretically possessing the means to control the behavior of the organization through their financial contributions, demands for its services, and formal representation through the Board of Governors and Board of Executive Directors. In practice, however, only a few of the major donor and client states exert significant influence over the institution. As mentioned above, five donor states (the United States, Japan, Germany, France, and the United Kingdom) represent the major shareholders. In the case of the IDA, which is heavily dependent upon donor contributions, these five states account for nearly $88 billion, or 71 percent of the IDA's cumulative subscriptions and contributions.

The most powerful donor state is obviously the United States, which in 2007 controlled 16.41 percent of the votes on the IBRD board (giving it de facto veto power over any charter amendment proposals) and

---

[7] For similar arguments, see Kapur 2002a; and World Bank Staff Association 2001a.

13.01 percent of the votes on the IDA board.[8] The United States itself merits more attention here due to its disproportionate power over the Bank. But its sources of influence, particularly the formal power wielded by the weighted voting system and IDA replenishment process, are by and large similar to those of the other donor states. We can thus generalize from the case of the United States some essential points about the relationship between the Bank and its donor states writ large while simultaneously understanding the unique leverage of the United States that makes the Bank appear so susceptible to U.S. pressure.

U.S. influence derives historically from its financial position during the Bank's formative years. Although the U.S. share of overall member state contributions to the institutions of the Bank Group has fallen over time, in the 1950s and 1960s U.S. input accounted for nearly 35 percent of the total paid-in capital of the IBRD and thus 35 percent of the votes on the IBRD executive board. Moreover, during the postwar economic recovery period, when the European member states were still net recipients of the Bank's funds, nearly 85 percent of the Bank bonds sold on private capital markets were denominated in American dollars and traded on U.S. markets.[9] This theoretically meant that the United States could influence the Bank's policy and practices by threatening to deny it access to the U.S. private capital market if the government decided not to pledge its backing of Bank bonds through callable capital. Without such support, the Bank would have been unable to earn the triple-A rating that made its bonds so attractive. Eventually, as the European economies bounced back and their currencies became fully convertible, the U.S. share of the total paid-in capital began to decline, and its hold over the Bank's access to private capital funds diminished as Bank bonds attracted European buyers.

However, just as the IBRD's financial dependency on the United States was decreasing, the creation of the IDA in 1960 opened another venue for leverage by the United States and other donor states. The IDA was created as a concessional lending arm to service the poorest developing countries who cannot afford to borrow from the IBRD and who lacked the credit ratings necessary to attract private capital. The IDA is funded in large part through donor state contributions, which are renegotiated every three years.[10] The U.S. share of this replen-

---

[8] The U.S. contribution to the IDA in the thirteenth replenishment round in 2002 (IDA 13) equaled 20.12 percent of all contributions. However, in IDA 14 (ratified 30 June 2005), the U.S. contribution temporarily dropped to 13.78 percent in FY2005.

[9] Gwin 1994, 7–9. See also Mason and Asher 1973; Ascher 1990; Brown 1992; Kapur, Lewis, and Webb 1997; Kapur 2002a; and the World Bank Staff Association 2001a.

[10] The IDA also gets a portion of its funds from repayment on past loans and contributions from the IBRD. Recent decline in middle-income country borrowing from the IBRD, however, has raised concerns that if IBRD profits fall, the IDA will become more

ishment has to be approved *every year* by the relevant authorizing and appropriations committees of the U.S. Congress. This gives Congress the opportunity to place demands on the Bank by threatening to with-hold funds or block IDA replenishment agreements if the Bank does not comply with its wishes. For example, in 1993, the chairman of the House authorizing committee informally told Bank management that the U.S. contribution to the tenth replenishment of the IDA (IDA 10) would not be forthcoming until the Bank fulfilled two conditions: the adoption of a public informational disclosure policy and the establish-ment of an Independent Inspection Panel empowered to hear com-plaints of any group negatively affected by the failure of the Bank to comply with its own policies.

Congress may also pass legislation that directs how the U.S.-ap-pointed executive director may vote on certain policies and projects. For example, in 1972, Congress passed the Gonzales Amendment, which prohibited U.S. executive directors in any of the multilateral development banks from voting in favor of the use of foreign aid to countries where U.S. private property had been expropriated by the national government.[11] In 1978, Congress mandated opposition to all loans for the production of export commodities that were in surplus on the world market and thus could harm American producers.[12] In 1989, in response to growing NGO concerns, Congresswoman Nancy Pelosi sponsored an amendment that requires the U.S. executive direc-tors of the International Financial Institutions to abstain from any vote on a loan that would have a significant impact on the environment and did not make publicly accessible an environmental assessment for the project at least 120 days prior to the board's vote.[13] More recently, during the IDA 14 replenishment process, the United States made several demands for new policies to ensure "results measurement" in IDA lending decisions, such as the strengthening of the Country Policy and Institutional Assessment (CPIA) process. The IDA 14 agreement,

---

reliant on donor contributions. Contributions from donor states currently amount to $18 billion of the $33 billion that will be made available to IDA borrowers FY2006 to FY2009 (IDA 14). The remaining funds come from internal Bank sources, including repayment on past IDA loans and transfers from the IBRD net income, and (more recently) IFC net income. Source: http://web.worldbank.org/WBSITE/EXTERNAL/EXTABOUTUS/IDA/0,,contentMDK:20189587~menuPK:413944~pagePK:83988~piPK:84004~theSitePK:73154.00.html, accessed 19 March 2006.

[11] Expropriation of United States Property; loan restrictions, 22 USC 284j (2001). This was a response to earlier expropriation of U.S. private property in Guyana and Peru. See Schoultz 1982; Ascher 1990; Brown 1992; and Gwin 1994.

[12] HR2506, sec. 514 (2001).

[13] HR2494, International Development and Finance Act of 1989, PL101-240 (1989), sec. 521.

signed in June 2005, also incorporated a larger "grants component" to all IDA lending (30 percent) and an increased amount of IDA funds dedicated to private sector development.[14]

There are limits on the hold of the United States over the Bank. A no vote or abstention by the U.S. executive director rarely blocks a board decision. A 1994 report from the U.S. General Accounting Office notes, for example, that between 1990 and 1993, the U.S. executive directors to the World Bank voted no twenty-two times and abstained ninety-eight times on IBRD or IDA loans proposed to the Board, because of an explicit legislative requirements or specific U.S. economic and policy concerns.[15] All 120 loan proposals were approved.

Nonetheless, one must not discount the informal influence of the U.S. government and the executive director, who more often than not exercise voice prior to an actual board vote. Voting on the executive board is largely by consensus, and thus the United States may be highly effective in persuading others to its position prior to any formal vote. For example, U.S. opposition to the Allende regime essentially stopped lending to Chile between 1970 and 1973.[16] As William Ascher wrote in 1990, "any signal of displeasure by the U.S. executive director has an almost palpable impact on the Bank leadership and staff, whether the signal is an explicit complaint or simply the executive director's request for information on a problem. . . . Criticism or even neutral comments about the Bank from the U.S. President, the Treasury secretary, senators, and others reverberates throughout the institution."[17]

U.S. influence via the IDA replenishment process is not always a sure way to influence the Bank. Threats to withhold IDA replenishments have been undermined by conflicts of interest between the United States and the other major donor states. In the mid-1990s, increased concern over U.S. attempts to tie aid contributions to conditions mandating that funds be used in part to hire American contractors led the European and Japanese governments to form an Interim Trust Fund within the IDA that would effectively deny U.S. companies a chance to bid on development aid projects.[18] The rise of trust funds in general, which are accounted for separately from the Bank's own

[14] Sanford 2005, 3–4.

[15] United States General Accounting Office 1994, 19.

[16] Ayres 1983; Ascher 1990, 124; and Gwin 1994. Sanford 1982 and Brown 1992, however, argue that U.S. opposition did not result in a freeze in Bank lending, but rather the Bank decided to reject loan proposals to Chile during those years because of concerns over their economic feasibility.

[17] Ascher 1990, 124. See also Gwin 1994, 56.

[18] United States General Accounting Office 1995a, 20.

resources, is a possible indication of where other member states have sought avenues of influence over the Bank's research and technical assistance outside of the normal IBRD and IDA subscriptions. The trust funds grant specified amounts of bilateral money for "special projects," allowing the donors more direct control over the substance of operations. Japan, for example, has actively used trust funds as a way to counter U.S. ideological influence over the Bank. In the early 1990s, the Japanese government funded the now infamous East Asian Miracle Report (discussed later), which was intended to challenge the "U.S. neoliberal" economic paradigm dominant in the Bank's research. Currently, Japan funds its own Social Development Fund.

Conflicts between donor states are indeed increasingly common. The thirteenth replenishment negotiations of the IDA were held up for over three months past the December 2001 deadline due to a dispute between the United States and its European counterparts over a condition the United States attached mandating at least 50 percent of IDA disbursements be in the form of grants rather than loans.[19] According to one official from the U.S. Treasury Department at the time, there was little hope of a consensus that would enable the United States to realize its interests.[20] In the end, donors agreed that grants would comprise 18–21 percent of all IDA 13 aid.[21]

All of this seems to indicate that the United States is not always able to impose its interests on the Bank. Jonathan Sanford points out that the European donors have demonstrated an interest in attaining greater influence over the IDA by increasing their relative shares of contributions and votes, thus balancing the U.S. influence derived from its financial leverage. He notes that the Europeans pushed very hard during the IDA 14 negotiations to increase the overall size of the replenishment, contributing more themselves even as U.S. donations declined. This may mean that "the European countries (EU members control over 31 percent of the vote in the World Bank) may wish to exercise a larger leadership role than before in the MDBs."[22] If the Euro-

---

[19] For that matter, the U.S. Treasury appears to be at odds with the U.S. Congress over the extent to which the United States should push for increased grants within the IDA. The European and Japanese position called for between 5 and 15 percent of IDA funds to be given in the form of grants. They oppose higher percentages out of concerns that borrowing countries will not have the incentive to properly use the funds or ensure the effective implementation and sustainability of projects.

[20] Comments of Brian Crowe, U.S. Treasury Department, to the Tuesday Group meeting at Oxfam International, Washington, D.C., 5 February 2002.

[21] Sanford 2005, 3.

[22] Sanford 2005, 4.

pean states should decide to act collectively, as they do in the Ministerial Rounds of the World Trade Organization, it could introduce a whole new dynamic to the politics of the Bank's board that challenges traditional understandings of U.S. dominance.

There is in fact growing evidence that the European donor states are starting to actively use their power of the purse to push their own agendas. Just prior to the 2006 annual meetings in Singapore, Britain's secretary of state for international development, Hilary Benn, announced that Britain would withhold a £50 million payment to protest the conditions the Bank attached to its aid. More specifically, Benn's attack was directed to Paul Wolfowitz's anticorruption measures, which included the suspension or cancellation of loans to countries. Benn, along with other European donors, strongly objected to Wolfowitz's apparent willingness to sidestep the board in these decisions. In a speech in London on 13 September 2006, Benn argued that "when problems arise, some people argue that we should suspect our aid or withdraw it completely. I don't agree. Why should a child be denied education? Why should a mother be denied healthcare? Or an H.I.V.-positive person AIDS treatment, just because someone or something in their government is corrupt?"[23] This European pressure was felt even more strongly in April and May 2006, during the Wolfowitz scandal, when the European donor states (led by Germany and the United Kingdom) openly threatened to redirect their aid monies away toward other aid organizations if the leadership crisis was not satisfactorily resolved.

Despite the signs of a growing European counterweight to U.S. influence that is creating a greater sense of conflicting principal preferences, the United States continues to possess a soft power over the Bank unmatched by other member states. This stems from the geographical and ideological vantage point of the United States. Despite strong objections from Keynes, U.S. Treasury Secretary Henry Morgenthau insisted in 1944 that the World Bank headquarters be located in Washington, D.C.[24] The close proximity to the White House and Treasury Department has facilitated behind-the-scenes interaction that has permitted the United States to promote its foreign policy interests within the international organization.[25] Indirectly, the use of English as

---

[23] Benn 2006.

[24] Mason and Asher 1973.

[25] The U.S. executive director, for example, is in daily contact with the Working Group on Multilateral Assistance, which consists of representatives from the State Department, Commerce Department, International Development Cooperation Agency, Federal Reserve, and Export-Import Bank, as well as the Treasury. Also, the U.S. Agency for International Development is given a mandate for the Early Project Notification Sys-

the Bank's primary official language and the heavy recruitment of staff trained in Anglo-American universities has strongly affected the character of consulting, research, technical assistance, and agenda setting.[26]

Moreover, the United States has historically had nearly free reign in the choice of the Bank's president, as well as a say in the appointment of its chief economist. In 1981, for example, the Reagan administration strongly pushed the nomination of A. W. Clausen to replace outgoing president Robert McNamara. A former commercial banker, Clausen was strongly sympathetic to the free market and laissez-faire economic ideology that characterized Reagan's domestic and foreign economic policies. Once in office, Clausen replaced chief economist Hollis Chenery with Anne Krueger. Krueger was a strict supply-side economist who replaced nearly the entire research and policy staff with likeminded individuals.

More recently, in the spring of 2000, then U.S. Treasury secretary Lawrence Summers (chief economist of the Bank in the early 1990s) voiced strong opposition to the Bank's chief economist, Joseph Stiglitz. In published articles and speeches, Stiglitz had criticized the "Washington Consensus" underpinning the Bank's thinking and had gone as far as to publicly demonize the International Monetary Fund (and the United States by association) for its handling of the East Asian financial crises.[27] Perceiving Stiglitz's position as undermining the U.S. support of economic development via export-led growth and free trade, Summers pressured then president James Wolfensohn to censure and then eventually dismiss Stiglitz in the months leading up to renewal of Wolfensohn's five-year term as president.[28]

The tide may be changing. The Wolfowitz scandal in April–May 2007 has indisputably eroded the soft power of the United States on the Bank's board. The unwillingness of the Bush administration to back down from its support of Wolfowitz in early May severely damaged relations within the board, producing splits between pro-Wolfowitz (United States and Japan) and anti-Wolfowitz (European) donor states. Even before this, Wolfowitz's nomination for the presidency by the U.S. Treasury Department in the spring 2005 incited contentious debate over the U.S. prerogative of selecting the president and the tacit agreement that the president always be an American. Although the

---

tem, in which it monitors the preliminary design of Bank projects in-country and alerts the U.S. executive director to potential problems. United States General Accounting Office 1994, 20.

[26] Kapur, Lewis, and Webb 1997, 2.

[27] Stiglitz 1999, 2000; Naim 2000.

[28] Wade 2001c, 2002.

Europeans have historically gone along with the U.S. choice (as they did again in 2007 with Robert Zoellick's nomination) in order to protect their right to choose the head of the IMF, this gentleman's agreement appears to be losing support. Perhaps more than any other time in the Bank's history, the conflicts between donor states are publicly visible, creating an unprecedented governance crisis that is producing within the Bank a pervasive sense of unease about the future.

Developing Country "Clients"

The predominance of the U.S. hard and soft power over the Bank overshadows that of the organization's other member states, in particular the borrowing states. Conventional wisdom lends little leverage to the developing countries that heavily rely on the Bank's loans and grants. Failure to comply with loan conditions, or defaulting on loans, is a strong signal to private lenders that the country is not "creditworthy," and many private capital vendors will not consider lending to a nation that does not qualify for funding by the Bank or the IMF. As a result, for many of the poorest countries of the world who would not under any circumstances qualify for private commercial loans or who cannot afford higher interest rates, the IBRD and IDA are among the very few sources of funding.[29]

Nonetheless, there are two important reasons to see this dependent relationship in reverse, giving borrowers the upper hand and compelling the Bank to pay attention to their interests. One overt form of power available to the Bank's largest client states is the threat of loan default. Default essentially translates into nonpayment on loan principals or interest, which reduces the Bank's annual net income. Such defaults happened in the past in the smaller member states (Congo, Liberia, Iraq, and Syria) with little impact on the Bank's total loan portfolio. However, as Bruce Rich argues, in the early 1990s, the real possibility of default by the Bank's largest borrowers, such as India, Brazil, and Indonesia, could have put between 11 and 13.5 percent of its entire portfolio in a nonaccrual status and leave the Bank with its first annual loss.[30] At the end of the fiscal year 2001, the total IBRD and IDA cumulative lending to India, Brazil, and Indonesia equaled nearly $116 billion, or nearly 24 percent of total IBRD and IDA cumulative lending.[31] By 2005, the IDA's top ten borrowers alone accounted for over $5 bil-

---

[29] Hancock 1989, 5. See also Kapur 2002a.
[30] Rich 1994, 185.
[31] World Bank Annual Report 2001, 126–28.

lion of the $8.7 billion lent by IDA in that year—over $1 billion of which was borrowed by India.[32] In such a scenario of loan default by the biggest IDA borrowers, the Bank would have to tap the callable capital of its major donor states—something it has never done. This would not only cause great concern and ire among the donor states, but would also risk the Bank's bond ratings on the private capital markets and thereby weaken its primary source of funds that help to reduce its dependence upon donor state contributions and enhance its relative autonomy.

A second form of influence available to borrowing countries comes from the Bank's own organizational culture, which will be discussed at length in the next section. Larger borrowing countries, cognizant of staff members' imperative to lend money and get projects approved, often resist conditions during loan negotiations. Likewise, once conditions are in place, many of the biggest and geopolitically important borrowers, such as Russia and Brazil, will not comply, under the logic that the Bank (as well as the IMF) will continue to release loan tranches anyway because of political and economic imperatives or reluctance on the part of staff and management to abandon programs in progress.[33]

Borrowing country influence over the Bank today is probably most visible in terms of the pressure stemming from the measurable decline in demand from middle-income countries at the same time that the Bank is facing increasing competition from private capital markets.[34] After all, it is a for-profit institution and a *bank*, which means its raison d'être is to lend money. Middle-income countries are thus the Bank's bread and butter; borrowing from the IBRD (the hard-loan window) and thus underwriting the Bank's primary source of financial autonomy and sustainability. The IBRD's profits not only allow the Bank to expand its lending and thus grow as an organization, but also in part fund the activities of the IDA, thus making the Bank less dependent on donor states.

However, middle-income countries such as China, Russia, and Brazil have recently weaned themselves from Bank funds and turned increasingly toward private capital markets, where commercial interest rates are declining and loans are more attractive than Bank funds that come with numerous strings attached (see below). According to an evaluation conducted by the Bank's Independent Evaluation Group in 2007, the seventy-nine borrowing countries classified by the Bank as

[32] World Bank Annual Report 2005.
[33] Nelson 1995; Storey 2000.
[34] Zhang 2004; Linn 2004.

middle income (meaning annual GDP per capita ranging between $1,000 and $6,000) have over the last twelve years repaid an annual average of $3.8 billion more than they have taken out in new loans. The report also notes that loans from the Bank accounted in 2005 for just 0.6 percent of the national investment of these middle-income countries, down from twice that amount in 1995.[35] Overall, IBRD disbursements have fallen 30 percent in real terms since 1995, due primarily to the steep decline in external sovereign borrowing in developing countries.[36] Such a dramatic turn of events has prompted the Bank to identify the renewal and expansion of services to middle-income countries as one of the three priorities of its recently drafted long-term strategy framework.[37]

Moreover, some of the largest borrowing countries of the Bank are now becoming potential lenders, and thus competitors to the Bank.[38] China itself has declared its intent to start lending more for development, particularly in Africa, where the Bank has placed heavy conditions on governance and corruption in its lending decisions. This competitive threat is quite credible, considering China's geopolitical interests in the region and its foreign currency reserves of over one trillion U.S. dollars. Likewise, President Hugo Chávez of Venezuela, in a characteristic fit of anti-Americanism, launched in the spring 2007 an idea for a Banco del Sur (Bank of the South). Chávez envisions the new development bank, funded and run by Latin American countries (largely with a current surplus of oil revenues), to displace the World Bank, IMF, and Inter-American Development Bank, which he perceives as dominated by the United States and the "Washington Consensus."[39]

Overall, these demand-side shocks and rise of unexpected competitors put the Bank in financial peril. In response, since the mid-1990s the Bank has sought to engender a more "client-focused" image, and accordingly been less willing to readily concede (beyond rhetoric) to demands by donor states and NGOs for increasing safeguard and

---

[35] World Bank Independent Evaluation Group 2007, xiii–xiv. See also World Bank Independent Evaluation Group 2006a.

[36] World Bank 2007a, vi.

[37] World Bank 2007a, vi.

[38] Resource dependency models identify the rise of competitors as a material resource pressure that threatens organizational security. For example, according to Barnett and Coleman (2005), the rise of potential competitors in the 1960s significantly increased Interpol's insecurity regarding state funding and thereby prompted Interpol to acquiesce to state demands to take on counterterrorism activities.

[39] See "Hugo Chavez Moves into Banking," *The Economist*, 12 May 2007, 39–40.

other loan conditions that repel big borrowers.[40] It has also visibly responded to borrower pressures by renewing its attention to large infrastructure lending and by allowing client countries to use their own auditing and procurement methods, over the strong objections of activists who see large infrastructure projects as the most likely source of ecological devastation and corruption. The credibility of client states' threats to stop borrowing (and in so doing, make the Bank more responsive to their demands) is reinforced by critical changes in private capital markets.

Private Capital Markets

Private capital markets are not "actors" that possess any formal delegation authority over the Bank. But as a whole, the market is capable of creating significant pressure. On the one hand, there is the Bank's financial dependence, in the form of the sale of bonds on the world's stock markets, which provide a substantial base of funds from which the Bank can lend to client countries. These earnings help to reduce the IBRD's dependence on member states' capital subscriptions, and thus buffer the organization from political interference leveraged through financial control. However, this also means that the Bank's authorizing environment includes the interest of private financiers, whose conservative Wall Street mentality has historically pushed the Bank toward areas of project lending and technical assistance that are perceived to produce tangible economic rates of return.[41] Particularly in the early formative years of the organization, before repayment on loans started to contribute to the base funding pool, many scholars believed this relationship with private capital narrowed the Bank's development agenda. Later, "Wall Street" interests were seen to counter demands for increased attention to social and human development issues, preferring the Bank focus on large infrastructure projects.

More recently, as discussed briefly above, leading governmental officials have noticed a new competitive relationship between the Bank and private capital markets that has affected the demand for its products. This is the result of the dramatic increase in private capital flows

---

[40] This was a critical issue during the Strategic Compact reform period (see chapter 6).

[41] Payer 1982; Kapur 2000a. As discussed in chapter 5, perceived competition from private capital flows also contributed to pressures for organizational reform in the Bank in the mid-1990s.

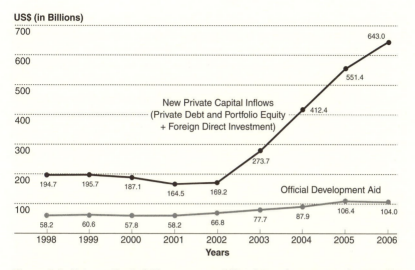

Figure 3.2. Private Capital Flows versus Official Development Aid, 1998–2006
Source: *Global Monitoring Report 2007* and World Bank Development Indicators 2007

to the developing world since the early 1990s. A report of the General Accounting Office in 1996 found that in 1994 the private sector accounted for 72.5 percent of new foreign resource flows to all developing countries, while the World Bank only accounted for 3.3 percent.[42] As demonstrated in figure 3.2, in 2006 private capital flows reached a record $643 billion and private remittances exceeded $200 billion, in comparison to net official development aid of $103 billion.

By the middle to late 1990s, conservative critics, including the U.S. Congressional Advisory Committee led by economist Alan Meltzer, were arguing that the increased availability of private capital meant that many of the Bank's lending services were no longer needed. Therefore, the Bank should shift its activities toward the disbursement of grants to the poorest countries that cannot attract private capital (in other words, where the finance gap still exists). This is a fate that could lead the Bank to near financial dependence on the IDA's donors (thus heightening its organizational insecurity). Yet the proposal is seen by those on the political right and left as a way to prevent the odious debt burdens that now plague many of the least developed countries.[43] These arguments have perhaps resonated more strongly in the United

[42] United State General Accounting Office 1996, 27.
[43] See, for example, the Meltzer et al. 2000; O'Neill 2001a and 2001b; and Lerrick 2006.

States than in other donor countries. As already mentioned, the push to increase the proportion of grants over loans was a major point of contention in the thirteenth replenishment round of the IDA. In the end, the United States backed down from its demand that 50 percent of IDA funds be disbursed as grants, primarily due to Japanese and European opponents who feared that greater financial dependence on U.S. replenishments would make the IDA more susceptible to U.S. political influence.

On the other hand, many proponents of the Bank (or at least, the opponents of the conservative critique) dismiss much of the argument that private capital flows are crowding out development aid. As many of the Bank's reports are quick to point out, the massive amounts of private capital are directed almost exclusively to a small number of developing countries (the largest emerging markets), leaving out the poorest regions of the world, which have become increasingly reliant on multilateral and bilateral development assistance as the primary component of their budgets.[44] Moreover, the Bank still maintains influence over private capital markets through several means. As mentioned above, they include its role in signaling the creditworthiness of developing country economies, as well as gathering and disseminating key economic and social data that foreign direct investors use extensively. Finally, through sectoral and structural adjustment lending, the Bank has in recent years paralleled the IMF's role in serving as a lender of last resort, helping to bail out economies in crisis and by default the foreign investors wrapped up in the quagmire.[45]

Nonetheless, the Bank's legitimacy has been weakened by the arguments of the political Right. The abundance of private capital flows as a viable alternative to Bank funds (especially for creditworthy middle-income countries) creates pressure on the Bank to increase grants and otherwise prove its relevance. In so doing, it has become more susceptible to the pressures of middle-income borrowers, resulting in numerous reports designed to demonstrate how it is restructuring lending and technical assistance to become more responsive to borrowers' needs.[46] Concerns over declining demand for IBRD lending and subsequent reliance on potential volatile private capital flows were a central part of the agenda of the annual meetings in Singapore in the fall 2006 and Washington, D.C., in the spring 2007.

[44] Gurria and Volcker 2001; de Ferranti 2006; World Bank 2006a; Muasher 2007.

[45] On the changing relationship between the World Bank and the IMF, see Polak 1994.

[46] There are a series of reports on the Bank's middle-income country strategies. See, for example, World Bank 2001b, 2004, 2007a; and World Bank Independent Evaluation Group 2007.

Organizational Competitors

The Bank's autonomy and influence within its external environment and its ability to secure scarce resources from donor and borrower states is also potentially threatened by the existence of other bilateral and multilateral development agencies.[47] The number of these organizations has proliferated in the past fifty years, leading some scholars to identify them as potential competitors of the Bank during a period when official development aid is in decline.[48] As a result, in the past ten years, there has been more attention to the need for these aid organizations to coordinate with one another—a difficult task for these complex bureaucracies, all driven by different mandates and political imperatives.[49] At the same time, all these institutions appear to be in a fight for sustained relevance in an era characterized by an abundance of easily accessed private capital and the increased tendency of donors to channel aid through their own bilateral agencies and trust funds, where they can more easily earmark monies.[50]

At the same time, the World Bank is clearly the leader of the pack, so the threat to its resources and relevance may not be as dire as often depicted in the popular media. In the words of many aid workers I interviewed, the Bank's bureaucratic size and financial resources "dwarfs all others in project lending," and as a result, the Bank's own actions often set the agenda for other aid organizations. Quite often, one project of the Bank will have a budget bigger than the entire aid portfolio of a bilateral organization, giving the Bank considerably more leverage than other aid agencies in dialogues with borrowing country governments to determine how aid will be directed.[51] Moreover, many of the Bank's most proximate competitors are the regional development banks that are set up on the same organizational model and share similar mandates (and sometimes staff), policy agendas, and philosophy of development.[52] Finally, to the extent that these other IOs rely

---

[47] Similar statements were made in several interviews with staff members of the European Union's Technical Assistance to the Commonwealth of Independent States (EU TACIS) and USAID (Moscow, October 1999, and Washington, D.C., May 2000).

[48] Miller-Adams 1999 and Kapur 2002a. This was particularly true in the 1990s, when overall official development assistance (ODA) stagnated and even dropped, in terms of overall donor contributions.

[49] Development Assistance Committee 1996.

[50] Weisman 2007b.

[51] Interview with USAID official, Moscow, Russia, October 1999.

[52] Hancock 1989. One may add here that many of these organizations share at one time or another the same staff, as many individuals move between the organizations during the course of their careers. The regional development banks set up on the World Bank organizational model include the Inter-American Development Bank (established

upon Bank-generated data in their own work, the kind of information the Bank decides to gather and its interpretation within economic and sector analysis reports represents a unique position of normative authority and power for the Bank within the overall international development regime.

However, growing concern over the ineffectiveness and misuse of aid has led to a larger debate not only on increased donor coordination, but also greater selectivity in aid activities in order to reduce overlap and inconsistencies and reign in mission creep. This restrains bureaucratic independence by forcing all aid organizations, the Bank included, more carefully to define and narrow their agendas and policies, as well as modify their operational practices to allow for greater communication, participation, and thus the input and oversight of other agencies.[53]

Nongovernmental and Civil Society Organizations

One of the most distinctive features of the Bank's current authorizing and task environments is the presence of several thousand international, national, and local nongovernmental (NGO) and civil society organizations (CSO), many of which are devoted to monitoring the activities of the Bank.[54] The influence of these NGOs and CSOs has been noticeable since the early 1980s, particularly since the aforementioned case of the activist campaign against the Bank-financed Polonoroeste road project in Brazil (see chapter 2). NGOs began lobbying national parliaments to use their "power of the purse" during IDA replenishment processes to hold the Bank accountable for its activities. This led to the first public hearing in the U.S. House of Representatives on the impact of multilateral development bank (MDB) lending on the environment, as well as the mobilization of media coverage and social movements in both industrialized and developing countries. This has hence cumulated into massive protests each year during the annual meetings of the IMF and World Bank. Innumerous watchdog organizations vigilantly monitor almost every aspect of the Bank's activity, in

---

in 1960), the African Development Bank (1964), the Asian Development Bank (1966), and the European Bank for Reconstruction and Development (1991).

[53] One example of such coordinated efforts is the jointly issued Millennium Development Goals of the United Nations, Organization for Economic Cooperation and Development, the IMF, and the World Bank. The eighth goal of the MDGs is increased aid coordination and selectivity.

[54] For a comprehensive list of national and international governmental organizations specifically designed to monitor and expose the activities of the World Bank, see the Bank Information Center website at http://www.bicusa.org.

issues ranging from compliance with policies on the resettlement of indigenous peoples, to gender advocacy, to the World Commission on Dams. In sum, NGOs and CSOs have not only been effective in pushing their own agendas, but have also assumed the constant monitoring and "whistle-blowing" functions that the states themselves have not always performed, and in some cases have called the states themselves to account for the apparent errant behavior of the Bank.

In the United States in particular, NGOs have been very effective in catalyzing congressional pressure on the Bank, thus affecting one central source of needed resources. Congressional lobbying has resulted in legislation intended to promote reform, directives on how the U.S. executive directors to the banks can vote, and several U.S. government studies, reports, and ad hoc oversight committees. The overall effect has been a greater demand for accountability on the effects of the Bank's loans, as well as specific operational policies, such as those requiring environmental and social assessments during the appraisal and implementation of projects.[55]

One recent example is the NGO participation in the drafting of the 2006 U.S. Foreign Operations Appropriation Bill (signed into law on 15 November 2005), which contains new legislation regarding greater transparency and accountability at the multilateral development banks. The law specifically requires the U.S. executive director to raise specific proposals for reform concerning loan oversight, audit functions, and internal whistle-blower protections, and to push for the Bank's adoption of these new rules. NGOs, such as Environmental Defense (led by senior attorney Bruce Rich) and the Bank Information Center (executive director Manish Bapna), were very influential in testifying before the U.S. Congress and working closely with Senator Dick Lugar, the lead author of the bill.[56]

These NGOs are often quite small and underfunded, and thus have virtually no direct means of threatening the resources of the World Bank. Yet the threat they pose to its external legitimacy and authority has affected the way the Bank portrays and pursues its operations.[57]

[55] Two watchdog organizations, the Bank Information Center (based in Washington, D.C.) and the Bretton Woods Project (based in London), report often on NGO campaigns and their impact upon changing Bank policies and practices. See www.bicusa.org and www.brettonwoodsproject.org. For a critical assessment of the growing NGO influence over the Bank, see Mallaby 2004.

[56] Foreign Operations, Export Financing and Related Programs Appropriation Bill of the 109th U.S. House of Representatives, Report 109-152. Signed into law 24 June 2005. Interview with Bruce Rich, February 2005.

[57] This concurs with the argument of Keck and Sikkink 1998 that the primary power of international NGOs derives from their ability to hold others to account, including states, corporations, and international organizations.

Perceiving the need to appear responsive to, and inclusive of, NGOs and civil society groups, the Bank now keeps close track of any NGO and CSO involvement in its activities and is quick to highlight the increasing percentage of projects in which NGOs and CSOs have played (even if marginally) a role.

As a result of successful parliamentary lobbying and increased interaction with the Bank through project participation, NGOs and CSOs can also be viewed as a source of new development norms and agendas. The environmental campaign described in chapter 2 is one example of successful NGO campaigns leading not only to new environmental and social safeguards, but also to an increase in relevant staff, units, and resources devoted to the sustainable development agenda in the World Bank—a process that has sparked an internal "socialization" around new environmental norms within it.[58] While many still dispute the degree to which the Bank has embraced and mainstreamed its environmental agenda, lending for stand-alone environmental programs has increased since 1993,[59] the number of staff in the Environmental and Socially Sustainable Development Unit has risen, and several *World Development Reports* and other research publications have focused on environmental, social, and participatory development ideas.

Evaluation Groups

A final significant source of pressure that affects the organization's ability to sustain resources and legitimacy are the various oversight mechanisms, or evaluation units. These groups, mostly autonomous or semiautonomous from the Bank, are all the more critical insofar as they are designed to look for policy incompliance and mainstreaming failures, and to hold the Bank accountable for its behavior. The most important of these groups are the Operations Evaluation Department (OED; now called the Independent Evaluation Group, or IEG) and Quality Assurance Group (QAG); also noteworthy are the Independent Inspection Panel and the Department of Institutional Integrity.

The Operations Evaluation Department (now IEG) was created by Robert McNamara in 1973. It is financially independent from the Bank and reports directly to the Board of Executive Directors. The role of the IEG has become significantly enhanced in the past decade as a result of the mounting external pressure for transparency and internal and external accountability at the Bank. The IEG's primary responsibilities

[58] Park 2005.
[59] Nielson and Tierney 2003.

are to evaluate completed projects (usually four to five years after completion) and report the findings to the executive directors, with the hope that the resulting lessons will feed back into the design and implementation of policies and lending operations. More recently, the IEG has tackled more systemic issues in the organization, conducting evaluation on "mainstreaming progress" in numerous areas of the Bank's development agenda, including the environment, governance, corruption, and gender.

The quality of the IEG's reports is generally highly regarded by those within and outside the organization, and it would seem that a negative evaluation would signal a damning indictment of the Bank's credibility and authority as an effective institution. Historically, however, there has been strong skepticism regarding the degree to which the OED/IEG acts independently, free from internal pressure to show positive results. William Easterly, a former Bank official, testified before the U.S. Senate Foreign Appropriations Committee in March 2006:

> Despite the use of the word "independent" . . . these evaluation units still remain housed within the organizations and use the same staff, which obviously compromised their independence. I know personally from my time at the World Bank of several examples of pressure being brought to bear from the rest of the Bank on the OED to alter its evaluations.[60]

There is equal skepticism regarding the extent to which its findings are taken into consideration by project managers within the organizational culture, which rewards project approval but until recently made little visible effort to hold managers accountable for the outcomes of projects. Nonetheless, IEG publications such as the *Annual Review of Development Effectiveness* are fully available to the public, which allows observant NGOs, civil society groups, and member states to use the Bank's data in attempts to critique its performance.[61] The IEG assiduously asserts its independence and claims that it has been a significant source of pressure for change in the Bank: "IEG has used its reports to urge the Bank to adopt a results-based management approach, even though Bank management was not yet ready to do so. A long-time external observer of IEG has told us that this "willingness by IEG to

[60] Easterly 2006a.

[61] For example, in preparation for the recent IDA 14 replenishment negotiations, the OED issued a series of reports on the effectiveness of the IDA in meeting several of its new agenda goals, including mainstreaming the environment, gender, participation, and governance in its overall lending portfolio and practices. Gwin 2001.

speak out is hardly new; rather, it has been a salient characteristic of the unit since its inception."[62]

The Quality Assurance Group (QAG) was established in 1996 in response to the critical internal report of the Portfolio Management Task Force (also known as the Wapenhans Report), which found that the Bank's declining performance on projects was due in large part to its neglecting to address implementation and sustainability at the design stage.[63] QAG's purpose is to monitor ongoing activities to assess this "quality at entry" and risks during implementation that may undermine the project over the long term. This attention has affected project management, as task managers and team members are now held more closely accountable for their actions during the design and implementation of projects. However, a critical distinction between the IEG's and the QAG's effectiveness in monitoring the Bank's behavior is that the QAG's reports (the *Annual Review of Portfolio Performance*, or ARPP) until March 2002 were confidential and thus not made available to outside actors who might put pressure on the Bank. Its findings, however, were *selectively* used within many of the Bank's public documents and IEG reports.[64] Since 2002, the ARPPs are available on QAG's website.

A third and very important immediate mechanism of oversight is the Independent Inspection Panel, created in 1993.[65] The Inspection Panel is empowered to hear the complaints of groups that live in an area affected by a Bank-financed project and believe that actual or likely harm to them is the result of the Bank's failure to comply with its own policies and procedures. The Inspection Panel is limited by the fact that cases cannot be heard without the approval of the Bank's board of executives and the borrowing country government,

[62] This statement is found in the IEG's list of Frequently Asked Questions, available at http://www.worldbank.org/ieg/.

[63] Wapenhans 1992 (the "Wapenhans Report"). QAG was created in response to the failed eighty-seven-point "Next Steps" reform initiative installed in 1993 under President Lewis Preston.

[64] Given the amount of leaked information in the World Bank today, early QAG reports, especially its official *Annual Reports on Portfolio Performance*, are not terribly difficult to obtain. This allows diligent researchers to compare the full findings and recommendations of the QAG reports to how they are selectively portrayed in public Bank documents and speeches. While the QAG reviews have indicated a significant improvement in project quality-at-entry and over portfolio performance—findings that are consistently highlighted in public statements—its more negative findings are often glossed over in official reports. Wade 2001d, for example, argues that QAG is much more firmly under the control of senior management, which need not bias the result per se, but certainly affects how those results are presented to the external actors.

[65] For a good overview of the Independent Inspection Panel, see Fox 2000; Fox and Treakle 2003.

which first pass judgment on the validity of the complaints. However, it has made rulings in high-profile cases that have resulted in significant changes to ongoing projects and in some instances cancellation of loans.[66]

Finally, President Wolfensohn in 1998 created an internal Oversight Committee for Fraud and Corruption to supervise the investigation of corruption in Bank-funded projects. The committee was later reconstituted and merged with the Business Ethics Office into the Department of Institutional Integrity (INT). INT is mandated to investigate allegations of fraud and corruption in operations as well as allegations of staff misconduct, and it reports directly to the president of the World Bank. The department itself has recently taken decisive action in investigating and punishing cases of staff fraud (characterized at times by staff as a witch-hunt).[67] The problematic role of INT is further discussed in chapter 4.

THE AUTONOMY AND INFLUENCE OF THE WORLD'S BANK

The increasing number of actors in the external environment seeking to shape the agendas and practices of the World Bank has led many scholars and staffers to argue that, as the title of a Staff Association newsletter put it, the "Bank Group is always navigating in political waters."[68] The newsletter portrays complex authorizing and task environments constituted by many interests producing incongruent pressures on the Bank, and thus provides a persuasive framework for understanding the roots of its organized hypocrisy.

However, it is important to recognize the degree to which the Bank possesses and exercises autonomy from its authorizing and task environments. This in turn roughly establishes the extent of its dependence on its environment and thus the nature of its response to these environmental pressures. In fact, the Bank has proven quite adept at buffering itself from external pressures and in some instances actually shaping

---

[66] One of the most prominent cases to come before the Inspection Panel was the Western Poverty Reduction Project in Quinghai, China. The plaintiffs in the case charged that the World Bank had, among other things, violated its own policies regarding consultation with local groups, environmental and social assessments, and information disclosure.

[67] Interview with Alison Cave, World Bank Staff Association, July 2005. See also Volcker et al. 2007 and Government Accountability Project 2007.

[68] World Bank Staff Association 2001a.

the external environment in its favor.[69] As predicted by resource dependency theory, this bureaucratic autonomy and authority has in part been engendered by the Bank—particularly by its organizational leaders—in key areas of its structure and activities through what Barnett and Finnemore list as the rational-legal, delegated, moral, and expert sources of authority in IOs.[70] So where has the Bank captured this autonomy and authority?

The first significant source of bureaucratic autonomy came early in the Bank's years, when John McCloy become the second president in 1947. As a condition for accepting the position, McCloy insisted that the Board of Executive Directors not interfere with daily operations.[71] This proved to have a lasting effect. Although the executive directors are formally endowed with the power to create and implement policy, in practice they are little involved in management and exercise limited oversight of daily operations.

The Bank's relative insulation from board pressure is due first to the complexity of its operations, where supervision of policies and programs requires extensive time and expert resources.[72] Consequently, the board relies heavily on the analytical reports, oral briefings, and carefully prepared project information and appraisal documents that many staff members agree are written specifically for "consumption by the EDs and the general public."[73] Moreover, although projects usually take well over a year to appraise and design, the board is supplied with many project documents only two weeks prior to the approval vote, thus leaving little time for adequate review.[74] In the early 1990s, the Bank also adopted a new "approval streamlining" process to facilitate the board's overview of the increasing number of project loans managed by the Bank. This new procedure allows for "smaller loans"

---

[69] Barnett and Coleman (2005) would call this "strategic social construction," although it is not entirely clear if the Bank's social constructions of development ideas and practices are always strategic acts to enhance the organization's autonomy and influence.

[70] Barnett and Finnemore 2004.

[71] Mason and Asher 1973, 49; Kapur, Lewis, and Webb 1997, 10. The U.S. administration apparently had a very difficult time finding someone willing to take the job, which put McCloy in an enviable bargaining position.

[72] Wapenhans 2000, 242; Woods 2001.

[73] This was repeated several times during interviews with Bank staff members, April–May 2000. With the Bank's new information disclosure policy adopted in 1993, staff must now make some project information available to the public. In response, the Bank started preparing short project information documents that contain brief summaries of the project's components and goals, heavily doctored in Bank jargon that one begins to quickly recognize after reading a handful of official reports. See also Ascher 1990, 127–28.

[74] Rich 1994, 194. See also Ayres 1983, 66; Kardam 1993, 1777; Kapur, Lewis, and Webb 1997, 2; Ascher 1990, 126; Caufield 1996, 102.

(usually under $50 million) or loans categorized as without significant environmental or social risk to be voted on without prior debate in a board meeting. Overall, in the words of several former senior managers, the Bank's management has taken the "mushroom" approach with the executive board: "keep it in the dark and feed it garbage."[75]

Despite widespread attention to the actions of the board during the Wolfowitz scandal, recent U.S. executive director Robert B. Holland III argues the board is ineffective in overseeing and directing the organization. In a letter of support of Paul Wolfowitz, published in the *Wall Street Journal* in April 2007, Holland stated:

> The board's structural ineffectiveness is compounded by the frequency of its turnover, with tenure averaging less that two years, hardly enough time to learn all the acronyms, much less who you can trust; the imperatives of gaining loan approvals for borrowing country directors (never once in four years did I witness one such director oppose any loans); and the comparatively high compensation enjoyed by many board members. Other parochial foreign policy interests, including those of the U.S. (especially in the form of a mind-numbing and influence-diminishing number of legislatively mandated voting requirements), are also a serious impediment to Board effectiveness. . . . Many board members would love to see the board's power relative to the president enhanced. All others should be horrified at the thought.[76]

A second source of the Bank's bureaucratic autonomy stems, ironically, from the interests and even dependence of the member states on the Bank. During each IDA replenishment process, a representative from the U.S. Treasury goes before the congressional appropriations committees to explain why support for the World Bank is in the interest of the United States. These statements usually argue that the Bank helps to keep overseas markets open to American exports, fosters stability and growth, and promotes American values. More importantly, however, the Bank's lending leverages U.S. foreign aid and provides lucrative opportunities for U.S. contractors. As Joan Spero argued in 1996, "the MDBs provide over $40 billion in assistance annually, on the basis of a U.S. contribution of less than $2 billion. As a result of their ability to leverage these funds, these institutions can address critical needs with resources that dwarf what the U.S. provide alone."[77] Yet it is also explicitly acknowledged that this ability to "address critical needs" is contingent upon the Bank's moral authority, derived from its

---

[75] Irwin 1990, 8; Daly 1994, 110.
[76] Holland 2007.
[77] Spero 1996. See also speeches by U.S. Treasury secretary Paul O'Neill (2001a, 2001b).

image of technical neutrality and independence from the whims of its most powerful states.[78] Member states thus must keep from being seen as intervening too deeply in the management of the Bank's activities, although many would argue that the United States has not always complied with this principle.[79]

A final source of autonomy and influence that has enabled the Bank to buffer itself from environmental pressures is the normative power derived from its "unique position as a generator of ideas about economic development."[80] During Robert McNamara's thirteen-year tenure (1968–81), he revolutionized the World Bank by quadrupling its staff and quintupling the amount of lending. One of McNamara's legacies is his creation of a leading international research institute within the World Bank, into which he recruited the "best and the brightest" of young economists. As a result, it now has a research division with a budget of over $100 million annually that far exceeds any private research institute or public university.[81] The Bank as an organization or through its staff disseminates this research through an astounding numbers of books, journals, articles, working papers, and reports. In addition to its flagship publication, the *World Development Report*, and the in-house *World Bank Economic Review* and *World Bank Research Observer*, the staff publishes over three hundred articles in academic and other professional journals each year that are cited 10–50 percent more that the average for economics articles.[82]

The Bank also promotes its ideas and practices through training programs for political elites and policymakers from around the world. The newly revamped World Bank Institute (formerly the Economic Development Institute) is one primary educational forum; there is an Annual Bank Conference on Development Economics and numerous other workshops, seminars, and exchanges. In addition, the Bank enjoys what Joseph Stiglitz calls an "asymmetry of information." It has almost unparalleled access to sensitive government data. Staff members may voice their development theories and strategies through policy dialogue and loan negotiations, as well as through economic and sector work used in economic reports on countries, Country Assistance Strategy papers (CAS), and the Poverty Reduction Strategy Papers (PRSPs) of its borrowing countries.[83]

---

[78] Gwin 1994, 54; Woods 2000b,135.

[79] Payer 1982; Ascher 1983, 1990.

[80] Wade 1996, 5. See also Escobar 1995 and Mehta 2001.

[81] Squire 2000.

[82] Squire 2000, 126.

[83] Stiglitz 1999, F585; Miller-Adams 1999, 12; and Stern and Ferreira 1997, 579.

The power the World Bank enjoys in shaping global ideas about development theory and practice is arguably unreplicated by any other development agency, think-tank, or university. This status gives it a critical platform from which to preach its own ideas, and thus mold international development in a manner that fits its organizational ideologies, goals, and practices. Wolfensohn's attempt in recent years to solidify the relevance and legitimacy of the Bank as "Knowledge Bank" only reaffirms the organization's commitment to this ideational source of autonomy and influence. Indeed, as the Bank's authorizing environment has become increasingly politicized in the post–Cold War era of globalization, it has sought to enhance its organizational security and buffer itself from external uncertainties and demands by highlighting its image as the world's elite development institution.

The Bank's World

The relative autonomy and power of the Bank, particularly in the crafting of development ideas and policies, implies that scholars must look not just at the interests of member states and other external actors to explain its behavior. As described in the two previous chapters, it is just as important to study the Bank's internal character: the dynamics of bureaucratic politics and organizational culture help us identify the sources of incongruent goals that contribute to organized hypocrisy and inhibit change. Yet, of course, these two worlds do not exist in isolation, but are instead mutually constituted. The evolution of the Bank's bureaucratic environment strongly reflects changes in its external political and financial environment. Thus, when defining and explaining the evolution of the formal and informal ideologies, norms, language, and routines that shape thoughts and actions within the Bank, one must do so with a view to the dynamic and historical path-dependent interaction with the world outside the organization. I tackle the explanation of bureaucratic politics and culture on two fronts: the ideological and intellectual environment and then the operational environment within the Bank.

The Intellectual Culture of the World Bank

It would be a mistake to say that the World Bank has one distinct ideology shared among its thousands of staff members, who themselves stem from an astounding diversity of political, cultural, and ethnic backgrounds. Yet it is impossible to deny that certain features of a dominant intellectual culture shape the way the organization as a whole conceives its core mission. This intellectual culture itself is not impenetrable, and has transformed over time in response to shifts in the material and normative environments as well as the particular philosophies and goals of the Bank's leaders. The Bank that was created sixty years ago is much different than the institution we know today. However, in the past two decades, its ideology has been marked by a triad of mutually reinforcing characteristics that have become embedded within the organization and have proven resilient in the face of pressures for change: apolitical, technocratic, and economic rationality.

The apolitical and technical pillars of the Bank's ideology are closely intertwined. The clearest origin of these elements is the Bank's own organizational mandate, which prohibits it from becoming involved in the political affairs of its member states or taking political considerations into account when lending.[84] This has shaped the Bank's approach to defining and pursuing development. From early on, it narrowed its range of activities to seemingly neutral or technical tasks, such as targeted lending for infrastructure and rural agricultural development or sweeping macroeconomic reforms and adjustment policies, while other development agencies endowed with different mandates pursued development based on rule of law, human rights, and democracy.[85]

Much of this bias in the Bank's approach is derived from the context in which it was born. Its apolitical, technical image was critical in its formative years for three reasons related to its external legitimacy. The first was the need to attract private commercial creditors, who were leery of buying bonds from the fledging international organization and thus demanded relatively conservative, solid lending to tangible projects with measurable rates of return. A second related reason was to attract clients for loans. Borrowing countries needed to perceive the Bank as a truly autonomous, multilateral organization that would not encroach upon their fragile sovereignties nor push the agendas of powerful states. Finally, as previously argued, an apolitical, technical approach to development was deemed necessary by donor states, who saw the neutral organization as a effective and acceptable

---

[84] Article IV, Section 10 of the IBRD Articles of Agreement: "the Bank and its officers shall not interfere in the political affairs of any member, nor shall they be influenced in their decisions by the political character of the member or members concerned."

[85] The distinction is especially true in comparing the World Bank or other MDBs to bilateral aid agencies, such as USAID. In the 1970s, USAID aggressively pursued rule-of-law reform and democratization programs as the heart of its development agenda, whereas the Bank until the mid-1990s explicitly steered away from any activity that might be associated with these issues.

way to pursue their own foreign policy goals (in veiled form) through multilateral lending.

Internally, this espoused adherence to apolitical, technical rationality serves organizational interests. The president and senior management can invoke the Bank's mandate as "an anchor and a shield, limiting the degree to which the Bank responds to external pressures."[86] As evident in the dramatic changes in the Bank's agendas over time, the organization's legal counsel have proven quite adept at interpreting the mandates to allow the Bank to respond to external pressures for change or evoke the mandates to resist demands.[87] Thus, changes or additions to agendas are closely correlated with the interests and initiatives of the organization's leaders. Likewise, as in the case of the current agenda of "good governance," when the Bank does respond to external demands for changes in policy, it can translate the mandates in a manner that not only permits the new activity but also establishes a legal framework that "fits" the new agenda to existing development paradigms, norms, and standard operating procedures (see chapter 4).

The interlinked ideological elements of apolitical and technical rationality naturally feed into the dominance of economic theory as the core of the Bank's development theories and practices. Gibbon argues that neoliberal economic ideas took hold in the early 1980s in the Bank because of a convergence of external interests among conservative private commercial lenders, northern manufacturers who favored the free market, laissez-faire ideology as a means of opening up southern markets for exports, and political imperatives within donor states who saw economic liberalization as a way of combating communism without resorting to military options.[88] Andy Storey and Robert Wade add that this constellation of external factors resonated within the Bank early on because they coincided with the its institutional self-interest in increasing the volume of its lending.[89]

This was especially true at two distinct periods in the Bank's history, during which the demand for its services appeared to be stagnating and the very purpose of the organization questioned by powerful actors within its authorizing environment. The first was in the late 1960s, at a time when technical assistance projects to aid the postwar

---

[86] Kapur 2002a; Ascher 1990.

[87] The apolitical mandate was strictly interpreted until the early 1990s, when an intersection of external and internal interests favoring an expansion of the Bank's agenda toward governance and law issues required a broader definition of "political" in order to justify lending in arguably sensitive areas of domestic affairs. See chapter 4.

[88] Gibbon 1995.

[89] Wade 1996 and Storey 2000.

reconstruction of Europe were no longer needed. In the search for a new raison d'être, President McNamara asserted that the Bank was in a unique position not only to reduce the gap between north and south by providing client states with the things that industrialized nations possessed (such as roads, electricity, and phones) but to alleviate the poverty that perpetuated underdevelopment by addressing basic needs, such as rural agricultural production, education, health, and overpopulation. Economic theory's claim to objective, reductionist reasoning based on sound, quantitative analysis and rigorous models directly appealed to McNamara's own personal obsession with numbers. It also allowed the Bank to construct universal models and standard blueprints for projects that could be quickly applied in any country at any time, thus enabling the Bank to rapidly expand its lending portfolio at a critical point in its "formative years."[90] Subsequently, the number of economists with the Bank rose dramatically in relation to the traditional core of engineers, architects, and other technical assistance specialists.

In the late 1970s and early 1980s, the Bank once again faced an external crisis, a decline in support from two of its most powerful member states, the United States and Great Britain. Under Reagan and Thatcher, the countries took a decidedly unilateralist approach in foreign policy and sought to decrease expenditures on foreign aid.[91] However, the domino debt crises in the Latin American economies beginning with Mexico in 1982 and the impending commercial bank crises with the United States opened the door for the Bank to reassert its importance by expanding its agendas beyond technical assistance projects to policy-oriented structural adjustment lending.[92] The resulting focus on macroeconomic stabilization and liberalization earned the renewed support of the United States and other major donor states. Under the U.S.-nominated president A. W. Clausen (a former commercial banker) and chief economist Anne Krueger (a supply-side economist), rapid staff turnover in response to this agenda heralded a new class of neoclassically trained economists who soon assumed positions of senior management.

Apolitical, technical, and economic rationality as the hallmark of the Bank's espoused ideology persists because such ideas have become

---

[90] Caufield 1996, 60–61; Wade 1996; Kapur, Lewis, and Webb 1997; and McNeill 2001, 8.

[91] One example of this was the Gramm-Rudman proposal in the mid-1980s that called for the reduction in U.S. contributions to multilateral institutions, and specifically to development aid agencies.

[92] Mosley, Harrigan, and Toye 1991, 1:47.

deeply embedded in its organizational structure and culture. The most obvious evidence is the Bank's hiring and promotion practices. One example is the Young Professionals Program, which recruits individuals under the age of thirty from elite schools and places them in a fast track to positions of higher management. These prestigious slots have until recently been reserved almost exclusively for those with advanced degrees in economics or finance.[93] The same trend existed in general staff hiring throughout the 1970s and 1980s. In a survey conducted in 1991, Stern found that of the 586 staff surveyed in the research and policy department, 46 percent had undergrad degrees and 55 percent had graduate degrees exclusively in economics or finance. Stern estimated the ratio of professional economists to noneconomists on the Bank's staff at ten to one. Moreover, these economists tended to share the same theoretical and methodological training, as 80 percent were educated in U.S. or British graduate programs that at the time were strongly biased toward neoclassical economics.[94]

The ideological socialization resulting from these hiring practices was reinforced during this time by promotional standards. Michelle Miller-Adams argues that the high placement of economists within the organization implies that "existing belief systems are reinforced when those who hold power within the organization seek out successors who have the same values and interests they do. Unintentionally, those principles that are used to identify successors become rewards and sanctions governing the whole course of socialization."[95] Miller-Adams further argues that this creates a self-selection bias in what type of individuals seek employment at the Bank. "Those who want to work at the World Bank come to believe the set of values and norms held by those who do work there; they then seek the training that will enable them to join the institution."[96]

Ironically, as the Bank's agendas expanded into areas requiring more diversified skills, it sought to reform its recruitment strategies. A pri-

[93] Nelson 1995; Stern and Ferreira 1997; and Miller-Adams 1999. A 1994 U.S. General Accounting Office report revealed that in 1988–89, 90 percent of the Young Professionals Program recruits were economists. Increasingly criticized for this bias, the Bank opened its recruitment process. By 1994, the number of entering young professionals with economics degrees fell to 63 percent. A recent interview with a young professional (a political scientist) confirmed this trend. Interview with Bank official, April 2005.

[94] Stern and Ferreira 1997.

[95] Miller-Adams 1999. Momani (2005) and Chwieroth (2007) make a similar argument in the case of the IMF, using archival and original data to show tremendous homogeneity and continuity in the IMF's hiring practices and professional socialization of staff.

[96] Miller-Adams 1999, 30. See also Berger and Beeson 1998 and Williams 1999. This observation was certainly confirmed in my own interviews at the Bank.

mary goal of the Strategic Compact reform in 1997 (see chapter 5) was to hire new staff in areas of activity targeted for improvement or mainstreaming (especially social, environmental, gender, and governance operational work).[97] Anecdotal evidence from interviews suggests that the Bank has encountered difficulties in attracting different professionals. A few staff members speculate that this may be due to resistance from entrenched economists who do not wish to relinquish their influence in the institution. Yet other staff members suggest that the organization is seen as a place in which economists dominate and all others are marginalized,[98] diminishing its image as an attractive place to work for noneconomists.

This last point is reinforced by what many inside and outside the Bank consider to be ideological uniformity in the organization's research and policy practices. In 1994, Susan George and Fabrizio Sabelli noted an absence of critical peer review and the practice of the Banks' researchers citing other research published by the Bank. They argued that this resulted in insular research and policy debate that rejected approaches at odds with the prevailing style, which favored quantitative, abstract models based on econometric analysis of large-n cross-country comparisons.[99] Michael Cernea (the first sociologist to be hired into the Bank in the 1970s) wrote in 1995 that noneconomic social science "did not land in an intellectual vacuum. It landed on territory long colonized by economic and technical thinking, both with entrenched tenure. It landed onto an in-house culture unfamiliar and resistant to this new socio-cultural knowledge and expertise."[100]

Research output is still dominated by one arm of the World Bank: the Development Economics Unit (DEC), which is also home base for the writing and vetting of the annual *World Development Report*. Jean-Jacques Dethier, a research manager in DEC, confirmed that a very large majority of the researchers in DEC are economics PhDs.[101] Two

---

[97] For detailed analyses of the Strategic Compact, see also Weaver and Leiteritz 2005; Nielson, Tierney, and Weaver 2006. Notably, while the overall number of staff has increased in these units, the available human resource data does not indicate the background (educational degrees) of these new hires. Several interviews with Bank staff indicated a prevailing suspicion that many of these hires were "economists in green clothing." Nonetheless, we cannot conclude that just because an individual has an advanced degree in economics or business that he or she is hostile to or ill-informed about environmental and social issues in development thinking and practice.

[98] Rao and Woolcock 2007.

[99] George and Sabelli 1994, 193.

[100] Cernea 1995, 15. For a similar account of the introduction of social development experts into the Bank, see Bebbington et al. 2006.

[101] Interview with Jean-Jacque Dethier, Budapest, April 2005, and Washington, D.C., July 2005. See also Dethier 2005, 2007.

DEC researchers, Vijayendra Rao (an economist) and Michael Woolcock (the sole sociologist in DEC), recently reiterated this point, arguing that "this creates a kind of disciplinary monopoly; as such, development policy at the Bank tends to reflect the fads, fashions,
controversies, and debates of one discipline." They go on to say that
this insularity has created as "argot within the Bank that is closely
aligned with the argot of economics, . . . creat[ing] high entry costs for
other disciplines."[102]

This dominance of economists and neoliberal, technocratic thinking
has strongly shaped the evolution of the Bank's "talk"—its espoused
development theory and agendas. Noneconomic social scientists seeking to get their ideas across within the organization must often strategically craft their ideas within the comfortable theoretical and technical
language of economics.[103] For example, in a 1993 study of the strategies
of internal policy advocates, Kardam argued that "sociologists [within
the Bank] should follow the example of environmental scientists in defining their work as a technical input to the economic analysis of projects, and to make it as quantitative as possible."[104] Moises Naim, former senior manager, argued that just as "solid technical writing is
more important than public eloquence, economic reasoning is re-
spected while 'soft' sociological-type analysis is belittled."[105]

This point is reiterated in more recent studies of internal norm entrepreneurs promoting social development issues.[106] In interviews for this
book, one staff member commented that the relative success in mainstreaming the governance agenda within operations was due to the
ability of staff within the Poverty Reduction and Economic Management unit to fit governance issues into theories of institutional development compatible with accepted economic theory. On the other hand,
the staff member argued, the Environmental and Socially Sustainable
Development unit had yet to have an impact on key policy and operational decisions because it was unable to put its ideas into testable
models based mainly on quantitative indicators.[107]

Ideological consistency is ensured by what Robert Wade and Robin
Broad characterize as the Bank's practice of "paradigm maintenance."[108] A large number of editors are employed to monitor all publi-

---

[102] Rao and Woolcock 2007, 2. For a general overview evaluation of the Development
Economics Department, see Deaton et al. 2006.

[103] McNeill 2001.

[104] Kardam 1993, 1779.

[105] Naim 1994, C-283.

[106] Bebbington et al. 2004, 2006; Vetterlein 2006.

[107] Interview with Bank staff member, October 2001.

[108] Wade 1996; Broad 2006.

cations issued as official documents. Susan George and Fabrizio Sabelli argue that these editors strategically replace negative language with euphemisms that the authors refer to as "Bankese."[109] Paradigm maintenance is reinforced by political interests outside the Bank, most noticeably the ideological preferences of dominant member states.

Paradigm maintenance is brilliantly illustrated in Robert Wade's account of the drafting of the Bank's *East Asian Miracle* report.[110] This 1994 report was a study of the astounding economic development of East Asia's "four tigers" (South Korea, Hong Kong, Singapore, and Taiwan), commissioned by the Japanese government in hopes of proving the merit of state intervention in economic growth. The first draft of the report provided evidence of the benefits of directed credit, subsidized exports, forced savings, restricted capital flow, controlled interest rates, and targeted tax plans. However, the report came under the close scrutiny of the Bank's senior management and editorial board, who feared that its prostate message would provoke the criticism of external private capital lenders and the conservative U.S. Treasury, which perceived the Bank's role as promoting stable, free, and open markets for foreign direct investment and trade. Moreover, there was internal resistance because the report's conclusions ran counter to the Bank's free market economic philosophy and threatened to place the Bank in a precarious position of seeming to support a development theory that contradicted its apolitical mandates. As a result, when the final report emerged, it had been heavily modified to dampen any "state-friendly" language and cast the East Asian economic growth as a "market-friendly" strategy compatible with the Bank's existing beliefs and espoused policies.[111]

Despite the Bank's proclaimed commitment to open consultation and debate, practices of paradigm maintenance are still easily found. A recent example is the 2000–2001 *World Development Report: Attack Poverty*.[112] Under its lead author, Ravi Kanbur, the first draft of the report argued that rapid economic growth did not necessarily alleviate poverty, but often left many of the poor behind. Building on the work of Nobel Prize winner Amartya Sen,[113] the report targeted empowerment of the poor as the key to development, indicating the need for networks, cooperatives, trade unions, and other forms of civil society

[109] George and Sabelli 1994, 212. Indeed, during one interview, a senior Bank manager remarked with some surprise that I appeared to be fluent in "Bankese."

[110] World Bank 1994a.

[111] Wade 1996. See also Rodrik 1994 and Nelson 1995, 147.

[112] World Bank 2000–2001.

[113] Sen 1999.

that allow the poor to articulate their interests and make state organizations more responsive to citizens. This approach ran counter to the laissez-faire ideology of the U.S. Treasury, which during the drafting of the report voiced strong opposition to the empowerment argument. As then Treasury secretary Lawrence Summers argued in a speech to the Council on Foreign Relations:

> any discussions of poverty reduction that do not lay primary emphasis on economic growth are like Hamlet without the prince. They are a symptom of what is morally urgent to avoid in development debates: the substitutions of attractive sentiment for clear-eyed analysis. Quite simply, rapid, market-led growth is the most potent weapon against poverty that man has ever known.[114]

Summers's statement coincided with a number of reports concurrently produced by the Bank that reiterated the rhetoric of "growth is good for the poor" and emphasized the central message of the benefits of globalization and free trade.[115]

Mounting pressure from the U.S. Treasury and the Bank's senior management pushed Kanbur to decide whether to revise the WDR, deemphasizing empowerment, or to protect the central argument, which would risk having the Bank push the report under the rug. Kanbur chose a third option, deciding to resign, believing the publicity might force the Bank to recognize the report as the work of an independent team. In the end, the WDR was revised to conform to the Bank's fundamental philosophy, with an added chapter on growth and reduced arguments on the importance of social safety nets and on the hazards of free market reforms.[116]

Paradigm maintenance in the World Bank is ultimately reinforced by a pervasive intolerance of open dissent. Many scholars trace this culture back to the mid-1980s, when tight control by Anne Krueger over the policy and research staff made it very clear that getting ahead in the organization meant toeing the party line.[117] This insistence on conformity has persisted despite very public claims by leaders that the Bank prides itself on pluralistic debate and self-reflection. In mid-1996, Wolfensohn, despite declaring that the Bank would become more

---

[114] Summers 1999.

[115] See, for example, World Bank 1998, 2000a, and 2002a, as well as several works by Bank research and policy staff, including Burnside and Dollar 2000; Dollar and Kraay 2002; and Dollar 2001.

[116] See Wade 2001a and 2002 for a detailed account of this incident.

[117] Mosley, Harrigan, and Toye 1991, 1:24; George and Sabelli 1994, 97; and Caufield 1996, 141.

open and transparent, sent a memo warning the staff that "criticism must be internal and constructive. . . . I will regard externally-voiced criticism of the Bank as an indication of a desire to find alternative employment."[118]

In the late 1990s, a number of publicized dismissals and resignations of high-ranking staff indicated that organizational censorship was increasing as the Bank became more sensitive to public protests.[119] A World Bank Staff Association newsletter in October 2001 tackled the question of freedom of speech within the Bank, arguing that arbitrary application of rules on sharing information with the public had created a culture of fear, uncertainty, and anxiety, resulting in plummeting staff morale.[120] David Ellerman, in the same issue, attacked senior management for "enshrining their Official Views" and making it clear that "those who argue against Official Views outside the organization—particularly with any public notice—are seen as traitors being disloyal to the organization itself."[121]

This intolerance of dissent and open debate naturally creates strong pressures for bureaucratic conformity. Moises Naim, a former senior manager, argues that this is especially true in the World Bank headquarters, in which a majority of the staff are foreign, with highly specialized, nontransferable skills and need to keep their G-4 visa status to stay within the United States. As a result, he argues, "the sensitivity of unwritten rules of behavior is amplified and . . . informal but deeply grounded routines, codes, and values create a very powerful organizational culture. Together with the significant autonomy the Bank enjoys vis-à-vis its clients, its culture makes promotion and job stability much more dependent on the person's internal reputation that on the opinions of those outside the organization."[122]

Finally, ideology is maintained by the habit of externalizing blame when policies founded on apolitical, technical, and economic rationality fail to produce the expected results. As Stiglitz notes, "when a particular prescription fails, the doctor always has an incentive to suggest that it was the patient's fault for not following the prescription precisely. One sometimes hears the defense of failed policies that 'the poli-

---

[118] Leaked memo from the Middle East and North Africa department, 1996, on file with author.

[119] The cases in point are the dismissals of chief economist Joseph Stiglitz, William Easterly, and Ashraf Ghani. See Wade 2002; Machan 2001; and World Bank Staff Association 2001b, 1–2.

[120] World Bank Staff Association 2001b.

[121] Ellerman 2001, 3. See also Ellerman 2006.

[122] Naim 1994, C-282. See also Irwin 1990.

cies were correct, but the implementation was faulty.'"[123] Staff members often escalate their commitment to floundering projects or policies because of their faith in the underlying rationale. Blame for failure tends to be placed on the implementation, more often than not attributed to corruption or a lack of political will in the borrowing country. A case in point is Larry Summers's reaction to criticism of the Bank's structural adjustment lending. Faced with evidence that adjustment had not led to dramatic growth rates and may have even undermined development, he answered: "oh well, the theory's right."[124] In the Bank, "it is hard to kill failed ideas of the past."[125]

The durability of the Bank's ideology, resting on the triad of apolitical, technical, and neoliberal economic rationality, has its roots in the interests of the Bank's most powerful principals, its organizational imperatives, and individuals who strive to maintain the external legitimacy, autonomy, and authority of the Bank. As Wade argues, "The Bank's legitimacy depends upon the authority of its views; like the Vatican, and for similar reasons, it cannot afford to admit fallibility."[126] The dominant ideology persists because of the tangible and conceivably changeable practices of hiring and promotion, paradigm maintenance, intolerance of internal dissent, and the conscious or unconscious habit of externalizing blame for the failure of ideas. All of this has the effect of compelling members to work within the boundaries of the dominant culture, which affects the way the organization interprets and acts upon new development ideas and problems. This culture also can lead to resistance to certain aspects of change that go against prevailing ideologies. Furthermore, the ideological elements of culture are internalized and reinforced through the Bank's norms and routines governing the expectations and behavior of actors in the daily management of operations.

The Operational Culture of the World Bank

In February 1992, Bank president Lewis Preston appointed Vice President Willi Wapenhans to head a Portfolio Management Task Force to look into the steady decline in the Bank's lending performance over the previous decade. In October 1992, the Wapenhans Report was is-

---

[123] Stiglitz 1999, F584.

[124] Internally circulated memo, 12 December 1991, on file with author.

[125] Berg 2000, 31.

[126] Wade 1996, 35. For an entire thesis on the analogy of the Bank to religion, see Cobb 1999.

sued (and later leaked to the public).[127] The report found a dramatic decrease in projects' return rates, an increase in cancellations, and a large amount of unspent or overly delayed disbursements. The authors attributed these results in part to forces outside the Bank's control, including the debt crisis, declining terms of trade, faulty macroeconomic policies, and political instability. Yet the core findings laid blame on institutional barriers to effective portfolio management. Specifically, the authors identified poor management of project design, implementation, and evaluation, the result of the organization's "approval culture" and "disbursement imperative," which rewarded staff for getting projects off the ground and money out the door, as opposed to an effective administration of loans that would focus on results. It is this operational culture that was targeted for reform during the Wolfensohn era (see chapter 5) as the Bank sought to become more "results-oriented" and focused on clients' demands and goals of alleviating poverty. Yet despite rather draconian measures to disrupt this culture, many of the underlying norms, habits, and incentive structures persist, influencing the way in which new policies and development agendas are (or are not) translated into operational priorities and practices.

The origin of the "disbursement imperative" in the Bank's operational culture is often traced to Robert McNamara, president from 1968 to 1981 and the most important shaper of the Bank's bureaucratic identity and culture.[128] As already mentioned, when McNamara entered office in 1968, the Bank was under increasing pressure to find outlets for its loans and services. It faced the real possibility of fading out of existence.[129] McNamara sought to rectify the situation by identifying new types of development activities. He initiated annual lending targets that over his thirteen-year tenure would increase lending from $1 billion to $12 billion.[130] Internal promotions were granted on the basis of the ability of operational staff to meet targets. As a result, staff members had a strong incentive to find "bankable" projects (particularly those that would require large loans), convince borrowing

---

[127] Wapenhans 1992. Ironically, despite the fact the many NGOs and academic scholars (including me) have copies of the Wapenhans Report, it is not officially available to the public through the Bank library or archives. It is still considered for internal use only.

[128] Finnemore 1996b, chap. 4.

[129] Mason and Asher note in the early 1970s that the Bank was actually collecting more money than it was lending (a "negative net transfer" problem), thus making it difficult to maintain its image as a development institution. Mason and Asher 1973, 308.

[130] Baré (1998) argues that McNamara's obsession with numerical targets was well documented in his previous position as general manager of Ford's assembly line and his planned deployment of troops in Vietnam when he was secretary of defense. See also Kapur, Lewis, and Webb 1997, 1184–85.

governments of their necessity, and get the projects designed and approved as quickly as possible.

The result was a bureaucratic environment in which development initiatives came not from the borrowing countries, but from Bank staff driven by organizational imperatives. "Theoretically, the Bank was supposed to finance projects requested by a borrowing government. In practice, the Bank sent out its own flying squads to find bankable projects. The government—apprised of the possibility of a project thus identified and designed by the Bank—would then ask the Bank to kindly study the financing."[131] Ellerman, Denning, and Hanna further argue that the tendency to identify and "sell" projects also stemmed from weaknesses within the borrowing countries, especially in Africa, which did not have the resources to design development projects that would qualify for financing. Therefore, there was a need to "vertically integrate the production of the input into [the Bank's] own operations"[132] so that it would have sufficient "deal flow" to justify its own budget.[133]

The internal pressure to lend means that, in practice, projects are pushed through the organization very quickly. They often lack adequate oversight by management and the Board of Executive Directors. Caufield notes, for example, that during McNamara's administration, 40 percent of all IBRD loans were approved in the last two months of each fiscal year.[134] Rich calls this the "bunching season," during which time it becomes nearly impossible to reach many operations staff or executive directors (confirmed by my own attempts to conduct interviews in June). Mentioning McNamara's former position as general manager of the Ford Motor Company, Rich likens this rush to "an assembly line approach to project preparation" in which there are "no brownie points for engaging in any policy discussion which might hold up the approval of a loan."[135] One consequence of this is the resistance to any new policy guidelines or requirements, such as costly and time-consuming environmental and social impact assessments, that may slow down the project cycle or deter borrowing governments from formally requesting loans.

According to interviews with staff, lending targets and the related disbursement imperative continue to strongly bias the Bank toward

---

[131] George and Sabelli 1994, 43. This was essentially what happened in the Bank-funded Russian and Legal Judicial Reform project that I investigated in Moscow in 1998–99.

[132] Ellerman, Denning, and Hanna 2001, 178.

[133] Tendler 1975, 103.

[134] Caufield 1996, 102.

[135] Rich 1994, 189–90.

project or program lending based on technical, economic reasoning that facilitates the construction and application of universal "blueprints" and thus reinforces the ideological tenets just discussed. This is consistent with Barnett and Finnemore's general observation that organizations seek to "flatten diversity" and find universal solutions that can be applied to any given task.[136] One consequence in the Bank is that operational staff members are chosen for missions not based on their expertise in a particular geographical area, but rather their technical skills or general knowledge of policy. In fact, according to interviews, the Bank has historically discouraged staff from developing area specialties, under the logic that such specialists tend to develop an "attachment" to their assigned countries and thus become incapable of providing neutral assistance.[137]

Moreover, McNamara's obsession with lending targets and the Bank's prevailing ideology affected project design by valuing technical inputs and outputs that can be quantitatively measured. Staff tend to design projects that show the number of specific things to be accomplished, such as number of students enrolled in a school-building project, with targeted outcomes that attempt to correlate such outputs with the organization's goals, such as overall reduction in illiteracy rates. This significantly biases projects toward development activities that can produce certain kinds of results, while steering them away from activities that may not produce immediate tangible effects.

Perhaps more striking is how this quantitative bias affects what information is taken into account during appraisal and design of projects. Theoretical and methodological backgrounds, reinforced through training practices, direct staff to pay attention to certain variables when assessing a project. Considerable weight is given to economic and technical factors that are easy to identify and measure, whereas complex political and social risk assessments that involve "soft" qualitative indicators are usually distrusted as unscientific. As a result, "the information generally selected for consideration in policy-making in the Bank excludes many political and socio-cultural considerations that shape the realities of social and economic change."[138] The current push

---

[136] Barnett and Finnemore 2004, chap. 2.

[137] Interviews with Bank staff members, August 2000, October 2001. One new Bank staff member remarked to me that she had been brought into the Bank for her extensive expertise on Latin American judicial systems, which would be increasingly important as the Bank expanded its activities in legal and judicial reform. However, once in the Bank, she was first assigned to public sector administration, with her first assignment in Tanzania. Interview with Bank staff member, Washington, D.C., April 2000.

[138] Nelson 1995, 146.

to focus more on "results-based" management of programs, as part of the principals' demands in IDA 14, may reinforce these cultural traits.

Time and resource constraints also prompt staff to rely on set categories or "labels" that can trigger standard responses. Ferguson's study of aid in Lesotho, for example, revealed that staff in the 1980s selectively gathered data and constructed development projects based upon the assumption that Lesotho was a traditional subsistence peasant society that only recently had turned to migrant labor, missing the critical fact that Lesotho's economy was actually based on cash crops. This misperception is attributed to the predilection to deductively design aid proposals around the prevailing organizational discourse and routines of the Bank rather than the specific context.[139] On the other hand, staff who are cognizant of these information distortions may gather relevant data on an informal level or portray that information in official project documents as consistent with apolitical, technical, and economic rationality. They do this in order to gain the acceptance or at least acquiescence of higher levels of management through which the project proposal circulates before reaching the board.[140]

A final point about the norms governing the identification, appraisal, and design of projects is the "strategic myopia" that affects selection and assessment. Needing to win approval for projects as quickly as possible, staff members are frequently overoptimistic (at least in writing) about how the project relates to broader development objectives, its expected output and the impact, and its sustainability.[141] As a result, as revealed in the Wapenhans Report and reiterated in later evaluations by the Operations Evaluation Department and Quality Assurance Group, staff members underestimate the risks during implementation that may undermine long-term outcomes. This often results in poor ratings of a project's performance, which are based in part on the deviation between outcomes predicted in the stated objectives of the project information document and the actual outcome as assessed by internal evaluation units.

This tendency to ignore risks is compounded by neglect of monitoring and evaluation (M&E) throughout the project life cycle—something that has received considerable attention in recent years in debates on engendering a learning and results-based culture in the Bank. The Wapenhans Report identified inadequate M&E as a key structural and cultural obstacle to reorienting the Bank's portfolio management

---

[139] Ferguson 1994, 26–29.
[140] Interviews with Bank staff members, August 1999, May 2000, and February 2002.
[141] Clements 1999.

toward results.[142] An incentive system that rewards staff for getting projects approved conflicts with norms that would promote supervision of projects once they are off the ground. Earlier studies and my own interviews reveal that staff members tend to leave projects soon after they have started, so as to pursue other lending lines. One project I studied in depth was on its fourth task manager only two and half years into implementation.[143] While some in the Bank assert that this neglect is not universal,[144] evidence from interviews and from official documents related to organizational reform indicates that staff turnover on projects remains a pervasive problem.

Despite reform rhetoric, many staff members still believe that institutional incentives reward individuals who get projects started, but do not hold them accountable for the long-term effectiveness of loans.[145] Moreover, the overall staff workload is quite high, as task managers in particular are often rewarded for the quantity of their loan portfolios rather than their quality.[146] Traditionally, the long timelines for projects (usually a minimum of four-year loan periods) have hindered the Bank's ability to link individual performance to project outcomes, and thus introduce mechanisms of accountability that can prompt staff to devote more time, resources, and attention to ongoing project management.[147]

Furthermore, M&E mechanisms, in facilitating organizational feedback and learning, are undermined by structural and cultural barriers. Ruth Levine, former Bank official now at the Center for Global Development, remarked recently on the weaknesses and disincentives for evaluation:

> Evaluation simply is not seen as the central business of the development banks. When material and human resources are stretched, short-term operational demands will over-ride the longer-term, more strategic imperative of evaluation and learning. As one indica-

[142] See, for example, various OED and QAG evaluations, as well as the assessment of the Strategic Compact, all discussed in greater detail in chapter 5.

[143] Interviews with Bank staff members in Washington, D.C., and Moscow, regarding the Russian Legal and Judicial Reform Project, September–November 1999.

[144] Interview with Maria Dakolias regarding legal and judicial reform projects in the Latin American and Caribbean region, May 2000. Staff turnover was much lower in this region.

[145] Caufield 1996, 214; Clements 1999, 1377; Blustein 1996; and Berg 2000. This was confirmed in interviews conducted in 1999, 2000, and 2001 in Washington, D.C. This may be changing as the Bank seeks to create more of a culture of "accountability."

[146] This was affirmed by nearly all Bank staff I interviewed during fieldwork conducted throughout 1999–2005. See also Caufield 1996, 214–15; and Naim 1994, 283.

[147] Naim 1994, C-283 and Wapenhans 1992.

tion, resources spent to design and implement impact evaluations were not even recognized as a separate item in the World Bank's budgeting system until 2005. Most task managers at the development banks can tell very sad tales about watching their evaluation budgets disappear during negotiations with either management or borrowing governments.[148]

Notably, the Operations Evaluation Department traditionally possessed few means to ensure that its conclusions had an impact on operational policies. Rich laments that in the early 1990s "many of the most damning indictments of Bank performance can be found in OED studies, yet OED is one of the most marginalized parts of the Bank; it is viewed by many Bank staff as a professional purgatory, a dumping ground for those that cannot be fired or who are exiled from operations, where the real action of moving money takes place."[149] When asked about the usefulness of OED evaluations, one Bank staff member told me quite bluntly, "We're all just too busy. [The reports] land on our desks, and five minutes later land with a big thud in the back of our file drawers."[150]

Evaluations conducted by project team members are also affected by incentives that lead to excessive optimism at the appraisal stage and to externalization of blame at a project's completion. Evaluations carried out during implementation, such as midterm reviews, tend to be much more critical and blunt, but are treated as strictly confidential and rarely shared beyond the immediate team. Final evaluations, on the other hand, are a different matter. Interviews with Bank staff members and other secondary studies indicate a lack of regard for project completion reports (now called "implementation completion reports"), which usually are conducted by the most junior member on the team.[151] The tendency of these reports to highlight successful components and

---

[148] Levine 2006, 4.

[149] Rich 1994, 171. This may be changing, as the OED has increased the size of its staff and Bank management is emphasizing the importance of monitoring and evaluation.

[150] Interview with Bank staff member, April 2002. The creation of the Quality Assurance Group, which evaluates projects in progress (as opposed to after the fact), may counter these tendencies. Mallaby argues in fact that QAG has had an observable impact on making staff more accountable for results, in fact "spreading a healthy terror among project managers" (2004, 167). Nonetheless, the effectiveness of QAG in changing staff incentives and behavior may be limited insofar as the evaluations are still largely kept internal and thus insolated from the additional oversight and accountability mechanism provided by external watchdog groups. Chapter 5 assesses the shift toward a "results-based" culture in more detail.

[151] Interviews with Bank staff members, August 1999, April–May 2000, and October 2001. See also Wapenhans 1992; Nelson 1995; Baré 1998; Berg 2000; and Wapenhans 2000.

hide failures is caused by pressure from project managers, who themselves are under pressure to give their projects good ratings. According to an internal survey, "management tends, often unfairly, to blame staff for poor project performance."[152] As previously mentioned, when performance results are widely publicized (internally or externally), there is a natural incentive to dismiss the lessons as due to the uncontrollable exogenous factors, downplay past errors, or use code words to suggest where faults might lay.

The result, broadly speaking, is an operational environment in which assessing the impact of a loan may be actively discouraged. Any focus on ensuring results is diminished and organizational learning is impaired. The roots of this pattern may actually be linked to external pressures on the Bank, notably the systemic pressure to demonstrate developmental effectiveness. Once again, Ruth Levine sums it up nicely:

> Those rare individuals within large bureaucracies who wish to undertake impact evaluation typically encounter daunting resistance. Program implementers may perceive evaluation as a threat, potentially leading to a cut-off of funding if results are not uniformly positive. At higher levels in an organization, managers who are responsive to demands by shareholders for "results, results, results" may prefer to promulgate anecdotes about success, without regard to the strength of evidence, rather than exposes the genuine lessons of experience—including the occasions when results were poor.

In general, evaluations tend to end with similar empty statements: "challenges still remain, but we are now prepared to address them."[153]

Conclusion

The Bank's world possesses strong intellectual and operational ideologies, norms, and routines that shape the Bank's bureaucratic politics, contributing greatly to our understanding of how development agendas, policies, and practices evolve within the organization. What the Bank does is not solely determined by external material and normative forces, and thus accounts that only analyze state interests, shifts in epistemic communities, or actions by NGOs remain thin and unpersuasive. Getting inside the organization allows us to assess the character and dynamics of organizational culture and bureaucratic politics,

[152] Caufield 1996, 252; Baré 1998, 323; and Clements 1999.
[153] Berg 2000, 33–38.

providing an excellent starting point for grasping the bureaucratic culture and goals that may or may not be consistent with environmental pressures. This in turn allows us, as outsiders, to identify where incongruent goals, within and between the environment and bureaucracy, occurs, and thus where organized hypocrisy is most likely to arise.

More critically, this dual level of analysis may enable us to explain when and where we can expect patterns of policy incompliance and mainstreaming gaps to expand or shrink. This requires a sophisticated understanding of organizational change that takes into account the myriad of push and pull factors outside, within, and between the external and internal environments of the Bank that facilitate or constrain talk and action. Here we must pay particular attention to the interests of member states and other external actors that impose countervailing demands. At the same time, we can look at the existing culture and entrenched bureaucratic interests that might resist change or push it in directions unintended by reformers.

The following empirical chapter is a case study of the dynamics of organized hypocrisy and change. Chapter 4 describes the Bank's embrace of good governance and an anticorruption agenda. Attention to good governance and anticorruption attained central status in the Bank's espoused development paradigm in the mid-1990s, marked by President Wolfensohn's famous "cancer of corruption" speech at the World Bank annual meetings in 1996. The idea of addressing governance and corruption was revolutionary at the time, challenging the organization's fundamental philosophy and approach to development. As a result, the incorporation of good governance and anticorruption into Bank theory and operations has been neither a spontaneous nor a natural process.

Instead, the governance and anticorruption agenda was initially met with, and is still confronted by, ideological and political resistance within and without the Bank. The process of mainstreaming the governance agenda and compliance with new anticorruption measures thus remains contested and incomplete, despite strong rhetorical support and increases in operational resources in recent years. Thus today, over ten years after Wolfensohn opened the door to these issues, incongruent goals in the authorizing, task, and bureaucratic environments of the Bank still contribute to organized hypocrisy in its governance and anticorruption work.

CHAPTER FOUR

Good Governance and Anticorruption: From Rhetoric to Reality?

GOOD GOVERNANCE and anticorruption are central to the theories and practices of global development today. The ambiguously defined, yet somehow morally indisputable concepts are widely viewed as the panacea for many development ills. Good governance and anticorruption measures are the keys to holding inefficient governments accountable for their actions. They are the preconditions for a market-friendly environment that attracts investment and ensures economic growth.[1] They are also the institutional means by which the poor can achieve the basic human security, become "empowered" to exercise their voice, and overcome the barriers to realizing the fundamental instrumental freedoms that constitute development.[2] Moreover, the presence of a sound and transparent public sector and the rule of law are increasingly asserted to be the foundations of a country's local capacity and willingness to implement and sustain development programs and policies.[3] Prominent programs and reports, such as the U.S.-led proposal for the Millennium Challenge Account and the United Nations Millennium Project Report, target good governance and anticorruption as the key means and end of development goals, and as the essential preconditions for the selective allocation and use of development aid.[4]

Surprisingly, despite the strong rationale and motivation visible today, the Bank's embrace of the governance and anticorruption agenda starting in the early 1990s was far from spontaneous. Donor states, freed from Cold War tensions, no longer shied away from these inherently political areas of development aid. Many borrowing governments, on the other hand, understandably resisted governance and anticorruption reforms as intrusions on their sovereignty. Internally,

---

[1] The empirical connection between "good governance" and economic growth rates, measured in terms of per capita income, is supported by numerous academic and Bank-sponsored publications by Daniel Kaufmann and Aart Kraay from the World Bank Institute. See, for example, Kaufmann and Kraay 2002a and 2002b; and World Bank 2007c.

[2] Sen 1999; Narayan-Parker 2000; Santiso 2002; and World Bank 2000–2001.

[3] Thomas et al. 2000; World Bank 1998, 2002b.

[4] United Nations Millennium Project 2005.

the obstacles of bureaucratic culture and politics proved equally daunting, reinforced by the divide in the external authorizing environment. On an intellectual level, governance and anticorruption issues ran head-first into the economistic, technocratic, and apolitical features of the Bank's intellectual culture. The foremost barrier to translating governance and anticorruption from rhetoric into action was internal opposition to the potential breach of the Bank's apolitical mandate. As one staff member argued, everyone knew in the 1990s that the governance-related reforms were neither apolitical nor particularly conducive to technical assistance. Yet until quite recently one no one dared to openly say the "p" word. This is despite wide realization inside and outside the Bank that the "myth of apolitical, technical assistance" is "the fig-leaf [that] has been wearing thin in recent years."[5]

As a result, the governance and anticorruption (GAC) discourse that finally emerged in the middle to late 1990s in the Bank was overtly driven by a economistic theoretical framework that lacked, in the words of one staff member, a "real working theory of the state."[6] According to the operations staff I interviewed, this in turn proved a significant barrier to implementation of the agenda, insofar as pursuing GAC projects is extremely difficult without the explicit analysis of the vested interests and political environments within client states. Governance and corruption issues as theoretically conceived also proved an ill fit with existing lending instruments and routines, clashing early on with the underlying norms and incentives informing traditional approaches to project management.

The emergence and institutionalization of GAC "talk" and "action" thus reflect a continuous tension within and between external and internal pressures. On one level, it appears that the gap between the espoused commitment to governance and anticorruption ideals is quite rapidly shrinking, implying a resolution of conflicting environmental pressures and a significant cultural change within the Bank. Between 1990 and 2006, for example, GAC appeared to be making significant headway in the Bank's lending, with total expenditures in public sector and rule of law reform totaling $2.9 billion, or 13.0 percent of all lending in 2005 (up from 0.6 percent in 1995) and the percentage of new projects with anticorruption programs increasing from 0.4 percent in 1995–96 to 5.0 percent in 2004–5.[7] Between 1990 and 2006, public sector governance and rule of law reform (the two main pillars of GAC work) accounted for close to $39 billion out of a total of $92.3 billion in cumu-

---

[5] Interview with Bank official, May 2000, Washington, D.C. See also Kapur 1998, 8.

[6] Interview with Mari Kuraishi, April 2000, Washington, D.C.

[7] World Bank Annual Report 2006.

TABLE 4.1
IBRD and IDA Cumulative Lending (by theme), Fiscal Years 1990–2006
(in US$ millions)

	IBRD	IDA	IBRD + IDA
	Public Sector Governance and Rule of Law		
Africa	480.27	9,057.50	9,537.77
East Asia and Pacific	5,067.73	1,133.18	6,200.91
Europe and Central Asia	7,926.64	1,134.18	9,060.82
Latin America and Caribbean	13,250.56	838.02	14,088.58
All Regions	26,725.20	12,162.78	**38,887.98**
	IBRD	IDA	IBRD + IDA
	All Themes[a]		
Africa	3,116.56	51,469.72	54,586.28
East Asia and Pacific	62,589.06	16,080.84	78,669.90
Europe and Central Asia	58,473.36	7,173.32	65,646.68
Latin America and Caribbean	87,277.10	5,110.39	92,387.49
All Regions	211,456.08	79,834.27	**291,290.35**
	IBRD	IDA	IBRD + IDA
	Public Sector Governance and Rule of Law as Percentage of Total Cumulative Lending		
Africa	15.41%	17.60%	17.47%
East Asia and Pacific	8.10%	7.05%	7.88%
Europe and Central Asia	13.56%	15.82%	13.80%
Latin America and Caribbean	15.18%	16.40%	15.25%
All Regions	12.64%	15.24%	**13.35%**

Source: *2006 World Bank Annual Report.*

[a] Other thematic categories include Economic Management; Environment and Natural Resource Management; Financial and Private Sector Development; Human Development; Rural Development; Social Development; Gender and Inclusion; Social Protection and Risk Management; Trade Integration; and Urban Development.

lative IBRD and IDA lending (13.3 percent; see figure 4.1). Moreover, governance and corruption assessments were more recently mandated within the key Country Assistance Strategy papers, new expertise has been brought into the Bank to tackle these issues, and a plethora of new formal policies exist to increase attention to and compliance with GAC measures. The key question here is why and how this happened. In particular, what set of external and internal factors converged to make the translation of the Bank's governance and anticorruption rhetoric into reality, as opposed to the more troubled translation of previous agendas such as sustainable development?

It is easy to find cynical answers to this question. Many inside and outside the Bank perceive GAC research and projects (particularly in the 1990s) to be variations on previous themes or "old wine in new bottles." The implication is that little has really changed in the Bank's neoliberal discourse and practice, and therefore the hypocrisy lies in the claim that a real transformation has occurred.[8] Others do see a significant change in the Bank's development paradigms, but continue to see distinct disconnects between the ideological and operational embrace of good governance and anticorruption. According to one member of the Bank's staff, the GAC agenda is "yet one more instance of where the Bank fails to match its rhetoric with its reality."[9]

This is indeed what Paul Wolfowitz appeared to think when he entered the Bank in May 2005 and adopted anticorruption as his number one development agenda. Wolfowitz's push for compliance with GAC measures and mainstreaming anticorruption work soon met resistance on several fronts, both internal and external to the Bank. In 2006–7, these conflicting pressures became apparent in the contentious drafting of, and very public debate over, the Bank's new GAC strategy paper. Thus, on one level, this story is about how the organized hypocrisy of the Bank—the gap between its rhetoric and its action regarding governance and anticorruption—first emerged and then slowly closed over time through a fascinating process of change within the world's Bank and the Bank's world. On a deeper level, the story is a critical investigation into where organized hypocrisy may still exist, and why.

The Evolution of the Good Governance and Anticorruption Agenda

Environmental Catalysts

The Bank's current embrace of a governance and anticorruption agenda can only be understood in the context of the organization's historical perspective on the role of the state in development. At the onset, the Bank's primary focus was the provision of funding and technical assistance for physical capital and infrastructure. This met the demands of a Europe recovering from World War II, as well as the belief that the key to effective growth was the provision of the tangible goods—roads, bridges, buildings, and so forth—that would enable successful state-building through targeted industrialization. In the 1970s, as concerns over equity and social development crept into tradi-

---

[8] Interview with Bank official, April 2000, Washington, D.C.
[9] Email correspondence with Bank official, June 2000.

tional ways of thinking, development paradigms shifted toward a "basic needs" approach that emphasized once again the object gap between the First and Third Worlds. Greater concern was given to the social dimensions of development, including education, health, and the provision of other basic social services, and the positive role and responsibilities of the state in providing them.

The turbulent 1980s, however, experienced an insurgence of neoliberal thinking during the Reagan and Thatcher administrations and the financial crises throughout Latin America. This prompted the Bank to refocus on macroeconomic (structural) adjustment.[10] The shift in development ideologies embodied a growing disapproval of state-led development strategies (such as import substitution industrialization) and a push for deregulation, privatization, and fiscal austerity. The prevailing sentiment was that "the government was best that governed least."[11] The resulting social and political costs of structural adjustment policies, however, produced a strong public backlash against the Bank and its sister institution, the IMF. Consequently, the Bank returned in the 1990s to an amalgamation of development strategies stemming in large part from a continued emphasis on structural adjustment. This time, however, it would be adjustment "with a human face" and with a much more nuanced approach to the role of government in socioeconomic development. In the 1990s, institutional language permeated development thinking and rearticulated previous development theory by stating that although corrupt, heavy-handed government was indeed detrimental to economic growth, "good" government was indispensable.[12]

In general, the recent literature on the good governance agenda and interviews with staff involved with early GAC work identify several external factors contributing to this shift in development thinking. The first factor is the failure of structural adjustment programs in Latin America and Africa in the 1980s.[13] In Latin America, rapid decentralization and privatization outpaced reform in the systems of accountability and civil service institutions, leaving considerable doubt as to how the new market-oriented environment would be effectively

---

[10] See Gwin 1994 and Stern and Ferreira 1997 for a discussion of how the United States in particular pushed a neoliberal agenda on the World Bank, as manifested in the appointment of Anne Krueger as chief economist and the appointment of Barber Conable, former U.S. congressman, as president of the World Bank.

[11] Nelson 1995, 289.

[12] Brautigam 1992; Nelson 1995; Blustein 1996; and Miller-Adams 1999.

[13] For a thorough analysis of the failure of structural adjustment programs, see Easterly 2001.

regulated and enforced.[14] By the late 1980s, for similar reasons, the Bank's adjustment policies in Africa were under heavy fire from the United Nations' Commission for Africa.[15] The inability of these programs to produce expected growth and the unanticipated result of social hardships due to budget cutbacks and rising unemployment led to question the logic of these aid policies. However, in a classic case of externalizing blame, the discrediting of structural adjustment faulted neither the aid organizations themselves nor their economic theories. Instead, senior officials at the Bank (and at the IMF) attributed many of the setbacks to political resistance. Borrowing governments were seen as reluctant to implement and sustain reforms in the face of strong domestic opposition. The response by the development aid community was thus not to dismiss the idea of structural adjustment, but to modify it according to "political realties."[16] According to the Bank's legal counsel, writing in 1991, "recognizing that early adjustment loans were often too optimistic about the implementation capacity of governments and their commitment to reform, the Bank has in particular directed its attention to measures that enhance government implementation capacity."[17]

A short time after open debate started on the failure of structural adjustment lending, the Bank and other aid agencies were facing a second challenge: the collapse of the command economies in East Central Europe and the former Soviet Union. The failure of initial Bank- and IMF-sponsored shock therapy programs in Poland and Russia to "get the prices right" and incite rational market behavior debunked the traditional neoclassical economic idea that a vibrant economy would emerge simply by reducing the regulatory role of the state and rapidly privatizing state-owned enterprises.[18] Shock therapy, based upon the tripartite plan of economic liberalization, stabilization, and privatization, had clearly neglected the need for change in both the formal and the informal institutional structures underlying economic exchange.[19] In a 1992 report, the Bank identified the absence of a legal system conducive to private sector development as one of the primary impediments to privatization and new investment. In 1996, the Bank published its hallmark *World Development Report* on the theme of the

---

[14] World Bank 1992, 4.

[15] Tshuma 1999.

[16] Miller-Adams 1999, 106. This was reiterated in my interviews with World Bank staff members Phillip Keefer, Pierre Landell-Mills, and Douglas Webb (World Bank, April–May 2000).

[17] Shihata 1991, 59.

[18] Murrell 1991; Williams 1998.

[19] Ahrens 2001, 61.

transition from plan to market, emphasizing the necessity of developing property rights and a market-friendly legal system (including arbitration and bankruptcy), as well as deeper institutional reforms in the banking and financial sectors.[20] This was reinforced by the harsh lessons of shock therapy, which had produced hasty and often corrupt privatization programs leading to looting of the assets of the formerly state-owned enterprises, frequently in collusion with the government officials running the privatization programs.[21]

Pushed strongly by external critics and a growing impatience by donor member states to "do something about Russia," the Bank was compelled to rethink its aid policies toward transitional economies.[22] Without a forthright admission of the failure of shock therapy, the Bank publicly recognized that the "first generation reforms" in East Central Europe and the former Soviet Union failed to bring about sustained socioeconomic growth and development because they ignored the political economy of institutional reform and the inability of traditional macroeconomic adjustment policies to change the incentive structures facing politicians, bureaucrats, and business leaders.[23] Thus, the "second-generation reforms"—newly labeled the "post-Washington consensus"—would address these deficiencies by focusing on strengthening the efficiency, accountability, and transparency of governing institutions (especially the legal, banking, and financial systems).[24]

The lessons of structural adjustment and shock therapy programs coincided with a critical paradigm or normative shift within economic theory itself. The growing popularity of new institutional economics, building on the Nobel Prize–winning work of Douglass North and on that of Ronald Coase and Oliver Williamson, caused a stir among development economists within academia and subsequently within the research department of the Bank. New institutional economics focuses primary on transaction cost analysis and a historical explanation of the evolution of market institutions to govern economic exchange. In particular, North's work outlines how complex exchange in modern market economies (as opposed to Third World economies) is a function of the ability of rational economic actors to transact within a framework of formal and informal contracts, which reduces uncertainty and introduces transparency and predictability into the enforcement of

[20] World Bank 1996.
[21] Wedel 1998.
[22] Interview with Bank staff member, October 2001, Washington, D.C.
[23] Santiso 2002, 24. See also World Bank 1997a.
[24] Naim 1995.

property rights and stable exchange in the market.[25] The role of the state here, as opposed to the laissez-faire notions within neoclassical economics, was to create, monitor, and enforce the institutions (including formal laws).[26]

This view of the state playing a benign governance role in the market coincided with the Bank's observations on the economic "miracle" of East Asia from the mid-1980s through the mid-1990s. Despite the Bank's rather liberal interpretation of the causes of the region's tremendous economic growth over the previous decade,[27] its 1993 report on the "East Asian Miracle" did admit that the state played a positive role in ensuring a "market-friendly environment" for foreign and domestic investment and export-led growth. This modest deviation from the laissez-faire neoliberal ideology of the Bank represented, in the words of one staff member, the "revenge of the institutional economists."[28]

Without conceding to a prostate development theory, the Bank began to embrace in official publications the relatively neutral language of institutional economics as a means of attributing past economic failures throughout the developing and transitional world to "poor governance" and "institutional deficiencies," including the weaknesses in checks and balances on corrupt and bloated government bureaucracies and the absence of the rule of law.[29] The success in East Asia (soon to be dispelled in the financial crises of 1997–98)[30] was seen as the result of "getting the institutions right," thereby providing the infrastructure necessary to "get the prices right." This once again deflected blame away from the Bank's own previous policies: after all, the fault was not in the theory, as once argued by former chief economist Larry Summers, but instead with domestic institutions' inability or unwillingness to fully implement needed macroeconomic restructuring. Little change was needed in the Bank's underlying theory of what would lead to economic growth and prosperity. Nonetheless, the introduction of new institutional economics into mainstream development paradigms opened the door to the language of good governance.

---

[25] North 1990, 34.

[26] North 1986, 1990; Eggertsson 1990; and Williamson 1994, 1996.

[27] The Bank's 1994 report has been strongly criticized for its blatant neglect of the interventionist policies of most East Asian governments, including the extensive subsidization of export industries, incentives provided for domestic savings, and aggressive fiscal spending in domestic education, health, and social welfare programs. For critiques of the Bank's interpretation, see Rodrik 1994; Wade 1996; Kapur 1998; and Stiglitz 2002.

[28] Interview with Mari Kuraishi, Washington, D.C., May 2000.

[29] Interviews with Phillip Keefer and Douglass Webb, Washington, D.C., April 2000.

[30] Stiglitz 2002, 91.

In the most general sense, the good governance and anticorruption agenda as articulated in the language of institutional economics was ushered into the mid-1990s within the broader context of globalization. Increased cross-border financial and trade flows, as well as the concrete processes of regional trade integration and the accession of Eastern European countries to the European Union, brought attention to the pressures for institutional and market policy convergence. According to Douglas Webb, a longtime Bank staff member, the governance agenda gained the ardent support of Part I member states and private capital markets, which saw the agenda promoting "market-friendly" language consistent with the support of liberalized trade and the development of institutions and policies that would facilitate foreign investment.[31]

Ultimately, the end of Cold War tensions also relaxed donor states' concerns about sovereignty that had formerly impeded international aid agencies from intruding upon politically sensitive areas of domestic reform.[32] Although the Bank itself was restricted to apolitical development assistance, many other aid agencies less encumbered by such mandates openly engaged in lending for the purposes of democratization. For example, the European Bank for Reconstruction and Development was established in 1991 to lend *only* to democracies in East Europe and the former Soviet Union. Other international organizations, such as the Inter-American Development Bank, Asian Development Bank, and U.S. Agency for International Development, also increased lending for rule of law development and the promotion of "democratic governability."[33] This cleared the path for the Bank to begin pursuing such activities over the objections of borrower states, albeit (as discussed later in this chapter) using the language of apolitical, technical assistance for "good governance reform."

Internal Advocacy of the GAC Agenda

The external conditions leading to the introduction of the good governance and anticorruption agenda says very little about how these ideas and policies were introduced, debated, and finally embraced in the Bank. In fact, what the preceding analysis overlooks is the internal shift toward governance and corruption concerns, which started as far back as the late 1970s. The ideas of governance and later anticorruption in

---

[31] Interview with Douglass Webb, April 2000, Washington, D.C. See also statements by Larry Summers (2000) as undersecretary of the U.S. Treasury.

[32] Kapur and Webb 2000; Santiso 2002; Bøås and McNeill 2004, 110.

[33] Santiso 2002, 28.

the Bank were actually developing even before the external shocks, normative shifts in epistemic communities, and increasing pressure from member states detailed above, although these environmental factors noticeably facilitated the rise of the governance and anticorruption agenda in the 1990s. Thus, the cultural and political environment within the Bank is a critical part of the explanation of when and how the governance and anticorruption agenda emerged.[34] It is also a crucial part of understanding the tensions with the intellectual and operational cultures that shaped how GAC issues were talked about and where they were or were not put into practice.

The initial interest in governance issues was first articulated in the late 1970s by a very small group of operational staff within the Bank, working within the African regional operational division. This group found that many of the reform failures in Africa were attributable to the Bank's own failure in recognizing and addressing the weakness of the public sector. Specifically, reform failures were seen to be due to pervasive corruption and the absence of efficient and sound public institutions capable of implementing and sustaining the objectives of development aid.

However, much like the response to a similar internal movement surrounding the environmental agenda, the initial reaction of management to requests by the operational staff was quite weak.[35] President Robert McNamara created a small public sector management task force in 1979 under the direction of Arturo Israel, but allocated very few staff, few resources, and little formal authority to the group. Even within this unreceptive environment, the group did manage to establish a Public Sector Management Symposium, comprised of a handful of staff members meeting annually to discuss the expansion of the Bank's work on public sector management.[36]

In 1983, the group succeeded in getting a small section on "good government" included in the *World Development Report*.[37] Yet again, however, this had little impact on the Bank's public discourse of development or its operational activities. Regional offices were encouraged, but not required, to set up units on public sector reform in their operations departments. According to Pierre Landell-Mills, a key figure in the early governance movement within the Bank, these regional offices (especially the Asian department) were very reluctant to reallocate re-

---

[34] This internal story of the emergence and mainstreaming of the governance agenda until the middle to late 1990s is also recounted in depth in Miller-Adams 1999.

[35] Interview with Pierre Landell-Mills, April 2000, Washington, D.C.

[36] Miller-Adams 1999.

[37] World Bank 1983.

sources to this new area and were not told to do so by any senior management directive.[38] In the absence of any willingness on the part of senior management to push the agenda and any effective internal oversight or control mechanisms, the public sector task force had virtually no means to influence operational policy or research directions in a significant way.

Nonetheless, the strong advocacy efforts of the small group eventually resulted in the creation of a central division for public sector management in 1981. Yet, even as the group began to make small inroads in operational work, the interest and support of management waned. A 2001 report by the Operations Evaluation Department on the governance agenda attributes this diminishing support to intellectual opposition, particularly the dominance of neoclassically trained economists within the Bank in the early 1980s. Many of these economists were recruited from academia with little or no experience in government and with little interest in or appreciation of noneconomic factors affecting development.[39]

Throughout the 1980s, much of the Bank's focus centered on the debt crises in Latin America. As a result, the focus in research and operations rested on macroeconomic restructuring through structural adjustment, which presumed that sound socioeconomic policies could be imposed by making aid conditional. To the extent that public sector reform was addressed at all, it was within the context of decentralization, the downsizing of civil service, and the reduction of public budget expenditures. Most often, these reforms were integrated into existing loan and grant packages as technical assistance. This happened despite the growing awareness by those in the operations unit working directly in the area that governance problems involved political dimensions that were not amenable to the technocratic fixes that, in much of the Bank's standard short-term infrastructural, macroeconomic restructuring, and capacity-building loans, were presumed to work.[40] Moreover, there was little attention to the actual ability or willingness of governments to implement and sustain those policies—a lesson that, according to staff I interviewed, would not be fully learned for several years.

Thus, in 1987, when newly appointed president Barber Conable initiated a large-scale reform of the internal bureaucracy, the fledging

[38] Interview with Pierre Landell-Mills, April 2000, Washington, D.C.

[39] World Bank Operations Evaluation Department 2001b, 19.

[40] Interviews with Pierre Landell-Mills and Richard Messick, April–May 2000, Washington, D.C. See also Miller-Adams 1999; World Bank Operations Evaluation Department 2001b.

public sector management division was eliminated altogether and the straggling public sector work was put into a single division with private sector work. Driven by the neoliberal ideologies of the chief economist's office (then under the leadership of Anne Krueger) and the open hostility to addressing what were seen as "political matters," private sector concerns soon completely dominated public sector work. This left the public sector management staff "orphaned" for the next several years.[41] Six years later, in yet another internal reorganization in 1992–93, the remaining public sector management group (in what was then named the Public Economics Division of the Development Economics Vice Presidency) was eliminated. The one remaining specialist in public sector management was relocated to the Human Resource Development and Operations Policy Vice Presidency.[42] A 1994 report on public sector management, intended for presentation to the Board of Governors, was never completed, "an indication of the low level of attention being paid by senior management to governance and public sector management" even by late 1993, when systemic pressures in favor of governance and anticorruption issues were beginning to converge.[43]

Despite the absence of clear support from within the Bank's internal hierarchy, the small group of public sector reform advocates achieved a significant breakthrough in 1989. In this year, the Bank's Council of African Advisors[44] sponsored a report that candidly rejected the standard economic explanations of Africa's failures in development.[45] Instead, *From Crisis to Sustainable Growth: Sub-Saharan Africa: A Long Term Perspective Study* argued that the region's difficulties were due to an entrenchment of kleptocratic elites who enriched themselves and their clans by looting public funds rather than striving to alleviate poverty.[46] The first draft of the report strongly criticized the Bank's management for its blindness to these political realities.[47] After an internal vetting, the report was strongly opposed by senior managers and member state

[41] Interviews with Pierre Landell-Mills and Richard Messick, April–May 2000, Washington, D.C.

[42] Interviews with Pierre Landell-Mills and Richard Messick, April–May 2000, Washington, D.C.; and interview with Pierre Landell-Mills, April 2000, Washington, D.C.

[43] World Bank Operations Evaluation Department 2001b, 20.

[44] The Council of African Advisors was a group of senior African political officials, including Ellen Johnson-Sirleaf (current president of Liberia).

[45] The paper was written originally as a ten-year progress report on an older initiative to improve African perceptions of the Bank and to suggest ways of improving its work in Africa. Phone interview with Pierre Landell-Mills, 11 June 2007.

[46] World Bank 1989.

[47] World Bank Operations Evaluation Department 2001b, 3.

representatives on the grounds that the language of the report was too political (according to the Bank's legal counsel), contained unflattering connotations for developing countries (according to the executive directors from China, Brazil, India, and several African countries), and smacked of "socialism" (according to the British government).[48]

The second draft of the report, written by staff member Pierre Landell-Mills, thus strategically adopted the language of "good governance," defined as "the exercise of political power to manage a nation's affairs."[49] Although the report was still met with some consternation by the board and senior managers, the language of good governance was already being used academically and was neutral enough to avoid the kind of reactions that the language of kleptocracy had invoked in the first draft.[50] At the same time, the published report argued that the hallmarks of the Bank's activity—private sector reform and the introduction of market mechanisms—were not sufficient for economic growth. Rather, even prior to these reforms, the primary need was to direct technical assistance and loans toward reforms geared at building an efficient public sector, a reliable judicial system, and an accountable political administration.[51] In a greater departure from the Bank's ideology and practice, the report advocated political pluralism, the rule of law, and the protection of human rights as key to the effective use of aid and socioeconomic development.

At the same time, this damning report was reinforced by an increasing awareness of aid fungibility and mounting criticism about the ineffectiveness of development aid over the previous decade.[52] The internal Wapenhans Report of 1992 (discussed in the previous chapter), circulated in draft form in 1991, claimed that much of the decline in the performance of the Bank's lending portfolios was in fact due to the kinds of governance failures in borrower countries identified in the 1989 report, *From Crisis to Sustainable Growth*. These included factors related to weak public institutions, the lack of adequate legal frameworks, weak financial accounting and auditing systems, uncertain policy frameworks, and closed decision-making processes leading to wide-scale corruption and waste.[53] In particular, the report openly chastised management for neglecting the aspects of governance that

[48] Phone interview with Pierre Landell-Mills, 11 June 2007.

[49] World Bank 1989, 60.

[50] Phone interview with Pierre Landell-Mills, 11 June 2007.

[51] World Bank 1989, xii. See also Klitgaard 1990.

[52] A summary of the internal debate and findings on aid effectiveness can be found in World Bank 1998.

[53] Wapenhans 1992, 4. See also Tshuma 1999.

represented key obstacles to the implementation and sustainability of development projects, as well as the need to engage measures to ensure borrowers' commitment and ownership.

Nonetheless, senior management continued to be extremely cautious with the emerging governance agenda. The obvious political overtones raised fears that integrating governance issues into reform agendas would be considered a breach of sovereignty in the Bank's client countries.[54] In fact, many of the governments in borrowing countries were openly hostile to this idea.[55] As a result of such resistance from borrowers and in the absence of focused pressure by donor states, management continued to sidestep governance and corruption concerns:

> For many Bank managers, denial was often the easy way out. They preferred to disregard obvious abuses and took at face value borrowers' claims of dedication of honest and efficient government. Signs of poor governance tended to be treated as though they were the outcome not of lack of commitment, but rather of weak capacity, which was to be tackled by structural reforms, technical assistance, and training.[56]

Paralleling this perceived resistance from the borrowing countries, the primary obstacle in the early 1990s to the integration of governance and corruption issues into the Bank's official development paradigm stemmed from internal debate over the fit of governance work with the Bank's charter mandates. In particular, Article IV, Section 10 of the IBRD Articles of Agreement dictates that "the Bank and its officers shall not interfere in the political affairs of any member, nor shall they be influenced in their decision by the political character of the member or members concerned."[57] The potential for the governance agenda to violate this mandate and clash with the Bank's carefully maintained image of a neutral technocracy, which was essential to the organization's external legitimacy and financial relationship with client countries, prompted considerable reluctance among senior managers. As a result, entering into the arena of governance reform required very careful articulation of how governance would be officially defined in the Bank's publications and what would constitute governance reform and the Bank's role in promoting it.

---

[54] Landell-Mills and Serageldin 1991, 307.

[55] Interview with Bank staff member, April 2000, Washington, D.C. See also Mallaby 2004, 180.

[56] World Bank Operations Evaluation Department 2001b, 7.

[57] Cited in Shihata 1991, 57.

In 1991, senior management asked Ibrahim Shihata, the Bank's general counsel, to issue a legal opinion that would interpret the scope of the governance agenda with respect to the Bank's Articles of Agreement. Shihata's response reflected the prevailing imperative of upholding the politically neutral facade: "The Bank's credibility and strength has traditionally depended on its status as a quintessential technocracy exclusively concerned with economic efficiency."[58] Facing increasing pressure from internal advocates and external sources (including Part I member states now quite interested in governance reform, especially in the post-Communist world), senior management pressured a very reluctant Shihata to issue a flexible interpretation of the mandate that would enable the Bank to openly discuss governance issues.[59] To do this, Shihata defined "political" according to the Oxford English Dictionary, as "belonging to or taking a side in politics or in connection with the party system of government; in a bad sense, partisans, factions, . . . and the political principles, convictions, opinions or sympathies of a person or party."[60] Accordingly, Shihata's legal interpretation permitted governance reforms to be funded by the Bank to the extent that they remained essentially apolitical, neutral, and fundamentally driven by economic (rather than partisan) motives. The legal opinion thus upheld a prevailing myth in the Bank's ideology that economic considerations could in fact be separated from the political sphere.[61]

This narrow yet ambiguous definition of the scope of the Bank's involvement in good governance reforms set a strong precedent for how governance issues would be talked about outside the Bank. Despite the explicit warning of earlier writings that the political dimension of governance reform could not be ignored, the Bank publicly did just that as it crafted its emerging governance agenda. In 1992, an internal task force on governance issued an official report in which it adopted a limited definition of governance, focusing specifically on the use of much more neutral language than that found in the 1989 report. In the 1992 report, governance is defined "as the manner in which power is exercised in the management of a country's economic and social resources for development."[62] The report identified four specific areas in which the Bank would be allowed to approach governance reform: public sector management, accountability, the legal framework for development, and information and transparency.[63] These areas

---

[58] Shihata 1991, 54.

[59] Interview with Bank staff member, May 2000, Washington, D.C.

[60] Shihata 1991, 70.

[61] See Nelson 1995 on the "myth of apolitical, technical assistance."

[62] World Bank 1992, 1.

[63] World Bank 1992, 2.

were somewhat more carefully defined in a subsequent report in 1994, describing the constitutive elements of governance as "epitomized by predictable, open, and enlightened policy making (that is, transparent processes); a bureaucracy imbued with a professional ethos; an executive arm accountable for its actions; and a strong civil society participating in public affairs; and all behaving under the rule of law."[64]

Internal advocates of governance issues were dismayed by Shihata's legal interpretation and these resulting reports. Interviews with staff members present during this time indicate that the Bank's departure from the explicitly political language held in earlier reports reflected not just the concern over the Bank's mandates and external image, as publicly stated, but also the ideological battle within the organization with economists who were strongly opposed to the injection of political theories into their models.[65] It was this resistance that strongly shaped the emerging language of governance reform, which was supposed to provide the "enabling environment" for the private sector and the checks and balances needed to ensure the capacity of governments to implement Bank-financed projects.

Moreover, in one of the most sensitive areas of governance—legal and judicial reform—the general counsel was asked once again to define the scope of the Bank's involvement. In response, Shihata declared that any legal and judicial reform sponsored by the Bank must demonstrate a direct and obvious link to economic development.[66] Moreover, in order to dissuade clients and critics of the notion that the Bank would be imposing politically sensitive governance reforms, Shihata argued that all such reforms must be initiated by the country itself in response to its own felt needs. The Bank could then only respond favorably to a request for such a reform project if it was found to be directly relevant to the country's economic development and to the success of the Bank's lending strategy for that country.[67] Thus, the language of client-driven country ownership of development projects became intertwined with the notion that the Bank would only take a *reactive* stance in facilitating limited governance reforms upon the formal request of borrowing governments.

The narrow interpretation of the Bank's mandates and the resulting limited definition of governance opened the door, but failed to really

---

[64] World Bank 1994b, 1.

[65] Interviews with Bank staff members, April–May 2000, Washington, D.C.

[66] This prompted Bank staff working on legal and judicial reform projects to engage in careful wordplay to justify certain components of projects that may have more direct political and social consequences (such as legal education and public awareness campaigns). Interviews with Bank officials, September–October 1999, Washington, D.C., and October 1999, Moscow.

[67] Shihata 1991, 89. See also Shihata 1995, 1997; and Vorkink 1997.

give a strong promotion for the governance agenda. As stated earlier, very few resources were allocated to governance research and operations. The 1992–93 organizational reforms under then president Lewis Preston came close to eliminating any institutional resources for governance. Nonetheless, the governance issue did not die, nor did Shihata's legal opinion close the door on the scope of governance activities. In the words of one staff member, Shihata's opinion did have a small positive effect, insofar as "an economic rationale can be found for almost anything."[68] However, what the governance agenda needed was not so much a legal opinion that would permit the Bank to venture into this new development discourse and respond to external interest, but rather a strong push from *within* senior management.

Breaking the Taboo: Wolfensohn and the "Cancer of Corruption"

The Bank today considers the time period up to the early 1990s to be the "prohibition era" for governance and anticorruption work (see figure 4.2).[69] The governance agenda essentially lay dormant until 1995, when James D. Wolfensohn was appointed as the new president. Wolfensohn, a former Australian national and a lawyer and investment banker by training, quickly earned a reputation within the Bank for his ambition to make his mark, his quick temper, and his open distrust of economists. Prior to Wolfensohn's arrival staff members were not encouraged to address (and were sometimes openly discouraged from addressing) governance and related issues in both research and operations.[70] Upon taking office, however, Wolfensohn unilaterally criticized the management's previous resistance to tackling corruption that lay at the core of the governance agenda. In 1996, in a famous speech given at the Bank's annual meeting in Hong Kong, Wolfensohn denounced the "cancer of corruption" and proclaimed his intention to make governance and corruption problems a priority.

Wolfensohn's ability to follow through on this purpose, however, was constrained by contrary pressures from inside and outside the organization. In a later speech given in 1999, Wolfensohn confessed:

> When I came to the Bank nearly five years ago, I was told we did not talk about corruption. Corruption was political. It was the "C-word." . . . But it soon became very clear to me corruption and the issue of press freedom, while they may have a political impact, are

---

[68] Interview with Ian Newport, May 2000, Washington, D.C.
[69] World Bank 2006b, 38.
[70] World Bank Operations Evaluation Department 2001b, 7.

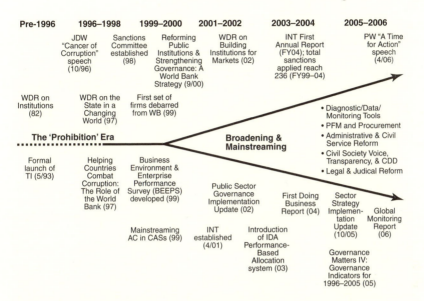

Figure 4.1. Visual History of the World Bank's Governance and Anti-Corruption Agenda. Source: World Bank. 2006. "Strengthening Bank Group Engagement on Governance and Anticorruption." Paper prepared for the Development Committee Meeting, Singapore (8 September 2006, p. 38), reprinted with permission of the World Bank.

essential economic and social issues, both key to development. *So we redefined corruption, not as a political issue but as an economic and social issue.* Corruption is the largest single inhibitor of equitable economic development, and in redefining the issue in this way our shareholder countries reacted very favorably. Indeed, six months later at a meeting of our development committee, ministers all made speeches about corruption and asserted that it was at the core of the problems that affect development.[71]

Indeed, the strong commitment from the new president appeared to be the tipping point for internal advocacy of the GAC agenda. According to Sebastian Mallaby, Wolfensohn's actions had the effect of breaking through the "intellectual dam" at the Bank, and "before long the Bank's research machine was gushing with new literature acknowledging the link between corruption and development."[72] Systematic attention by senior management to governance, especially corruption

---

[71] Wolfensohn 1999, A39 (emphasis added).
[72] Mallaby 2004, 176.

and the rule of law, finally became evident after 1996. This is in large part due Wolfensohn's appointment of Joseph Stiglitz as chief economist, a scholar famous for his work in institutional economics and an open critic of the Bank's past structural adjustment policies.[73] Stiglitz's promotion to the top research position led to a dramatic shift in the research focus of the Bank, including the hiring of many new staff trained in institutional economics, legal reform, and public administration (mainly finance).

These internal staff changes in turn ushered in a series of major publications indicating that governance and anticorruption issues had finally found firm ground in the Bank's official development discourse. In particular, the 1997 *World Development Report: The State in a Changing World* presented for the first time the Bank's embrace of good governance within its most widely read publication. That same year, the Bank published an official anticorruption strategy in a report entitled *Helping Countries Combat Corruption: The Role of the World Bank.*

In 1998, a critical report entitled *Assessing Aid* provided a powerful economic rationale for the Bank's governance and anticorruption agenda. The report argued that the effect of aid on economic growth was neutral or even negative until countries with "good" economic management were statistically distinguished from those with "poor governance."[74] The study found that with good management, an additional 1 percent of GDP in aid increased growth in per capita income by 0.5 percent and reduced the level of poverty by 1 percent. In countries with poor governance ratings, aid was not found to be effective

---

[73] Stiglitz initially established his career in research devoted to information economics, a field closely related to the emerging discipline of new institutional economics. Upon becoming chief economist of the World Bank, Stiglitz became an open critic of the "Washington Consensus." See Stiglitz 2000 and 2002.

[74] The measurement of "good governance," of course, is a hotly contested issue. For detailed discussion of governance measures by World Bank staff members, see Isham, Kaufmann, and Pritchett 1995, 1997; Keefer and Knack 1997; Kaufman, Kraay, and Zoido-Lobaton 2000; Burnside and Dollar 2000; Knack 2000; Collier and Dollar 2000, 2001; Kaufmann, Kraay, and Mastruzzi 2003. See also the World Bank 2000–2001. For the most part, the Bank's official research (which almost exclusively cites other Bank research in support of its conclusions) offers six main indicators of governance: (1) voice and accountability, which includes civil liberties and political stability; (2) political stability; (3) government effectiveness, which includes the quality of policymaking and public service delivery; (4) the quality of the regulatory framework; (5) the rule of law, which includes protection of property rights and independence of the judiciary; and (6) control of corruption. The governance indicators are measured according to an aggregate of ratings compiled by international firms such as Freedom House and Transparency International. For a full list of governance performance indicators and explanations on how they have been compiled and measured, see http://www.worldbank.org/wbi/governance/govdata/.

due to a higher chance of its being misused, pocketed, or distorted due to local institutional "incapacity" to deliver public services effectively. This study represented a watershed moment for the governance agenda, which resonated strongly at a time of strong external critiques of aid effectiveness. *Assessing Aid* articulated a specific economic justification, stated in convincing quantitative terms, for allocating aid selectively on the basis of governance performance.[75]

By 1997, attention to governance concerns had gained enough traction intellectually to start to gain entry into the Bank's broader analytical and operational work. The first step was to give governance an "institutional home" and increase the number of staff working on governance issues. During the 1997 Strategic Compact reorganization, a thematic group on Poverty Reduction and Economic Management (PREM) was created and endowed with a number of staff keenly interested in governance issues.[76] PREM includes a separate division for analytical and operation work on the public sector, headed by its own director and sector board. By 2001, the staff of this group (PRMPS) reached fifteen specialists in areas of public expenditure management, tax administration, judicial and legal reform, public administration, institutional assessment, and decentralization. In addition, the expansion of the legal department of staff devoted to stand-alone legal and judicial reform helped to broaden the governance agenda. "Rule of law" reforms quickly became an extremely popular component of the governance agenda. In essence, by 1997–98 the good governance agenda seemed to have found a "home" within the Bank's internal bureaucracy, thus setting the stage for mainstreaming the agenda.

An Intellectual Battle Won . . . or Lost?

Endowed with a clearer mandate and institutional resources, the GAC agenda quickly took pride of place in the Bank's public discourse. However, considerable debate exists on the extent to which the Bank's prominently displayed support of good governance really represents a significant departure from the organization's neoliberal, antistatist ideology. As demonstrated above, external and internal resistance to earlier political definitions prompted internal governance advocates to

---

[75] This study has resounded strongly with the current U.S. administration, which is highly critical of the effectiveness of development aid. Prior to his resignation, U.S. Treasury secretary Paul O'Neill (building on the findings of the Meltzer commission report) made a specific proposal for scaling back U.S. contributions to development aid organizations, including the World Bank, and making aid specifically conditioned on the ability and willingness of borrowing clients to meet a strict set of governance criteria.

[76] Interview with Rick Messick, April 2000, Washington, D.C.

pursue a narrower definition of good governance. Although packaged in the guise of a "post-Washington consensus," it contains very few critiques of past neoliberal policies.[77] Even within operations, the key Country Assistance Strategy papers that set the reform agenda for borrowing countries continue to highlight the traditional venue of neoliberal reform policies under the label of good governance. These proposed policies include the familiar calls for trade liberalization, fiscal restraints, prudent macroeconomic management, deregulation, and privatization.

Even in the Bank's official publications, the conception of the role of the state in socioeconomic development remains largely antagonistic, fitting well to preexisting organizational norms and laissez-faire ideology.[78] Indeed, the Bank continues to uphold in its official discourse a view of governance and the rule of law as things that constrain state action in the economy rather than creating room for a proactive role.[79] The state possessing "good governance" is a passive actor, providing public goods, a benign policy environment, macroeconomic stability, and investment in people and infrastructure. This is much in line with the underlying goals of the neoliberal policies and structural adjustment conditions employed in the 1980s. In this sense, governance reform rests on curbing arbitrary state actions and corruption, achieved by subjecting state institutions to greater meritocratic competition and bureaucratic downsizing, and making the states more responsive to citizens' needs by enhancing participation and decentralization. In the 2000–2001 *World Development Report*, the overwhelming focus of the good governance agenda is how to constrain states from encroaching upon private property rights, engaging in excessive regulation, pursuing poor macroeconomic policy, and restricting trade.[80] Only recently did the Bank's official definition of "corruption" shift from "the abuse of public office for private gain" to a definition that recognizes corruption as also prevalent in the private sphere.

The internal governance advocates I interviewed between 2000 and 2005 argue that the strategic framing of governance in terms amenable to the Bank's resistant economists worked insofar as governance ideas made significant inroads into the Bank's discourse. The choice of linguistic, theoretical, and methodological ways for talking about governance and corruption seem to matter. And once "on the table," staff

---

[77] Kiely 1998; Miller-Adams 1999; and Cohn 2005.
[78] Gillies 1996; McAuslan 1997; Faundez 1997; Miller-Adams 1999; Naim 2000; Santiso 2002; and Pincus and Winters 2002.
[79] Brautigam 1992.
[80] World Bank 2000–2001.

members argue, ideas can be debated and definitions can be broadened. Yet even three years after the PREM unit was created as the main home for governance work, staff continued to complain that the Bank's *official* view of the state noticeably lacked a theory of politics and had no forthright examination of power.[81] This has affected the way in which governance concepts have been articulated and diffused inside the Bank. Much of its research and operations continue to focus on the technocratic ingredients of state capacity, while ignoring overtly political or cultural factors.

Thus, strategic framing to gain intellectual entry has in effect changed the original idea of governance imagined by early advocates. The Bank in its governance work "does not dwell on the more intangible (and analytically difficult) social foundations that determine state legitimacy and authority, without which the best of designs for improving state capability are bound to flounder."[82] Even by 2005, resources for political stakeholder analysis were scarce.[83] Blunt talk of politics is more common today, but it is a recent phenomenon. Research on governance focuses almost exclusively on demonstrating (through sophisticated statistical, large-n models) the causal effects of the quality of governance on development prospects and aid effectiveness. Staff members readily dispute this apolitical and technocratic approach when speaking off the record. However, they also explicitly recognize this strategic articulation as necessary for governance to gain a prominent position among the Bank's competing policy paradigms.[84]

Translating the Governance and Anticorruption Rhetoric into Reality

Breaking Through the "P" Barrier: Internal Obstacles to Mainstreaming the Governance Agenda, 1996–2000

Generally speaking, staff members working on governance and anticorruption projects are quick to point out that the GAC discourse that emerged in the mid-1990s did not easily demonstrate how the complex concepts could be translated into practice. In fact, the emerging GAC talk appeared to impede operational mainstreaming in two key ways.

---

[81] Interview with Mari Kuraishi, April 2000, Washington, D.C.

[82] Kapur 1998, 8.

[83] Interview with Bank staff member, July 2005, Washington, D.C.

[84] This point was reiterated in several interviews with Phillip Keefer, Rick Messick, Mari Kuraishi, and Linn Hammergren, in addition to several other Bank staff members who wish to remain anonymous. April–May 2000 and July 2005, Washington, D.C.

The first is the persistence of an apolitical stance on governance reforms that has affected internal decisions regarding resource allocation, including staff hires and the development of skill sets and policy tools necessary to effectively tackle governance and corruption issues. Specifically, the theoretical and methodological framework that emerged to justify the Bank's foray into governance and corruption had the real effect of adapting the issues to prevailing economic models, thus precluding the perceived need to hire more social scientists and to develop the policy tools and skill sets necessary to address the *political* economy of governance reform. The second reason concerns the neglect of practical means and incentives for staff to actively push governance and anticorruption reforms on reluctant client states, especially in light of the persistence disbursement imperative and approval culture and the new pressure for an enhanced "client-centric" focus in the Bank's operations.

Even in official publications one can find implicit critiques by operational staff regarding the mechanistic, technocratic, and apolitical language permeating the official rhetoric, insofar as it "places enormous faith in the powers of formal rules, organizational structures, and technological innovations to reorient behavior of economic actors in developing countries."[85] This, in the view of many operational staff, leaves the Bank's notion of governance ahistorical and overly confident in the ability of aid providers to design and predict the direction and pace of institutional change.[86]

Those faced with the dubious task of constructing concrete governance and anticorruption reforms in the mid-1990s complain quite openly that the economists who dominated the intellectual articulation of the agenda still thought too much in terms of rational choice and incentives. These economists failed to see that both political and economic institutions are culturally and historically derived and driven by informal processes that are neither transparent nor easily captured by external agencies seeking to redesign local institutions.[87] One staff member attributes this myopia to the economists' interpretation of new institutional economic theory, which serves as the foundation of the governance agenda.[88] While Douglass North focuses heavily on the slow evolution of informal institutions (including norms, culture, and other intangible aspects of a political economy), the Bank's particular

---

[85] Burki and Perry 1998, 13. See also World Bank 2000a, 17.
[86] Philip 1999 and Schacter 2000.
[87] Interview with Rick Messick, April 2000, Washington, D.C.
[88] Interview with Phillip Keefer, April 2000, Washington, D.C.

view of institutional development emphasizes the building of formal institutions that can be facilitated through externally driven aid. Explicitly missing here is the recognition that institution-building in developing countries does not start on a *tabula rasa*.[89] Rather, there is a "persistence of dysfunctional organizations rest[ing] on vested interests, incentive structures, and ingrained patterns of behavior and expectations, none of which will be reversed automatically."[90]

Nonetheless, internal critics are quick to point out that this is predictable behavior on the part of the Bank. In the words of one staff member, "There is a very human tendency to stick with what you know how to do—an economist's idea of public administration does tend to be long on the structural adjustment aspects (privatize, decompress wages . . .) and short on organizational reengineering." The same staff member went on to comment specifically on how this has affected the legal and judicial reform projects in the Bank: "While they [economists at the Bank] have read their Douglass North, I don't think they have read very closely—otherwise they might be less confident that a new law would change the incentive structure and provoke new behavior—of the type predicated in their formal theories."[91] Yet even when such projects fail to produce immediate results, the Bank is slow to admit the fallacy of its approach. "There is simply no proof that top-down approaches do not work."[92]

The reallocation of staff resources necessary for mainstreaming of the governance agenda was thus quite slow, according to internal evaluations published in 2001. Many staff members at that time attributed this delay to the continued dominance of economists in key managerial positions (including vice presidents, network heads, and country directors), as well as the pervasive cynicism regarding "social and political scientists." In the words of one economist in the research department, "Why do we need political scientists? We're not interested in voting behavior."[93]

Indeed, until quite recently, the number of social scientists within the Bank has been extremely low in comparison to economists, engineers, and business and finance specialists. According to staff interviews, the noneconomists that have been employed sporadically throughout the research and operations departments have been put to

---

[89] Stark 1992.
[90] Linn Hammergren, personal correspondence, July 3, 2000.
[91] Linn Hammergren, personal correspondence, July 3, 2000.
[92] Interview with Bank staff member, April 2000, Washington, D.C.
[93] Interview with Bank staff member, April 2000, Washington, D.C.

work on grassroots level issues, leaving an absence of systemic work on the sociology and politics of institutional development at the level of policy formation. According to the 2001 OED evaluation of governance mainstreaming in the Bank:

> Good governance is the product of complex political, social, economic, and cultural factors. Good analysis of governance problems requires skills in all these areas. However, to date the Bank is preeminently an organization of economists and is dominated by economic thinking. Its 100-odd social scientists are deployed almost exclusively at the project level to undertake beneficiary analysis and oversee work on participation and involuntary resettlement. The Bank's handful of political scientists are largely marginalized.[94]

Moreover, despite the widespread recognition by country team members that politics matter deeply in the Bank's projects (especially in governance and anticorruption reform), its apolitical mandate constrains how openly they may discuss these issues in operational work. While political matters on the ground are the matter of intense discussion behind closed doors, the staff members do not have a practical or acceptable framework for talking about them in public forums, including the drafting of technical assistance papers and other project documents.[95] "Political analysis is treated as a luxury and is not debated openly."[96]

As a result, the internal advocates of governance issues (many of whom see themselves as marginalized social scientists) succeeded most in promoting governance issues in operations when they couched governance issues in terms that appealed to the "economist types" occupying senior management.[97] This is very similar to the experience of staff attempting to promote social development programs. In an internal memo, a sociologist working with the Environment and Socially Sustainable Development unit (ESSD) argued that the group's ideas on community-driven development would have no hope of "getting

---

[94] World Bank Operations Evaluation Department 2001b, 54. Even by 2001, when the governance agenda had been fully embraced in Bank publications, the total number of people employed in the public/private sector of the Bank came to 125, out of the total staff of 6,411 at the Bank's headquarters. Moreover, despite the visible increase in legal and judicial reform as one of the primary pillars of governance reform activities, the number of legal and judicial specialists in the Bank is estimated to be around fifteen individuals. World Bank 2001a, 64 .

[95] Interview with Mari Kuraishi, April 2000, Washington, D.C.

[96] Interview with Pierre Landell-Mills, May 2000, Washington, D.C.

[97] Cernea 1995; Woolcock 1998; McNeill 2001; and Bebbington et al. 2004.

on the table unless we can find a way to appeal to the SHTs [snooty Harvard-types] in senior management."[98] In the words of another staff member, "In the Bank, noneconomists are treated like second-class citizens."[99]

Many of the staff members I interviewed argued that this hegemony of economic ideas explains much of the narrow focus on the effects of governance on growth and aid's impact, rather than a wider concern with equity and justice. Moreover, it explains why research thus far has been dominated by quantitative, cross-national studies and quantifiable measures of governance with surprisingly few qualitative case studies. Because governance reform requires high levels of social and political knowledge about the borrowing countries, the Bank's ideologically driven choice of new staff and research agendas has impeded the ability of operational staff to translate ideas about governance into viable reform projects.

Moreover, governance-labeled projects are often narrowed to focus on aspects that can easily be portrayed as "apolitical," or that at least have economic consequences that are more direct than their political ones, even if doing so detracts from the potential impact of a proposed project. Components that are too blatantly political may be explicitly avoided by project teams or weeded out by country directors who must approve proposals before presentation to senior management and the Bank's board of directors: "Difficult institutional components of projects are often the first to be dropped in a pinch."[100] Moreover, the types of biases present in governance research have tended to neglect unquantifiable political, social, and cultural aspects. As a result, the diagnostic tools such as the new Public Expenditure Reviews and the Institutional and Governance Reviews that are intended to inform project management were not initially considered useful by operational staff.[101]

The institutionalization of governance issues and the allocation of staff in 1997 within the newly created PREM thematic network did not result in an immediate increase in governance projects or directly affect operational practices. The PREM network did take a proactive role in leading an internal discussion group and developing diagnostic re-

---

[98] Internal email, 2002, on file with author.
[99] Interview with Bank staff member, April 2000, Washington, D.C.
[100] World Bank 2000a, 53.
[101] World Bank Operations Evaluation Department 2001b; interviews with Bank staff members, April 2002 and June 2004.

ports ("toolkits") and practical guidelines for best practice.[102] However, under the new matrix management system installed during the 1996–97 Strategic Compact reform (see chapter 5), the ability of PREM to ensure a place for stand-alone governance reform projects is not assured. Instead, as in previous years, it depends on the willingness of powerful country directors to prioritize governance issues in the Country Assistance Strategy (CAS) papers and to hire PREM or related specialists through an internal contracting system to work on these issues.

Moreover, the PREM group's influence over operational decisions is unclear. Instead, operational decisions, including the allocation of resources between different sectors of lending, continue to be controlled within the country departments. By late 2000, nearly five full years after Wolfensohn's cancer-of-corruption speech and four years after the *World Development Report* devoted itself to the topic of good governance, there was an inadequate allocation of resources to the professionalization of staff in governance and corruption issues. At one point, the budget for public sector training was actually cut. In a internal survey in 2000, only one-third of staff believed that they have sufficient training on governance and institutional issues, and only 13 percent considered the Bank to have enough specialized staff to do the required work.[103]

One of the most evident obstacles to mainstreaming in this period was the clash between the nature of governance projects and the Bank's disbursement imperative and approval culture. This was not just due to perceived client state opposition, but a more widespread conflict with the existing operational culture. Interviews with staff in 2000–2002 indicate that there was continued reluctance to tackle governance and institutional development projects, which tend to be smaller (in terms of loan size), require more intensive monitoring, and, most critically, are less likely to demonstrate quick, positive results.[104] In an organizational culture where staff members continue to be rewarded for getting large loans approved rather than successfully implemented, governance projects are sometimes avoided. The appraisal time for governance projects is usually longer and often quite politically sensitive, requiring staff members to engage in contentious negotiations between political factions over issues such as legislative and

---

[102] To date, however, this has not had a significant impact on operational practices. In a 2001 survey of project task managers, 72 percent of the respondents admitted to never having used these toolkits. World Bank Operations Evaluation Department 2001b, 25.

[103] World Bank Operations Evaluation Department 2001b, 25.

[104] Interviews with Bank staff members, April–May 2000, Washington, D.C.

public sector reform in what is supposed to be an appraisal for apolitical, technical assistance.[105]

Governance reform projects have thus seriously challenged the organization's conventional way of conducting business. Governance projects often require cross-sectoral lending, which necessitates considerable intra-bureaucratic coordination between multiple divisions that normally may have to compete for scarce internal resources. QAG and OED evaluations of governance reform also reveal that the use of traditional lending instruments, focused primarily on measurable inputs and outputs and packaged within a standard four-year project timeline, have proven inadequate to achieve sustainable outcomes in institutional development.[106] Most governance projects exceed the four-year implementation period because of the inherent complexity of governance reforms that require extensive new legislation in sensitive areas such as property rights law, education, and taxation.[107] Implementation is most often impeded by resistance from groups in borrowing countries with vested interests in the institutional status quo, thus adding an indisputable political barrier to the technical implementation of governance reforms. Overall, "long-term institutional concerns do not fit easily into the traditional investment project with limited scope and the need to disburse against actual project expenditures."[108]

The rhetorical imperative that governance reforms be "client-driven" (initiated by the borrowing country) also runs counter to the culture within the Bank that rewards staff members for proactively seeking new clients and "selling" new projects. Most governance projects are portrayed as client-driven, using carefully worded language within official public documents to highlight when and how governments officially solicited the advice and funds of the Bank's staff. However, in interviews with staff members, it was clear that many governance projects are actively marketed to key public officials colorfully deemed "political champions" of reform. Governance reforms are thus seen within the Bank as primarily "supply-driven," neither generating nor building on a domestic political will for reform.[109]

---

[105] Interview with Bank staff member, September 2001, Washington, D.C. See also the case study of the Russian Legal Reform Project in Weaver 2003.

[106] World Bank Quality Assurance Group 2001. See also World Bank Operations Evaluation Department 2001b, 52–53.

[107] In the Russian and Legal Reform Project, the project team members I interviewed talked at length about the difficulties in getting new legislation passed through the Russian Duma and the subsequent delays in the project implementation timeline.

[108] World Bank Quality Assurance Group 2001, 39–40.

[109] This was certainly a major problem with the Russian Legal and Judicial Reform project, initiated in 1996. Bank staff had actively sought a political champion for the pre-

At the same time, in eagerness to get projects "sold" to borrowing governments and approved by internal management, staff members are often overoptimistic about the capacity and willingness of governments to sustain governance reform. Reliance on the aforementioned domestic "political champions" to push through reforms often backfires when these individuals or groups fall from power or face fierce opposition from other domestic actors with high stakes in maintaining the status quo: an inevitable feature of most public sector reform and anticorruption campaigns.

In this way, the Bank's existing culture of moving money quickly has collided with the need to establish a broad enough demand for reform on the part of the borrowing country (called "client ownership") to ensure successful implementation of the project loans after they are approved. As the OED report argues, "true ownership of reforms is probably unlikely in cases where a country, desperate for funds, is willing to say whatever the Bank wants to hear in order to trigger release of a tranche, and then lapse into inaction or even reversal of reforms."[110] This general malady of "clientitis" implies that within the approval culture of the Bank it is very difficult to get staff to scrutinize the sincerity of a government's commitments, and even more difficult for staff to take action that might put approval of a project in jeopardy.[111]

Overall, by the end of the 1990s and a few years into the millennium, the mainstreaming of the governance agenda in Bank operations appeared far from complete. Most certainly, interviews with staff working on governance research and operations revealed a high level of frustration with an internal cultural and political environment resistant to new ideas and practices. According to one staff member, "We talk and talk about the importance of 'good governance.' But in the end, what do we do? Not much. It's the same old Bank."[112]

---

conceived project, eventually finding Ruslan Orekhov, deputy chief of the Yeltsin administration. Orekhov, however, did not stay long in power (a common fate among politicians in the Yeltsin era), and implementation soon suffered from the opposition of the Russian Duma and relevant ministries. Interviews with key Bank participants in the Russian and Legal Judicial Reform Project, Moscow, September–October 1999; and Washington, D.C., August 1999 and April–May 2000. See also Schacter 2000, 7; and the World Bank Independent Evaluation Group 2006b, 34, on the problem of overreliance on "political champions."

[110] World Bank Operations Evaluation Department 2001b, 29.

[111] Interview with Linn Hammergren, April 2000, Washington, D.C. See also comments on the persistence of "clientitis" in the evaluation of the Strategic Compact, discussed in the next chapter.

[112] Interview with Bank staff member, October 2001, Washington, D.C.

Tackling the "C" Word: Anticorruption Policy Compliance and Mainstreaming

> Let's not mince words: we need to deal with the cancer of corruption. . . . Let me emphasize that the Bank Group will not tolerate corruption in the programs that we support; and we are taking steps to ensure that our own activities continue to meet the highest standards of probity.
> —*James D. Wolfensohn, 1996*

President Wolfensohn eloquently articulated the Bank's anticorruption ideals in his 1996 speech at the World Bank and IMF annual meetings in Hong Kong. Yet the anticorruption agenda faced incongruent goals, impeding the translation of Wolfensohn's commitment to "zero corruption" into a clear set of enforced policies and mainstreaming in the Bank's practices. From the start, attention to corruption challenged the Bank's apolitical mandates and operational environment. Managers feared that if they raised issues of graft and bribery, they would provoke client governments' opposition during a key period in which demand for loans (especially in middle-income countries) was already in decline.[113] The anticorruption agenda also countered the existing disbursement imperative and "clientitis" of the Bank's culture, which had over several decades contributed to a high level of tolerance for corruption in loan programs. This culture was deeply rooted, despite a growing awareness among operational staff that corruption inevitably meant wasted funds and undermined the long-term effectiveness of development projects.[114] Moreover, on a more pragmatic level, operational staff lacked effective tools for actually implementing Wolfensohn's plans for fighting corruption.

In some instances, management and staff thought that corruption and poor governance were in fact defining attributes of underdevelopment. Therefore, withholding or canceling loans to countries that failed to meet standards for good governance and corruption busting seemed counter to the very purpose of the Bank. In the absence of client states' support for domestic anticorruption reform, the Bank could only push the anticorruption agenda by making loans conditional (which many consider ineffective in changing client governments' behavior), implementing costly and time-consuming auditing and procurement mea-

---

[113] Pound and Knight 2006, citing interview with Robert Holland, U.S. executive director to the World Bank.

[114] Bretton Woods Project 2006a.

sures (with costs passed on to reluctant clients), or canceling loans, which threatened the Bank's financial interests.[115] According to Dennis de Tray, the Bank's former country director for Indonesia, canceling or withholding projects and loans out of concerns about corruption would "hurt those the Bank is supposed to be helping. . . . If we are not careful in the way we deal with corruption, we will set up even sincere and committed leaders for failure and could end up creating just the failed states we are trying to prevent."[116]

The reticence of much of the management and staff to follow through on the new anticorruption agenda can thus partially be explained as a pragmatic response to what they considered an idealistic or naive goal given the reality of the countries to which they were lending. While the effects of corruption on development and the effectiveness of aid were well understood, the deeper causes of and cures for corruption were not, and thus a distinct strategy for addressing a sensitive and complex political issue in lending operations proved elusive. De Tray's qualified reaction, quoted above, is featured in Sebastian Mallaby's account of staff working in Indonesia, one of the Bank's most corrupt client states. Mallaby describes the response of staff to Wolfensohn's cancer-of-corruption speech:

> The boss had attempted to change the development agenda; he had stood up at the annual meetings and stunned people with his bold language. But then the Bank staff "at the coal face" had listened, considered, and formed their own opinion: his pronouncements were irrelevant. The majority of the Bank's Jakarta office could see no good way of turning anticorruption rhetoric into actual policies. The most they would do was talk more openly about corruption, but in a patient, Indonesian kind of way. They were not willing to resort to the nuclear option of canceling big projects.[117]

In sum, political opposition from client governments, cultural fissures within the Bank, and real pragmatic concerns prevented the full embrace of Wolfensohn's anticorruption agenda. In the words of one former staffer, the Bank's approach to fighting corruption could be described as the "three-monkey policy": "see nothing, hear nothing, say nothing."[118]

At the same time, one cannot easily conclude that the Bank's apparent hypocrisy was intentional. In fact, during the years following

[115] Mallaby 2004, 181–82.

[116] These candid remarks were made by de Tray (2006) after his retirement from the Bank, in February 2006 in a public speech at the Center for Global Development.

[117] Mallaby 2004, 183.

[118] Quoted in Bretton Woods Project 2003.

Wolfensohn's speech, he initiated several formal policy and staff changes intended to contribute to the anticorruption mainstreaming. In 1997, the Bank published its first key strategy report on how to fight corruption.[119] In addition, as part of the Strategic Compact reorganization launched in 1997, management announced that it planned to increase the number of financial managers and procurement specialists to help identify misuse of funds in projects.[120] In 1998, Wolfensohn set up an internal investigative unit to audit loans for evidence of corruption and set up a twenty-four-hour telephone hotline to allow staff and members of the public to report corruption. At the same time, the Bank established a "sanctions committee" to respond to the hotline information and punish companies and individuals found guilty of bribery and graft. In 2000, Wolfensohn turned this committee into the Department of Institutional Integrity, whose primary function now is to investigate allegations of corruption in Bank-funded contracts (debarring guilty companies from future contracts) as well as suspected corruption inside the Bank's staff.[121] Throughout this period, the World Bank Institute (under the leadership of Daniel Kaufmann) published extensive research findings on the scope and nature of governance and corruption problems and the impact on aid's effectiveness. On a formal level, by 1999, it thus appeared that the Bank was firmly embracing the anticorruption agenda and taking the necessary steps to translate the agenda into action.

Hypocrisy Exposed: The U.S. and NGO Campaign against the Bank

At the same time that these important internal changes were unfolding, there was a noticeable shift from relatively diffuse to more concerted external efforts to monitor and shape the Bank's governance and anticorruption activities. On a systemic level, the political and normative environment by the late 1990s had noticeably changed in favor of aggressively addressing corruption. Major international organizations, such as the Organization for Economic Cooperation and Development, the United Nations, the Council of Europe, and the Organization of American States were passing anticorruption conventions. International NGOs started to focus their multilateral development

[119] World Bank 1997b. See also the follow-up evaluation conducted in 2004 (World Bank Operations Evaluation Department 2004b).

[120] Financial management staff would increase from thirty-four in FY1988 to eighty-eight in FY 1999 (a 159 percent increase) and procurement specialists grew from forty-six in FY1997 to eighty-two in FY1999 (a 78 percent increase). United States General Accounting Office 2000, 14.

[121] United States General Accounting Office 2000, appendix 1; Finer 2003.

bank (MDB) campaigns around high-profile cases of corruption, especially in very visible and symbolic infrastructure and extractive industry projects. These NGOs likewise continued to lobby the U.S. Congress, as they had done consistently (and successfully) in the past to push the environmental agenda. This time, however, the NGOs engaged the U.S. power of the purse to push for new legislation that would more carefully monitor and sanction MDB activities to counter corruption.

Among the donor states, the United States was particularly receptive to concerns about corruption in development aid, leading to more extensive oversight of the Bank. In late 1999, not long after Congress commissioned the scathing Meltzer Report, Congress also directed the U.S. General Accounting Office to investigate efforts to mainstream and enforce the anticorruption measures that had been installed in the Bank since 1997. The GAO's report, published in 2000, was entitled *World Bank: Management Controls Stronger, but Challenges in Fighting Corruption Still Remain.*[122] While the report was far from a damning indictment, it did offer damaging critiques based upon the Bank's own internal assessments. In particular, the report noted that staffing changes were far from sufficient to meet the new goals, with only 14 percent of projects engaging specialists in financial management and procurement. Moreover, the report expressed concern about ongoing project management, finding that risk assessments and mitigation processes were weakly followed, and that management often understated or did not disclose known risks related to the borrower's implementation capacity.[123] Mainstreaming gaps also surfaced with respect to the Bank's stated commitment to including governance and anticorruption concerns in the critical Country Assistance Strategy (CAS) papers. According to the GAO's review of thirty-one CAS papers in early 2000, only 25 percent included a discussion of corruption-related risks or the role that progress on corruption-related issues would have on lending decisions. On this same note, only 40 percent of the CAS papers were rated as satisfactory or better in addressing corruption risks, and many CAS lacked comprehensive procurement reviews and financial accountability assessments.[124] In all, the interviews the GAO staff conducted with the Bank's officials revealed that "the Bank had for years been reluctant to address corruption risks openly and directly with borrowers."[125]

[122] United States General Accounting Office 2000.
[123] United States General Accounting Office 2000, 14–15.
[124] United States General Accounting Office 2000, 21–22.
[125] United States General Accounting Office 2000, 21.

Following the release of the GAO report, the U.S. Congress in 2001 passed new legislation mandating the GAO conduct an annual review of the financial operations and auditing processes of the multilateral development banks. The GAO is now required to report to the Foreign Appropriations Committee (which authorizes release of U.S. funds to the Bank and other MDBs) on whether the MDBs are taking adequate steps to prevent the misuse of development funds in borrowing countries and within the institution itself.[126] In 2003, the GAO released a second report entitled *World Bank Group: Important Steps Taken on Internal Control but Additional Assessments Should Be Made*. The report again gave a mixed judgment and recommended stronger enforcement of project-auditing policies.

The findings of the new GAO report were reinforced at the same time by public statements by former Bank insiders, who cast doubt on the ability and willingness of the Bank to act upon the new anticorruption mandates. In July 2003, Joseph Finer published in the *Washington Post* an article on the Bank's efforts to fight corruption. Finer quotes Peter Eigin, founder and president of Transparency International, the corruption watchdog organization with which the Bank works closely in the construction of its governance indicators. Eigin formerly worked in the Bank, but left in 1991 when his demands for more attention to corruption were ignored. While Eigin depicted the Bank's progress in tackling corruption in a mostly positive light, he spiced his remarks with a striking comment about the nature of culture and change in the Bank: "It's very hard to change a large organization like the World Bank, and they're still working through this. . . . They were pretty bad, and allowed [corruption] to become a major problem. There's been a total change in policy, but to change from policy to total implementation is a long way to go."[127]

In the same article Finer also quoted former insider William Easterly, now an economist at New York University. Easterly worked for the Bank until the late 1990s, when his public criticism of its past structural adjustment policies led to pressure for his resignation. In his comments to Finer, Easterly referred implicitly to the Bank's culture of "clientitis" and prevailing pressure to lend as reasons for shortfalls in the enforcement of anticorruption policies. He argued that "if the client is important enough geostrategically or one they want to cultivate in the

---

[126] Foreign Operations, Export Financing, and Related Programs Appropriation Act (PL106-429), section 803(a). For a more detailed description, see United States General Accounting Office 2003.

[127] Finer 2003.

long run, [the Bank] will continue lending to them, despite long histories of corruption. They continue forcing loans down that pipe."[128]

In the summer of 2004, the Washington-based Government Accountability Project (GAP) published an investigatory report entitled *Challenging the Culture of Secrecy: A Status Report on Freedom of Speech at the World Bank*.[129] GAP's evaluation of the Bank's internal whistle-blower policies contradicted Wolfensohn's rhetoric about the effectiveness of internal mechanisms designed to enable staff to report instances of corruption in lending projects and internal operations. GAP reported that despite the formal policy changes and the construction of the new "hotline" reporting system, staff members were still highly discouraged from speaking openly, and whistle-blower protections were weak and rarely enforced. In particular, the report notes numerous instances in which staff members who dared to report corruption frequently became victims of reprisal and often lost their jobs.[130] In one case, according to the GAP report, President Wolfensohn personally retaliated against a whistle-blower in the Financial Sector Vice Presidency and convinced the vice president to withdraw his complaints. The vice president was initially reassigned in his duties and then denied permanent status at the conclusion of his probationary period.[131]

The GAP evaluation lambasted what it saw as the "Trojan horse whistleblower laws" and a pervasive "culture of secrecy" that contradicted the Bank's carefully crafted image as an open, transparent, and accountable institution. Most notable in the GAP report was the direct blame placed on management for the ineffectiveness of internal mechanisms to fight corruption:

> The intangible element of leadership commitment to announced reforms normally is key to determining how seriously institutional staff take it, and how much is accomplished. Unless a leader demonstrates commitment through highly visible public actions, would-be whistleblowers may dismiss the charges as public relations gestures or empty rhetoric, and the changes may not disrupt ingrained patterns of management secrecy enforced by retaliation.[132]

In the same period in which the GAP report was being drafted, the U.S. Senate Foreign Relations Committee, chaired by Senator Richard

---

[128] Finer 2003.

[129] Government Accountability Project 2004. GAP is a nonprofit organization dedicated to promoting transparency and accountability in domestic and international governmental bureaucracies, with a specific focus on the construction and enforcement of "whistle-blower" protection policies.

[130] Government Accountability Project 2004, 8 and 16.

[131] Government Accountability Project 2004, 25.

[132] Government Accountability Project 2004, 33.

Lugar (R-Ind.), launched a series of hearings on corruption in the multilateral development banks.[133] The hearings themselves included testimonies from academic experts; NGO representatives from Environmental Defense, the Bank Information Center, and Transparency International; and the U.S. executive director to the World Bank (then Carole Brookins).[134] The testimonies provided startling statistics about the scope and nature of corruption in development aid. Jeffrey Winters, an academic expert on Indonesia, estimated that the Bank had participated passively in the corruption of nearly $100 billion in loan funds since its inception. Winters had actually been a key actor early on in blowing the whistle on corruption in the Bank's loans in Indonesia. At a press conference in Jakarta in 1997, Winters claimed that one-third of Bank loans in Indonesia had been stolen. The Bank vehemently denied the allegations. Yet within the year, two internal reports were leaked that fully supported Winters's claims, estimating that the total amount of loans stolen in Indonesia to be more than $8 million.[135] Manish Bapna, executive director of the Bank Information Center, further estimated that 30–40 percent of recent World Bank structural adjustment lending was also wasted due to corruption.[136]

All the speakers at the May 2004 congressional hearings supported what internal advocates in the Bank already knew about the bureaucratic obstacles to mainstreaming the anticorruption agenda. In large part they attributed tolerance of corruption to embedded institutional incentives, specifically the prevailing pressure to lend, and from the fundamental moral hazard in the structure of the MDBs, which by and large does not hold the institutions accountable for the proper or effective use of their loans.[137] Bapna argued that "while MDBs profess 'zero tolerance' for corruption in their projects and programs, this rhetorical commitment has not always been meaningfully implemented. Pressure to lend and a 'culture of loan approval' have inhibited a 'culture of accountability' from taking root. . . . As a result, there is little if any internal or external accountability for anticorruption results."[138]

All the speakers also called for fostering corruption expertise and diagnostic tools within the Bank, increased focus on particularly vul-

[133] Government Accountability Project 2004 notes that the 2004 congressional hearings were in part a response to the 2003 GAO report and a subsequent story in *Washington Times Insight* magazine on an investigation into whistle-blowing disclosures of corruption at the Inter-American Development Bank in late 2002 and early 2003. GAP 2004, 5.

[134] Rich 2004; Bapna 2004; Boswell 2004; Brookins 2004.

[135] Winters 2004, 3; Bapna 2004, 3. See also Mallaby's account of Winters in Indonesia in 1997 (Mallaby 2004, 184–85).

[136] Bapna 2004, 2.

[137] See especially Winters 2004, 2–3; and Bapna 2004, 8.

[138] Bapna 2004, 2. See also his longer description of institutional incentives on p. 8.

nerable areas such as extractive industries, the promotion of media and civil society groups in monitoring corruption, and disclosure in all MDB operations, including executive board meetings.[139] They also called upon the U.S. Congress to expand the legislation passed in 2004 that demanded greater transparency and accountability standards at the MDBs[140] and to use the IDA replenishment negotiations as leverage to push for strengthened information disclosure policies to enhance external oversight of all MDB activities.

Many of these concerns and recommendations were reiterated at a second hearing of the U.S. Senate Foreign Relations Committee on 21 July 2004. This hearing focused specifically on the role of the U.S. Treasury (the main liaison between the Bank and Congress) in overseeing anticorruption measures in the MDBs. The hearing included testimony on the now infamous Lesotho case, in which the client government was in the process of prosecuting a number of contracting companies for bribery and graft related to the Bank-funded Highlands Water Project.[141] Quite remarkably, Senator Lugar also took direct aim at the U.S. Treasury itself for its own weaknesses in overseeing the Bank's efforts to enforce compliance with new anticorruption measures. In February 2004, Lugar forwarded a specific allegation of corruption to the Treasury Inspector General's office. The Treasury failed to take concerted action, claiming uncertainty about its jurisdiction in MDB matters and "lack of resources since divestiture of Congressional funds to Homeland Security."[142]

As a result of the 2004 hearings and continued campaigning by a coalition of NGOs led by GAP, Congress passed the Leahy-McConnell Amendment as part of the Consolidated Appropriations Act of 2004 (Section 581). The amendment requires the U.S. Treasury secretary to report to Congress on the MDBs' progress toward greater transparency and accountability. Later legislation in the FY2006 Foreign Operations appropriation bill (drafted in 2005) mandates the U.S. executive directors to the MDBs to support clear and public anticorruption procedures that are coordinated across all MDBs, including staff financial

---

[139] Bapna 2004; Boswell 2004, 4. These points were later reiterated by John B. Taylor, undersecretary of the Treasury for international affairs in his testimony before the Senate Foreign Relations Committee on 21 July 2004. See Taylor 2004.

[140] See Sections 580 and 581 of the U.S. Congress Consolidated Appropriations Act FY2004 (PL108-199).

[141] For a description of the controversy surrounding the corruption on the part of Bank-contracted firms in the Lesotho Highlands Water Project, see Bretton Woods Project 2003.

[142] Lugar 2004. See also Bretton Woods Project 2004.

disclosures procedures, stronger whistle-blower protection policies, and the establishment of independent ethics and auditing offices.

Despite these dramatic examples of the most powerful member state enacting measures to pressure the Bank to enforce the anticorruption agenda (a external goal convergence that we might expect to reduce organized hypocrisy), critics remained unconvinced that these new laws had compelled substantial change in the Bank's behavior. One such instance is in the now very sensitive case of internal whistle-blower policies, which watchdog NGOs have identified as crucial in transforming the culture of secrecy and promoting transparency and accountability in Bank lending. GAP remains highly critical of the manner in which the "best practices" whistle-blower policies have been carried out. In March 2005, the U.S. Treasury released its required report on the Bank's progress in implementing various anticorruption measures. GAP's response was quite cynical:

> The good news is that Treasury is using its bully pulpit to press for change. The bad news is so far the reality is not close to the rhetoric. MDB whistleblowers still proceed at their own risk in policies that are more like traps than protection. Treasury praises long-pending Bank promises of still-secret plans to create whistleblower policies. Secret transparency reforms are an oxymoron.[143]

Thus, by the end of Wolfensohn's presidency in May 2005, doubt still lingered about the sincerity with which the Bank enforced the new rules and proactively pursued the identification and punishment of corruption. On the surface, however, the evidence was encouraging. In February 2005, the Bank released its first annual report on the investigations conducted by the Institutional Integrity Department and the Sanctions Committee, claiming that more than two thousand cases of fraud and corruption (internally and in Bank-funded projects) had been investigated and closed since 1999.[144] Public sector lending took over the largest share of Bank loans, at over 20 percent in 2006,[145] and the Bank's governance indicators were prominently used in new performance-based aid allocation systems. Between 2002 and 2004, all CAS papers were reported to "explicitly or implicitly" recognize corruption concerns. By 2005, governance assessments were mandated in PRSPs and the diagnosis section of all CAS reports.[146] Staff working in countries at high risk for corruption were told to devise specific anti-

---

[143] Government Accountability Project 2005.
[144] World Bank 2005.
[145] World Bank 2006b.
[146] World Bank 2006c.

corruption plans, to mitigate the "fiduciary and reputational risks" to the Bank's projects.

At the same time, however, groups within the Bank were beginning to talk quite bluntly about the ineffectiveness of past apolitical approaches to governance and anticorruption reforms. A Sector Strategy Implementation Update, released in March 2006, came to a sobering conclusion about the actual compliance with the mandate to include GAC assessment in the all-important CAS papers:

> while all CASs comply with the mandate to treat governance, the majority of CASs deal with governance in a perfunctory manner and still do not adequately assess the developmental or fiduciary risks or corruptions. . . . three reasons for this are weak commitment of governments to governance reform, disincentives for Bank country teams to analyze more fundamental institutional and political drivers of corruption and poor governance, and the tendency to compartmentalize and treat governance as a sector rather than as a cross-cutting theme.[147]

Likewise, the IEG's *Annual Review of Development Effectiveness* in 2006 reported limited changes in the governance perception indicators in countries where the Bank had been funding public sector reforms since the mid-1990s.[148] This report attributed the ineffectiveness of GAC reforms to the "limits of technocratic support" and "failure to align with political realities"—sentiments shared in reports by several watchdog NGOs.[149] In general, there was a clear recognition that "insufficient understanding of the political economy of reforms has led the Bank . . . to push reforms that stand little chance of success. Therefore, an assessment of the political landscape with respect to proposed anticorruption reforms is essential for designing effective programs."[150]

Even with this evidence of organizational learning, staff I interviewed in Washington in July 2005 still perceived significant bureaucratic resistance and cultural inertia to hinder more systemic attempts to mainstream the anticorruption and governance agendas. Resources for corruption diagnosis and reform projects remained thin despite a plethora of new analytical "toolkits" and proposals. Staff who report directly to country directors still believed that they faced conflicting priorities in an institution that espoused commitment to punishing

---

[147] World Bank 2006d, 29.

[148] World Bank Independent Evaluation Group 2006b, 34.

[149] World Bank Independent Evaluation Group 2006b, 34. See also Coopération Internationale pour le Développement et la Solidarité 2006 and Cornett 2007.

[150] World Bank 2006c, 10.

corruption while continually rewarding "client responsiveness" and large loans.[151] Thus, by 2005, despite a seeming convergence in external pressure and an observable effort internally to develop feasible mainstreaming strategies, there continued to be critical goal incongruence inside the Bank, perpetuating organized hypocrisy. Sebastian Mallaby, in a column in the *Washington Post* from 2006, aptly summarizes the perceived hypocrisy:

> Speeches are one thing, action quite another. The Wolfensohn bank developed state-of-the art corruption indexes, which are now used by the U.S government to identify which countries deserve extra foreign assistance; it created a department to investigate malfeasance in bank projects. But the anticorruption unit was understaffed and ineffectual, and the bank did not build on Wolfensohn's cancer talk by curing of corrupt borrowers consistently. Excuses were found. Lending frequently continued.[152]

PAUL WOLFOWITZ AND THE ANTICORRUPTION CRUSADE

> *Rick.* How can you close me up? On what grounds?
> *Captain Renault.* I'm shocked, shocked to find that gambling is going on in here!
> *Croupier.* Your winnings, sir.
> *Captain Renault.* (*sotto voce*) Oh, thank you very much.
>
> —Casablanca *(1942)*

Much like his charismatic predecessor, Paul Wolfowitz ("Wolf II" according to staff) signaled his commitment to resolving hypocrisies in the anticorruption and good governance agenda very early when he took over the reins in May 2005. And in many ways, Wolfowitz's intent was genuine. Between November 2005 and the end of June 2006, he canceled or withheld loans on at least nine major loans or debt relief packages due to concerns over corruption or poor governance in the recipient countries.[153] He openly critiqued weaknesses in the Depart-

---

[151] Interview with Bank staff members, Washington, D.C., July 2005.

[152] Mallaby 2006.

[153] This list includes the well-known Chad-Cameroon oil pipeline case. Under the previous agreement with the Bank, which partially funded the construction of the pipeline, the Chad government was supposed to allocate most of the oil export revenues to social and human development programs. In late 2005, the Chad government announced that it would not comply with this agreement (which it deemed an intrusion into its sovereignty), but would instead use the oil profits to purchase arms. In response, Wolfowitz froze the bank account in Britain where Chad's oil revenues were being held (and managed by the Bank). Other major loan cancellations or delays involved Kenya, Congo, India, Bangladesh, Uzbekistan, Yemen, Argentina, and Cambodia.

ment of Institutional Integrity under the previous administration, revealing a large number of backlogged cases and promising resolutions as quickly as possible. Wolfowitz also espoused a commitment to allocating more staff resources toward governance and anticorruption work, both in project lending and in internal oversight functions such as financial disclosure and auditing of staff activities.

Nonetheless, in February 2006, the sincerity of Wolfowitz's commitment to weeding out corruption was called into question by external critics, once again over the sensitive issue of internal oversight and whistle-blower protection policies. The controversy concerned a report commissioned by Wolfensohn before he left the Bank in May 2005. The report, written by American University law professor Robert Vaughn, was intended to address weaknesses in existing whistle-blower protections that had been identified in the previously mentioned GAP report. The Bank received the Vaughn report in June 2005, but Wolfowitz refused to release it to the public despite repeated calls to do so by NGOs and the U.S. Senate Finance Committee chairman, Charles Grassey.

In February 2006, the Global Accountability Project leaked the report with scathing statements regarding the Bank's rhetoric about transparency and accountability. GAP once again took issue with the secretive manner in which financial disclosures, audits, and whistle-blower policies were enforced, which "enables the Bank to evade taking action."[154] In late March 2006, the Senate Foreign Relations Committee launched another set of hearings, entitled "Multilateral Development Banks: Promoting Effectiveness and Fighting Corruption." The testimonies again included development experts from think tanks, NGOs, and the U.S. Treasury. In his opening speech, Chairman Richard Lugar made specific reference to the need to keep a vigilant watch on the MDBs to ensure that new transparency and accountability mechanisms enacted in response to past U.S. pressure did not become symbolic policies disconnected from institutional practice.[155]

In April 2006, coinciding with the IMF's and the Bank's annual meetings in Washington, Edward Pound and Danielle Knight published an article in *U.S. News & World Report*.[156] Their article was based upon their own four-month investigation of the Bank and focused on the

---

[154] Bretton Woods Project 2006b; Mekay 2006; Pound and Knight 2006.

[155] Lugar 2006.

[156] In the same month, a coalition of seventy-four civil society organizations and NGOs from around the world presented a petition accusing the Bank of knowingly employing corrupt corporate contractors in its lending projects even with formal policies in place designed to disbar such companies from bidding on Bank work. Eurodad 2006; Food & Water Watch 2006.

Department of Institutional Integrity. They reiterated many points of prior critics on the lack of transparency, pervasive secrecy, under-resourced anticorruption units, and pressures to lend. Yet the bureaucratic hesitancy to follow Wolfowitz's lead may also have stemmed from something else, according to Pound and Knight: "Inside the Bank . . .Wolfowitz has a bit of a rebellion on his hands. Internal critics complain that he is focused only on corruption. Development, not corruption busting, they say, is the principle mission of the Bank. The resentment runs deep."[157] Robert Calderisi, a former staff member, depicted staff resistance somewhat differently: "they [staff] have learned to be 'realistic' and believe the Bank would go out of business if it reacted to every illegal act committed by borrowers." With respect to Wolfowitz's unilateral cancellation of loans, which he did with little or no consultation with staff, Calderisi notes that "staff detect purism or opportunism rather than sober policy at work."[158]

On 11 April 2006, Wolfowitz delivered his most prominent speech on anticorruption in Jakarta, Indonesia—the country in which he had formerly served as U.S. ambassador. The speech, entitled "Good Governance and Development: A Time for Action," was strongly reminiscent of the cancer-of-corruption speech delivered by Wolfensohn ten years earlier. Yet Wolfowitz's speech was remarkable in two ways. First, it directly accused the Indonesian government, once a darling of the aid community for its economic growth record, of high levels of corruption. Breaking with the clientelistic culture of the Bank, Wolfowitz clearly implied that even the most important borrower governments would not be immune from criticism. Second, Wolfowitz gave a strong public endorsement to the governance and anticorruption agenda as key priorities. He implicitly admitted that the gap between rhetoric and action still persisted, and outlined a clear plan for mainstreaming the agenda within the institution itself. Wolfowitz proclaimed that the Bank would invest in more professional expertise to address corruption and hire more governance specialists to work directly in operations, including key lending areas such as judicial reform, civil service reform, the media, and public services. He also discussed the construction and deployment of "anticorruption" teams to country offices and changing project design procedures (including more decentralization to the community level) so that the assessment processes would be better equipped to address "the incentives and opportunities to fight corruption right from the start."

---

[157] Pound and Knight 2006. See also Williamson 2006.
[158] Calderisi 2006.

After the speech, in comments to reporters, Wolfowitz made a third notable remark. He announced his intention to take on directly the bureaucratic environment of the Bank, where vested interests, incentive structures, norms, and operational habits had previously stymied efforts to enforce the governance and anticorruption agendas. Wolfowitz specifically targeted the Bank's disbursement imperative and approval culture, arguing that he wanted managers to know that they would be rewarded "as much for saying no to a bad loan as for getting a good one out the door."[159] In making this statement, Wolfowitz set himself up for tackling one of the most daunting challenges facing any leader of a large organization: changing its culture.

Mainstreaming against the Tide: The New Governance and Anticorruption Strategy

One of the most remarkable results of Wolfowitz's aggressive push for the anticorruption agenda in 2006 was the visible pressure from numerous sources to pull back. At heart was not a rejection of the agenda itself, whose broad goals and values had by and large been accepted in the international community and the Bank itself by 2005. Rather, what was at stake was a widespread discontent with the seemingly punitive and arbitrary methods employed by Wolfowitz. In essence, the ideals of the GAC agenda had taken hold, but the specific practices of GAC reforms were still largely disputed, and thus operational mainstreaming remained incomplete.[160]

By this time, the contrary pressures came not only from borrower governments, who resisted governance-based conditionality and the perceived intrusions on their sovereignty. Critically, a core group of European donor states sided against the United States and Japan in their objection to Wolfowitz's heavy-handed methods for pushing the anticorruption agenda. In particular, the European donors perceived Wolfowitz's choice of loan cancellations or suspensions (decisions largely made unilaterally without consultation with the staff or board) to be suspiciously aligned with U.S. geopolitical objectives and selectively applied without due process.[161] European donors and several

---

[159] Quoted in Dugger 2006. Wolfowitz also announced his intention to increase the staff of the Department of Institutional Integrity from fifty-three to sixty-five, and to increase its budget by almost $5 million.

[160] See Marquette 2003 and 2007 for a general overview of the Bank's anticorruption campaign under Wolfensohn and Wolfowitz.

[161] Stiglitz 2007, 82.

borrowing member states also questioned the Bank's mandate in this area, and (like staff) the desirability of punishing corruption through withdrawal of funds. The British secretary of state for international development, Hilary Benn, aptly summarized the European point of view: "we must work with these governments. Not around them. Nor ignore them."[162] The general sentiment was that Wolfowitz had gone too far, to the point of forsaking the Bank's "true" development work. Sanctioning corrupt governments by withholding loans only punished the poor, and it was simply wrong to "make the poor pay twice."

These growing concerns among European donors and the Bank's major borrowers resulted in a formal request in April 2006 by the Board of Executive Directors for a new governance and anticorruption strategy paper, to be presented at the 2006 annual meetings in Singapore. Most saw the insistence on a new GAC strategy as a desire on the part of the member states to "see the method in [Wolfowitz's] meddling" and to exercise greater board oversight.[163] Officially, the GAC strategy paper was intended to "address past ineffective initiatives, and ensure more systematic and consistent treatment of governance issues across countries, to attain measurable and demonstrable improvements."[164] It sought to review staffing skills and the incentives guiding managers and staff to "engage proactively on the ground in governance issues," fixing the hitherto "inconsistent application of governance and anticorruption concerns across country programs," and to "effect results-oriented change at the front lines of Bank ground operations."[165]

The "bruising" reception received by the GAC strategy paper during the September 2006 annual meetings in Singapore reflected the growing divide on the Bank's board between the major donor states (European states versus the United States and Japan). At a minimum, the Development Committee's six-hour debate signaled that essential disagreements on the means of pursuing the GAC agenda were not resolved by the new strategy paper.[166] The European donors' dissent reinforced the vocal opposition of important developing countries, including India and China (the Bank's two largest borrowers). China threatened to halt future borrowing if Wolfowitz did not rein in his

---

[162] Benn 2006.

[163] "Double-Edged Sword: The Bank's Anticorruption Effort Has Critics on the Inside," *The Economist*, 14 September 2006. See also Behar 2007a.

[164] World Bank 2006b.

[165] World Bank 2006b, 6.

[166] Bretton Woods Project 2006b. The Development Committee is the principal advisory board to the Board of Executive Directors, made up of government ministers from member countries.

anticorruption investigative practices or pursued his plan to circumvent corrupt governments by developing direct relations with civil society groups, the media, national parliaments, and the private sector. China's threat was purportedly echoed by at least two more Asian countries that are essential to the Bank's continued lending.[167]

Inside the Bank, rebellion was also brewing. Increasingly, operational staff were noting the hypocrisy of Wolfowitz's crusade, reflecting sentiments widely expressed by nearly half of the thirty-two hundred participants in the external consultation surrounding the draft GAC strategy paper between November 2006 and February 2007. The ability of the staff to promote good governance and anticorruption reforms was undermined by the widespread perception that Wolfowitz (and by association, the Bank) failed to practice what he so ardently preached. Wolfowitz himself attained the presidency through a U.S.-controlled selection process completely lacking in transparency, meritocracy, and accountability. Moreover, Wolfowitz was not only a product of cronyism, but a perpetuator of it. Since coming to office, he had appointed, awarded generous salaries, and granted unprecedented authority to several "special advisors" from a narrow pool of conservative Republican loyalists.[168] For staff, the worst offense was the appointment of Susan Rich Folsom (wife of George Folsom, president of the International Republican Institute) to the directorship of the Department of Institutional Integrity (INT). Folsom was selected by Wolfowitz for the job despite an open search for the position that produced a short list of highly qualified candidates (she was not seen as qualified by the selection committee). Once in the position, staff members note, she used the INT to engage in an "internal witch-hunt" to root out corruption among staff, as opposed to investigating corruption in procurement contracts and in countries.[169] This only contributed to the growing distrust and resentment of staff and management toward Wolfowitz. Thus, even before the scandal broke regarding Wolfowitz's involvement in the secondment, promotion, and salary deal for Shaha Riza, there was already a clear sense that Wolfowitz did not have the moral high ground from which to push the good governance and anticorruption agenda.

---

[167] Behar 2007b, citing an internal email written by Hsiao-Yun Elaine Sun, the Bank's China manager.

[168] This included Kevin Kellems (former communications director for Dick Cheney), appointed to Directors of Strategy for External Affairs, and Robin Cleveland (former associate director of the Office of Management and Budget), appointed as special counselor to Wolfowitz.

[169] Interview with Alison Cave, president of the World Bank Staff Association, July 2005. Suzanne Rich-Folsom resigned in January 2008.

Conclusion: Hypocrisy, Post-Wolfowitz

The governance and anticorruption strategy paper was formerly approved by the board on 21 March 2007. The final draft reflects several of the concessions Wolfowitz was forced to make.[170] Specifically, the GAC paper made it clear that the Bank would remain engaged in countries with serious corruption problems, suspending loans only in "exceptional circumstances" with approval of the board.

The irony here is that the growing momentum behind the GAC agenda, both internal and external to the Bank, may be a key driver of the organized hypocrisy that we will continue observe. Specifically, as mentioned before, the momentum is manifested in a strong consensus about the importance of promoting good governance and fighting corruption for overall socioeconomic development. At the same time, there is considerably less agreement on the appropriate role of the Bank in pushing these agendas and the specific means of doing so in aid operations.

Thus, while governance and anticorruption issues have come a long way from "prohibition to prominence," with significant evidence of mainstreaming and growing compliance with new mandates (such as attention to GAC in CAS papers), there remain fundamental elements of goal incongruence that make the resolution of organized hypocrisy a chimera. This is once again tied to the political nature of the Bank's authorizing and task environments and the imperative of lending that defines the Bank's reason for existence. As Nathaniel Hobbs at the London School of Economics argues, the Bank's organized hypocrisy is inevitable. The sheer implausibility of implementing and enforcing the kinds of supervision and auditing measures that would be needed to monitor governance performance and corruption in every project preempts the full translation of talk into action. But more importantly, the Bank will continue to face the necessity of talking a "no corruption talk" to appease donors and NGOs but playing a "tolerate corruption game" to sustain the demand of borrowers.[171]

The more immediate dilemma will be reestablishing the Bank's legitimacy in the wake of President Wolfowitz's own hypocrisy. For Robert Zoellick, Wolfowitz's successor, getting the Bank's governance and anticorruption agenda back on track will be one of his most important and difficult tasks. Further pushback from member states is already evident. In July 2007, shortly after Zoellick took office, nine of the exec-

---

[170] World Bank 2007b; and Bretton Woods Project 2007.
[171] Hobbs 2005, 27.

utive directors wrote to Zoellick to protest the Bank's role in publishing the new 2007 governance indicators. The countries, which included China, Russia, Mexico, and Argentina, disputed their governance rating and argued "the Bank should reconsider whether it should be in the business of producing this kind of analysis at all." In reaction, according to the story in the *Financial Times*, "some Bank officials see the letter as the beginning of an attempt by developing countries, in particular those with authoritarian governments, to capitalize on the ouster of Wolfowitz to roll back the Bank's governance agenda."[172]

Furthermore, according to the October 2007 Volcker Commission investigation of the Department of Institutional Integrity, perceived resistance on the part of important borrowers (particularly the middle-income countries that have become so critical to the Bank's long-term strategy) will reinforce the cultural resistance to the GAC agenda. The report clearly identifies the push and pull of internal and external pressures that continue to inhibit GAC compliance and mainstreaming:

> [There is] continued concern, shared by some on the Board of Executive Directors as wells parts of the Operations staff responsible for shaping and implementing project lending, that a strong anticorruption effort would somehow be anti-development and "penalize the poor twice." There is a tendency as well to shrink from confrontation with borrowing countries who are members of the World Bank Group and sovereign countries in their own right. That tendency is reinforced by a culture of the Bank that favors seeking out lending opportunities rather than simply responding to borrowing countries' initiatives and felt needs.[173]

In the wake of the recent leadership crisis and transition and perceived persistence of organized hypocrisy, major reforms will certainly be expected. President Zoellick will undoubtedly at some point articulate a need and perhaps a strategy to reorganize the priorities, culture, and behavior of the Bank. And herein lies some promise: the "shock" recently experienced at the Bank may present a real opportunity for dramatic ideas to be proposed and acted upon, ranging from important changes to the Bank's governance and leadership selection process to new internal structures and rules for lending.

At the same time, there are two potential pitfalls to reform. The first danger lies in finding consensus on the direction of reform. It is not difficult to get everyone to agree that the Bank needs to be reformed, but it is exceedingly difficult to achieve agreement on what the exact

---

[172] Guha and McGregor 2007.
[173] Volcker et al. 2007, 8.

objectives should be. Incongruent goals in strategic reform programs are thus common features for organizations, which, at a minimum, must *appear* responsive to the multiple demands of politicized authorizing and task environments by adopting numerous and often conflicting reform goals. In this case, as argued in chapter 2, strategic reform programs can produce or perpetuate organized hypocrisy and inadvertently set themselves up for failure.

The other pitfall is in implementing effective reforms that necessitate not only navigating the dangerous political waters around the Bank, but also the cultural waters of its bureaucracy. Change may easy to enact on paper. Yet where reforms seek changes in organizational behavior that clash strongly with embedded ideologies, norms, and operational routines, substantial change will be very difficult to achieve. Revamping the formal governance of the Bank, in terms of member states' voting power on the executive board or rewriting the rules for selection of the president, will undoubtedly be politically contentious. Yet as the results of the last major reorganization clearly show, engineering change "beneath the tip of the iceberg" might be the hardest job of all.

CHAPTER FIVE

The Poverty of Reform

THE WORLD BANK today is "overstretched and underloved."[1] Deprived of the Cold War rationale driving previous aid expenditures and faced with growing budget constraints, financial support for the Bank has both dwindled and come with more strings attached. In the past fifteen years, donors have demanded that the Bank address a complex array of emerging international issues, from reconstruction after conflicts and natural disasters to the prevention and treatment of AIDS. The resulting mission creep challenges core organizational skills, mandates, and scarce resources. Simultaneously, competition from private capital flows and other multilateral and bilateral aid agencies has diminished the demand for the Bank's services, particularly from the "bread and butter" middle-income countries, while increasing calls for greater coordination among donors and selectivity of development assistance. Self-appointed watchdog organizations maintain a bright spotlight on the Bank's behavior, particularly when it falls short of proclaimed policies and best practices.[2]

When James D. Wolfensohn became World Bank president in late 1995, he was intent on making his mark on the institution. In 1996, Wolfensohn proposed an ambitious reform plan, entitled the "Strategic Compact." The Compact (as it became known) entailed a $250 million, thirty-month "renewal" of the Bank. The core objective, according to official statements, was to reestablish the Bank's preeminent position as the world's leading development agency by instigating a massive transformation in the way the organization goes about its core mission of promoting economic growth and alleviating world poverty.

As with previous attempts at reform, transforming the Bank proved more easily said than done. Although official statements paint a rosy picture of the Compact's achievements, external and internal assessments after its completion in 2001 highlight shortcomings and unintended consequences. Reports and interviews attribute many of the de-

---

[1] Wilks 2001.

[2] For a scathing review of the role nongovernmental organizations in monitoring the behavior of the World Bank, see Mallaby 2004.

ficiencies to conflicting demands in the external political environment, which compelled reformers to adopt contradictory goals: a hallmark of the organized hypocrisy that had propelled demands for reform in the first place. Yet the more critical findings of postreform analysis center upon the internal processes of change, in particular the "tenacious survival capacity" of vested interests within the Bank's bureaucracy and the inertia of organizational culture.

Organizational culture is perhaps the most puzzling and complicated variable to analyze in a study of reform processes and outcomes, if only because culture does not lend itself easily to observation and measurement. And yet sociological theory gives enormous weight to culture in explanations of organizational change. In general, organizational culture indelibly shapes the process of reform, defining the extent to which the change of formal structures and rules can disrupt informal values and incentives to incite meaningful changes in bureaucratic behavior. Indeed, Wolfensohn and his management team wrote the Compact initiative with the intent of dismantling the aspects of the "old" culture that contributed to the Bank's declining effectiveness and tarnished image. Cultural reengineering was expected to introduce new ideas, norms, and incentive structures that would reorient the staff around new, desired behavior.

How can we explain the dynamics of change in a way that enriches our understanding of, not just the origins and nature of the Bank's hypocrisy, but also the policy-salient question of what enables or constrains attempts to resolve hypocrisy? Answering this question requires a sophisticated study of IO reform that fully accounts for the dynamics outside, within, and between the political environments of the Bank.[3] This approach analyzes not just the *demand* side of reform (who wants which reforms, and whom we might expect to prevail, given power disparities), but also the *supply* side: how multiple and often contradictory reform goals are articulated in a reform plan, what shapes its implementation, and what factors explain outcomes that perpetuate or reduce areas of organized hypocrisy.

This chapter attempts to tackle these issues by examining the most recent major reorganization effort in the Bank, implemented between 1997 and 2001. I begin with the catalysts for reform, which in this case hinged upon a convergence of external and internal impetuses for change. Four external factors appear to be significant: a discernible change in the interests of the Bank's principal member states, competi-

---

[3] One exception is Kapur 2002b.

tive pressure from increased private capital flows, a broad paradigm shift within the broader international development regime and epistemic community of scholars, and the activism of watchdog NGOs. These factors cumulated in a resounding external demand for reform, albeit with very different ideas regarding the desired results. Yet because the Bank is a relatively autonomous international organization able to buffer itself from external demands, a comprehensive initiative did not emerge until a change in organizational leadership and a core coalition of internal advocates pushed for reform from the inside, articulating explicit targets and the strategies for getting there.

Past these precipitating causes, the particular dilemmas encountered in implementing and realizing the Compact goals can be traced back to conflict among external and internal factors outlined throughout this book. Wolfensohn's attempt to respond to the Bank's critics led to an expansion of its development agendas and a complicated set of goals in the reorganization that often worked at cross-purposes. The reform period, from 1997 to 2001, was thus a period of "mission creep," leading to heightened scrutiny by external critics and a high degree of uncertainty, anxiety, and demoralization among organizational staff. Critically, however, the process of change revealed something significant about the internal life of the Bank. The reform program was strongly shaped by its bureaucratic and cultural environment, which propelled change in a path-dependent direction that was not always congruent with the interests of external actors or even the intentions of internal reformers.

This chapter begins with a section examining the factors that catalyzed the Compact. This section also briefly revisits chapter 3's description of the bureaucratic and cultural environment of the Bank. At the onset of the Compact this environment was implicitly (if not explicitly in some instances) targeted for change. The following section briefly summarizes the methods and goals of the Compact as well as its portrayed successes. It also highlights the tensions and conflicts encountered during the implementation of the Compact. Particular attention is given to areas where reformist goals clashed with one another and where bureaucratic interests or culture impeded goals, producing unintended results, including continued organized hypocrisy. The chapter ends by tempering the fatalistic conclusions of the analysis, exploring where there may be promise for reform. Here I investigate current proposals for change, specifically linking the discussion to organized hypocrisy by investigating where reform demands today may incite change that resolves or exacerbates pressures contributing to hypocrisy.

Triggering Reforms at the World Bank

External Catalysts

Dramatic shifts in the authorizing and task environments in the early 1990s stimulated widespread pressure for reform in the Bank. The most prominent catalyst came in the form of a shift in the preferences of major donor states regarding their financial support for, and demands on, the Bank. Much of the political rationale for development aid disappeared after the collapse of communism in 1989–91.[4] Domestic budget constraints and waning public support for foreign aid compelled governments to cut back commitments and streamline the multilateral development banks. National parliaments justified such cutbacks by pointing to reports of declining effectiveness of aid and to the "bureaucratic flab" of overpaid and undertaxed international bureaucrats. Ironically, during the same period, donor states' demands on the Bank multiplied. As bilateral aid dried up in the early 1990s, Part I member states attempted to leverage their diminishing funds by pressuring the Bank to address their new, post–Cold War foreign policy objectives, ranging from the transition of post-Communist economies, to the rebuilding of postconflict societies, the fight against HIV/AIDS, and debt relief. At the same time, donors' contributions, especially to the IDA, were conditioned on changes in organizational structures and mandates.[5]

These pressures were (and continue to be) complicated by a breakdown in consensus among the donor states about the direction of reform. No longer lashed together by the need to maintain a common front against communism, the United States and its European and Japanese counterparts split over the purpose of lending. In particular, the welfare-oriented and state-led industrial policies of these latter states clashed with the U.S. promotion of neoliberal, laissez-faire policies considered critical to opening up emerging markets to U.S. trade exports and foreign investment.[6] The Bank's management (and especially

[4] United States General Accounting Office 1996, 19.

[5] This is evident in the successive replenishment negotiations of the International Development Agency. See, for example, Ascher 1990; Brown 1992; Gwin 1994; and World Bank Staff Association 2001a.

[6] Kapur 2002b; Pincus and Winters 2002. See also Robert Wade's account of the writing of the *East Asian Miracle Report*. As described in chapter 3, this report was commissioned by the Japanese government and intended to disrupt the American hegemonic influence over the Bank's ideology by providing evidence of the benefits of state-led industrial development in the dramatic economic growth of emerging markets of East Asia (Wade 1996). These conflicting donor interests are still readily apparent. For example, the thirteenth replenishment negotiations of IDA in 2002 revealed a strong division

President Wolfensohn) sought to appease the primary benefactors with a series of confusing agendas and rules that have only diffused the organization's core mission and strategies.[7]

As described in chapter 3, borrower states also contributed to reform pressures. Although the number of borrowing country governments increased with the collapse of the Soviet Union, their demand for the Bank's services stagnated in the 1990s. Potential borrowers were unhappy with strict loan conditions (including costly safeguard and fiduciary requirements) and poor evaluations of, and social opposition to, prior structural adjustment lending.[8] Moreover, borrowing governments were quick to complain about the Bank's bureaucratic procedures, which led to delays and red tape during appraisals of loans.[9] Alternative sources of aid and private investment capital (see below) enhanced the credibility of the "exit threat" by major borrowers, particularly middle-income countries.

In addition to state influence, there were also important nonstate actors and systemic changes that contributed to pressure for reform. They included increasing competition from other international development organizations and trends in private capital flows. Although the Bank remains the largest source of official development funds, the presence of other regional and bilateral development banks and aid agencies proffering similar assistance was dampening dependence on the Bank by the mid-1990s. Internal discussions of reform also identified the emerging knowledge base and pools of expertise in these other development organizations as a source of competition.[10] More critically, the presence of so many other voices in the field necessitated increased communication and coordination between agencies to reduce redundant and sometimes conflicting aid programs. This challenged the Bank to be more selective and open to cooperation with other agencies in its lending. It also encouraged senior management to define the Bank's "comparative advantage" as the premier international center

---

between the major donor states on the extent to which IDA funds should be disbursed in the form of grants rather than interest-free loans. Comments by Brian Crowe of the U.S. Treasury Department to the Tuesday Group Meeting at Oxfam International, Washington, D.C., 5 February 2002.

[7] Many observers directly blame President James D. Wolfensohn for this perceived "mission creep." See, for example, Einhorn 2001; Fidler 2001; and Wade 2002. For a general discussion of the increasing politicization of the Bank's authorizing environment, see the World Bank Staff Association 2001a; as well as Kapur 2000a and Woods 2000a, 2000b.

[8] Stiglitz 1999; Storey 2000.

[9] World Bank 2001c, 1.

[10] "The Matrix Environment at the World Bank: Orientation for New Staff," Fall 2001, PowerPoint presentation, on file with author.

for development information and expertise, thereby honing its relative power, influence, and claim to resources in the international development regime.[11]

Another factor driving organizational reform, directly connected to shifting demand for the Bank's loans, was the tremendous increase in private capital flows. By the mid-1990s, these flows (including commercial bank loans, foreign direct investment, and portfolio investment) to developing regions of the world equaled nearly five times the amount of total official development assistance.[12] This amounted to abundant, essentially unconditioned private sources of money for revenue-earning infrastructure, transportation, and energy projects that traditionally represented the bulk of the Bank's lending. Although this finance goes to few emerging markets and generally avoids the poorest nations,[13] critics argued that this trend indicates that the Bank was no longer needed to provide the capital to facilitate foreign investment and economic growth in developing nations.[14] When the private capital flows suddenly reversed after the financial crises in East Asia, Russia, and Brazil in 1997–98, demand for loans from the Bank temporarily rebounded. Simultaneously, however, the crises and contagion created yet another new challenge for the Bank: using development aid to cope with the aftermath of economic crisis and massive capital flight.

Meanwhile, a change in the ideational environmental of aid posed another factor. The Compact's authors noted that "the development paradigm was shifting, and the Bank risked losing its leadership role."[15] Scholars within the international development regime (many of whom work within, or as consultants for, the Bank) criticized the neoclassical economic orthodoxy underpinning the so-called Washington Consensus driving the Bank's lending strategies.[16] The failure of past structural adjustment policies to engender equitable and sustainable growth, particularly in Africa, converged with attempts to find viable theories for addressing the former Soviet Union's economic transitions. The slowly emerging "post-Washington consensus," cen-

---

[11] This argument is embodied in the World Bank's Comprehensive Development Framework. See Wolfensohn 1999. For a discussion of coordination between development agencies writ large, see the key report by the OECD Development Assistance Committee (1996).

[12] Author's calculation, using data from the World Development Indicators and International Financial Statistics, 1990–2000. See also Weaver and Leiteritz 2005.

[13] Gurria and Volcker 2001; de Ferranti 2006.

[14] See, for example, Meltzer et al. 2000; Ierly 2002; and Lerrick 2002, 2006.

[15] World Bank 2001c, 1; and interview with Bank official, April 2000.

[16] Stiglitz 1999; Naim 2000; Gore 2000; Storey 2000; Kanbur 2001; and Krugman 2002.

tered on Douglass North's theory of institutions, replaced the old tenet of "getting the prices right" with "getting the institutions right."[17]

Concern also grew surrounding aid fungibility and the prevalence of corruption . As described in the previous chapter, development theories began to emphasize good governance and a sound financial, regulatory, and legal infrastructure as the "capacity-building" prerequisites to increased investment, trade, and economic growth.[18] Likewise, progressive theories emphasizing the social and environmental dimensions of development pushed the Bank to evaluate its commitment to socially and environmentally sustainable development. This resulted in demands for more attention to the participation of civil society in defining and implementing development strategies and calls to refocus on the goal of alleviating poverty as first set out by Robert McNamara in the mid-1970s. The cumulative effect of the rapidly changing normative environment was a number of substantially different development issues that challenged the economic, apolitical, and technical rationality underlying the Bank's traditional approaches.

Perhaps the most critical source of outside pressure for reform in the early 1990s came from watchdog and advocacy groups, as discussed in chapter 3. The cumulative effect of these nongovernmental organizations and social movements was demonstrated in the "Fifty Years Is Enough" campaign during the fiftieth anniversary of the Bank in 1994. Since the 1980s, these groups have damaged the external legitimacy of the Bank by documenting the devastating effects of its projects and the gaps between its policies and actual practices. Through successful lobbying of national parliaments and direct engagement with the Bank, this transnational NGO and CSO movement has effectively pushed for reforms to make the Bank more open, transparent, and accountable for its practices. Moreover, the sheer visibility of NGO actions has attracted greater media notice and thus public attention to the Bank's activities.[19] This in turn has prompted donor member states to more closely monitor the Bank's behavior, as described in chapter 4 in the case of the Bank's anticorruption campaign. Increased NGO and donor state vigilance has also enabled reform-minded individuals *within* the Bank to advocate change and in some instances has prompted strategic coalitions between staff and outside actors.[20] One

[17] North 1990. See also internal discussions of the post-Washington consensus in Picciotto and Wiesner 1998 and Burki and Perry 1998.

[18] Kapur 2002a attributes this also to a decrease in inhibitions about sovereignty after the Cold War, thus permitting involvement in previously "taboo" areas of lending that may be perceived as encroaching upon the political terrain of client states.

[19] See, for example, Danaher 1994.

[20] See, for example, accounts of the evolution of the "participatory" and "social development" agenda. Cernea 2004; Vetterlein 2006.

very visible response to the NGO campaigns is the management's espoused commitment to a participatory development approach that includes consultations with national parliaments, NGOs, civil society groups, and local indigenous populations. The result is a widening of the Bank's development paradigm and greater demands upon project management that often conflict with prior demands for increased selectivity, cost-effectiveness, and efficiency in lending.

Internal Catalysts for Reform

It is difficult to say whether these external factors alone would have prompted a major reorganization at the Bank in the mid-1990s without impetus from within. Indeed, many of the outside demands for reform were precipitated by information leaked from inside the organization. The most critical information came from the report of the Portfolio Management Task Force in 1992 (see chapter 3). The report was commissioned by former president Lewis Preston and headed by a longtime senior manager and vice president, Willi Wapenhans. The report uncovered shocking statistics regarding the effectiveness of the Bank's programs. Specifically, the number of projects judged unsatisfactory at completion had jumped from 15 percent in 1981 to 37.5 percent in 1991. The share of projects with major problems had grown to 20 percent in 1991. Moreover, borrowers' compliance with conditionality agreements reached an all-time low, with only 22 percent of all legal agreements fulfilled in 1991.[21]

The Wapenhans Report identified several external causes of this declining performance, including poor macroeconomic policies in borrowing countries, volatility of commodity prices, and waves of debt crises. Critically, however, the report did something quite surprising: it specially attributed declining performance to the Bank's organizational culture, particularly the preoccupation with blueprint models, the "clientitis" of staff, the "approval culture," and "disbursement imperative."

The leak of the Wapenhans Report coincided with a number of other dissenting reports and commentaries published by current and former staff members that also disparaged the entrenched organizational culture.[22] This only fueled external scrutiny by the Bank's external prin-

[21] Wapenhans 1992, 9.

[22] See, for example, the contributions by Willi Wapenhans and Moises Naim to the 1994 Bretton Woods Commission report (see Naim 1994 and Wapenhans 1994), as well as the "farewell lecture to the World Bank" by Herman Daly (1994). These critiques were once again reified by another internal report in 1997, shortly after the launch of the Compact, by the newly created Quality Assurance Group (QAG). It found that there was a persistent imperative to "sell" projects, the related absence of any selectivity, and the

cipals. In a 1996 report, the U.S. General Accounting Office (GAO) argued that the Bank was continually misdirecting aid away from the countries most in need, promoting loans based on poor economic analysis, and not being proactive enough *during* project implementation in resolving problems. The GAO report pointed out that only 51 percent of projects in sub-Saharan Africa between 1985 and 1993 had been given satisfactory ratings, a dismal record attributed in part to the Bank's own performance as well as to the borrowing governments.[23]

None of this came as a surprise to anyone within or outside the Bank, but the subsequent leak of the internal report gave external and internal critics considerable arsenal. The initial response of management to the Wapenhans Report was a set of eighty-seven action plans entitled "Next Steps." This weak proposal included reporting and training exercises that had little discernible impact on the Bank's development paradigms and practices.[24] Efforts to strengthen reforms were weakened by the illness of the president, Lewis Preston.

When James D. Wolfensohn replaced Preston as president in late 1995, he immediately signaled his intent to reform the Bank. He proclaimed that he had read nearly fifty books critical of the Bank[25] and wanted to work toward an open, transparent, and results-oriented culture that would improve the Bank's effectiveness and its public image. In a speech delivered to staff in March 1996, he severely criticized senior management, pointing to internal surveys that showed that nearly 40 percent of staff had little confidence in managers and that a "glass wall of cynicism and distrust" pervaded staff-management relations.[26] Soon thereafter, Wolfensohn created a series of "renewal task forces" within the organization. Many inside and outside the Bank believe them to be a major catalyst for a comprehensive reform effort.[27]

---

bias toward large blueprint loans aligned with perceived Bank lending priorities that did not fit the needs or interests of the borrowing countries. The report concluded that "institutional amnesia is the corollary of institutional optimism and, despite the lessons of experience, Bank staff are overoptimistic and tend to propose overambitious operations that are beyond local implementation capacity." World Bank Quality Assurance Group 1997, 1.

[23] United States General Accounting Office 1996, 42–47.

[24] See the two reports by the United States General Accounting Office (1994 and 1995b) evaluating the "Next Steps" reform attempt, as well as Caufield 1996, 260–61.

[25] World Bank Staff Association 2001a, 1.

[26] Internal memo from a meeting between Wolfensohn and senior management on 12 March 1996, on file with author.

[27] Interview with Bank staff members, April 2002; and interview with Bruce Rich, 15 January 2002. See also Rich 2002, 34–37.

The Strategic Compact

The Strategic Compact was designed to transform the very identity of the Bank. The Compact, as it was called, promised a "renewal" of development ideas and practices to improve the effectiveness of aid, to make the Bank more responsive to borrowing governments, and to enhance its transparency and accountability. In sum, the reforms were expected to reestablish the Bank's relevancy and legitimacy in the post–Cold War world. Funded by a temporary (three-year) $250 million increase in the administrative budget, they were built on four objectives or "pillars" entailing extensive restructuring of the Bank's formal structure and reengineering its underlying culture—and thus reorienting the behavior of management and staff—around the desired image of the "new" Bank.

The first pillar of the Compact was characterized as "Refueling Current Business Activity." The core element was a dramatic decentralization of management and staff away from the Washington headquarters to the mission offices in the field. The objective was to reinvigorate demand for the Bank's services, distance it from the blueprint model of lending, and become more responsive to the specific interests and needs of borrowing countries. Reform architects also expected that decentralization would mitigate the image of staff as "inward-focused," meaning that they were overly occupied with pleasing their superiors in Washington. One very important component in achieving this client-oriented focus was to place greater control of the administrative budget in the hands of the country directors (CDs). Country directors have more direct contract with borrowing country governments and civil society groups and thus are in a better position to respond to the needs of borrowers. Under the new rules, the CDs contract out for specific staff services (such as conducting environmental impact assessments and ongoing project evaluations) through work program agreements. As a result, staff bid against each other for certain jobs, thus creating a competitive internal market that was expected to improve the quality, efficiency, and cost-effectiveness of project management.

The second pillar of the Compact, entitled "Retooling the Development Agenda," was designed to reallocate resources away from traditional lending areas (such as large infrastructure projects) toward neglected sectors now given priority, such a social, environmental and governance-related projects. This part of the reorganization also sought to build bridges for organizational learning between the Bank's units, connecting research and operations units that previously lived "on separate planets."[28] Four new "thematic network" units were created to help translate new development ideas and research findings into operational policies. These networks centered on the areas of Environmental and Socially Sustainable Development (ESSD), Human Development, Finance and Private Sector Infrastructure, and Poverty Reduction and Economic Management (PREM).

The related third component of the Compact envisioned a shift in the persona of the Bank from a lending institution to a "Knowledge Bank." The Bank's original stance as the leading source of capital to developing countries had eroded over time. Many experts inside and outside believed the Bank's influence now depended less on its financial might than on the power of its ideas. Thus, Wolfensohn recognized that the Bank's comparative advantage vis-à-vis other international organizations and private sources of capital would rest upon its position as the global producer of development information and expertise. The plan involved the creation of the Global Development Network, which, along with the thematic networks mentioned above, would foster collaboration and knowledge-sharing within and without the organization. Early Compact documents also see the Global Development Network and the thematic networks creating internal feedback loops and learning mechanisms that would enable the Bank to respond to shifts in the interests of its principals as well as theoretical and empirical discoveries within the broader international development community.[29]

To tie it all together, the last objective of the Compact redrew the basic lines of administrative authority within the Bank in a complex "matrix management system," designed by a team of expensive consultants hired from the Harvard Business School. The matrix system included the decentralization of staff mentioned above. Under an initiative entitled "revamping institutional capabilities," the system also set firing, hiring, and other promotional goals for human resources that would supposedly realign staff toward new development agendas. Resources were also reallocated toward monitoring and evaluation with the intention of improving weak areas of portfolio management.

Evaluation of the Strategic Compact Results

In 2000, Wolfensohn commissioned an internal review of the Compact reform initiative. Not surprisingly, the official reports released to the public in 2001 portray the Compact as a success. The primary assess-

[28] Interview with senior Bank official, April 2002.
[29] For a good critical discussion of the "Knowledge Bank" and the Global Development Network, see Stone 2003.

ment report placed on the Bank's external website in March 2001 (notably missing the detailed appendices, which I had to obtain from an internal source) emphasized the dramatic improvement in portfolio lending performance as compared to the dismal statistics in the Wapenhans Report ten years earlier. The statistics provided in the executive summary and main body of the report certainly seemed to support this change. For example, project design and implementation planning apparently improved, with QAG evaluations showing a jump in ratings of project quality-at-entry from 78 percent satisfactory or better in 1996, at the start of the Compact, to 89 percent in 1999. Likewise, the report indicated a decline in the number of ongoing projects considered "at risk" and upturns in estimates of the sustainability of development projects and of their impact on institutions. OED evaluations of the outcome of exiting loan projects in 1999 indicate 77 percent with satisfactory or higher ratings, up from 65 percent in 1993 (see tables 5.1 and 5.2). There was an even larger improvement in the quality of the Bank's nonlending economic and sector work, including assessments of technical assistance. Overall, progress appears in almost all of the Compact's targeted areas of lending performance.

Moreover, the Compact's official assessment pointed to a more "client-focused" organizational culture. The assessment highlights success in meeting client demands to streamline bureaucratic procedures and decrease the costs and time to prepare, appraise, and approve projects. On average, the number of months from project concept to approval by the Bank's Board of Executive Directors declined from just under 24 months in 1996 to around 14.5 months in 2000.[30] The decentralization effort was singled out as an even more significant step toward improving responsiveness to borrowing countries. The number of individuals in field (mission) offices increased to nearly 30 percent (approximately twenty-five hundred) of the Bank's overall staff. Nearly one-half of country directors by 2001 were based in mission offices— an increase from only three in 1997 to twenty-eight (out of a total of fifty-three) in late 1999 (see table 5.3). The authors of the report directly attributed an increased dialogue with borrowing governments to the enhanced presence of staff in the field.

[30] World Bank 2001c, annex 1, p. 7. Similarly, the time taken from project appraisal to negotiations, primarily spent on internal Bank processing of the project, dropped from 5.8 months for projects approved in FY1996 to 2.9 months for projects approved in FY2000 with subsequent decline in cost of lending preparation with a small increase in project supervision expenditures. The report claims that much of this efficiency gain comes from the elimination of multiple (white, yellow, green cover) draft reports and reviews that previously circulated throughout the Bank hierarchy (World Bank 2001c, annex 1, p. 7),

TABLE 5.1
Project Performance Ratings, Fiscal Years 1990–2001

Exit FY	Number of Projects	% Satisfactory Outcomes	% Likely or Better Sustainability	% Substantial or Better Institutional Development Impact	World Bank Performance		Borrower Performance		
					% Satisfactory Quality at Entry	% Satisfactory Supervision	% Satisfactory Preparation	% Satisfactory Implementation	% Satisfactory Compliance
1990	176	67	46	33	57	74	68	61	43
1991	211	67	48	36	64	79	73	65	53
1992	226	66	46	31	70	77	75	68	60
1993	233	65	45	29	58	72	71	61	58
1994	267	63	42	27	57	69	74	59	55
1995	241	68	46	25	60	72	78	59	66
1996	228	69	46	35	63	73	78	60	70
1997	234	72	52	36	70	73	80	61	73
1998	273	72	49	38	67	78	80	62	78
1999	272	72	55	39	71	73	79	62	75
2000	253	76	72	50	72	87	83	65	78
2001[a]	131	82	70	56	78	85	86	75	81

Source: World Bank Operations Evaluation Department 2001d, tables 7–11.
[a] The data represent a partial IBRD/IDA lending sample (131 out of 275) and reflect all OED project evaluations through October 15, 2001.

Furthermore, according to the official evaluation, decentralization enabled staff to improve coordination with other aid agencies and focus more on local capacity-building exercises, both of which were connected to the improved potential of countries to sustain development objectives past completion of the project. The report also stressed the increase in the participation of local groups within borrowing countries in design and implementation of projects. To promote this "participatory development" strategy, sixty-five NGO specialists (staff serving as special liaisons with NGOs and civil society groups) were hired in the field offices by 2001. There was also an increased level of civil society and NGO participation in the construction of Country Assistance Strategy papers (although the reports do not comment on the quality or impact of that participation).

The overall success of the Compact is qualified to some extent in the official assessment. The authors of the report remark that the reform fell short in a few areas due to uncontrollable factors associated with the East Asian financial crises in 1997–98, the need to respond to the aftermath of conflicts in the former Yugoslavia and East Timor in 1999, and the growing demand for debt relief that diverted the Bank's resources to the Heavily Indebted Poor Countries (HIPC) Initiative.[31] Perhaps more interesting are the authors' observations about the *unintended* consequences of Compact, noted in the appendices to the official assessment and revealed in subsequent internal memos and interviews. It is widely known that the Compact led to extensive layoffs and budget constraints. The report notes, and interviews strongly confirm, a general malaise, stress, sense of work overload, and fatigue over change within the organization.[32] The reform also resulted in considerable staff uncertainty and anxiety resulting from perceived mission creep and lack of clarity on the Bank's core mission. One internal memo vividly described a growing distrust between President Wolfensohn, the senior management, and staff.[33]

In reading the long assessments and appendices and in talking with dozens of staff members about the reform process, it was difficult

---

[31] World Bank 2000b.

[32] World Bank 2000b, 6; 2001c, 4 and annex 8. One specific example of this overload was the increase in unrecorded staff overtime, growing to 25 percent of total recorded work time in early 2000, indicating that the proclaimed efficiency gains have not been fully realized (World Bank 2001c, 14). More importantly, staff attitude surveys indicate a pervasive fear of losing one's job and a resulting rise in distrust between hierarchical divisions, with only 18 percent reporting a favorable level of mutual trust between staff and senior management in 1999 (World Bank 2001c, annex 8, p. 9).

[33] This was articulated in a leaked memo from the Middle East and North Africa Department, on file with author.

TABLE 5.2
Project Performance Ratings Weighted by Projects, Fiscal Years 1996–1999 and 2000–2001 Exits

Sector Group	Number of Projects		Outcome % Satisfactory		Sustainability % Likely or Better		Institutional Development % Substantial or Better	
	FY96–99	FY00–01[a]	FY96–99	FY00–01[a]	FY96–99	FY00–01[a]	FY96–99	FY00–01[a]
Sector Group								
Agriculture	206	63	67	69	45	49	38	43
Economic Policy	83	15	77	87	56	93	28	47
Education	90	34	74	82	44	75	28	47
Electric Power and Other Energy	67	31	64	58	47	57	38	52
Environment	24	13	71	69	54	69	42	46
Finance	66	15	67	80	56	87	44	67
Health, Nutrition, and Population	59	26	63	73	49	56	31	46
Mining	9	3	78	100	67	67	78	67
Multisector	15	5	73	100	33	75	7	33
Oil and Gas	22	13	73	62	64	58	36	38
PSD/Industry	45	20	58	58	55	63	36	42
Public Sector Management	56	33	84	82	65	84	45	55
Social Protection	48	25	83	92	35	86	42	52
Telecommunications	18	6	78	100	72	100	56	83
Transportation	90	48	85	93	61	87	53	76
Urban Development	55	21	74	90	44	71	31	48
Water Supply and Sanitation	54	13	55	69	36	75	25	46

TABLE 5.2 (cont.)

	FY96–99	FY00–01[a]	FY96–99	FY00–01[a]	FY96–99	FY00–01[a]	FY96–99	FY00–01[a]
Network[b]								
ESSD	228	76	68	69	46	53	38	43
FPSI	414	168	70	78	52	75	41	58
HD	194	85	73	82	43	72	31	48
PREM	171	55	79	82	59	84	33	50
Region								
Africa	304	111	57	66	34	51	31	41
East Asia and Pacific	153	57	81	80	59	71	43	61
Europe and Central Asia	130	90	82	81	65	81	45	53
Latin America and Caribbean	215	62	81	81	60	79	44	53
Middle East and North Africa	78	26	71	88	44	92	29	60
South Asia	127	38	68	89	51	81	32	63

Source: World Bank Operations Evaluation Department 2001d.

[a] The data for FY01 exits represented a partial IBRD/IDA lending sample (131 out of 275) and reflects all OED project evaluations through 15 October 2001.

[b] *Network Codes:* ESSD = Environmentally and Socially Sustainable Development; FPSI = Finance, Private Sector, and Infrastructure; HD = Human Development; PREM = Poverty Reduction and Economic Management.

TABLE 5.3
World Bank Staffing Trends

A. Decentralization of IBRD/IDA Staff

	6/30/97		6/30/98		6/30/99		6/30/00		6/30/01	
	Actual	% of Total Staff	Actual	% of Total Staff	Actual	% of Total Staff	Actual	% of Total Staff	Actual	% of Total Staff
Washington appointed	7,165	82.4	7,509	81.1	7,145	78.1	6,906	76.6	6,410	75.3
of which Washington based	6,809	78.3	7,101	76.7	6,711	73.4	6,490	72	6,006	70.6
of which outside Washington	356	4.1	408	4.4	434	4.7	416	4.6	404	4.7
Country office appointed	1,529	17.6	1,753	18.9	1,999	21.9	2,112	23.4	2,097	24.7
Total	8,649	100.0	9,262	100.0	9,144	100.0	9,018	100.0	8,507	100.0

B. "Refocusing the Development Agenda": Shifting Staff Skill Areas; IBRD Washington-AppointedStaff by Job Families

Job Family	6/30/97	6/30/01	Net
Accounting/Admin & Budgeting/Auditing	560	530	−30
Economics	727	755	28
Energy/Mining/Telecommunications	85	82	−3
Environment and Social Development	112	169	57
External Affairs	42	117	75
Finance	247	355	108
Human Development	131	167	36
Human Resources	146	167	21
Information Technology	485	694	209
Infrastructure	146	176	30
Investment	37	27	−10
Legal	91	109	18
Management	471	465	−6
Operations & Evaluations	573	636	63
Public/Private Sector	112	125	13
Rural	69	51	−18
Others	3,131	1,786	−1,345
Total	7,165	6,411	−754

Source: World Bank Human Resources Vice Presidency 2001, 10, 64.

not to pick up on a pervasive tone of skepticism. Despite the overhaul of bureaucratic structures and rules, most staff members remark on the inability of the Compact initiative to fully disrupt and reengineer the organizational culture of the Bank. To many of these individuals, this was never a realistic goal, at least not within three years. To an outside observer, it brings organizational culture and bureaucratic politics to the forefront in understanding the complex set of opportunities and constraints that shape the process of reforming international organizations.

BEYOND STRUCTURE: THE CULTURE OF REFORM[34]

> Changing the culture of any organization is a lengthy and complex process. The change process itself is influenced by the culture in place. If the latter is strong—when shared beliefs, values, and norms consistently drive behavior—the change process is even more difficult. Such is the current situation in the Bank.[35]

These words, written in a memo regarding the attempt to reorganize the Bank under president Barber Conable in 1987, ironically echo the sentiments of the various assessments associated with the most recent reform effort.[36] Despite an explicit recognition in the early Compact planning documents of the need to address and change the organizational culture,[37] the evaluation reports issued after the completion of the Compact period in 2000 consistently note the tenacity of underlying incentive structures and norms shaping the expectations and behavior of staff. The persistence of such culture is compounded by the fact that the reform goals themselves contained inherent contradictions, sending conflicting signals to staff and management. Specifically, there were two clearly opposing goals of the Compact. The first was to streamline the bureaucracy and become more attuned to borrowing governments' interests by decreasing the cost (in time and money) of project design, appraisal, and oversight. The second was to be more responsive to the critical demands of vigilant NGOs, civil society organizations, and their attendant national parliaments in donor states.

---

[34] This section of the chapter draws and expands upon an earlier analysis of the Compact in Weaver and Leiteritz 2005.

[35] "The Culture of the World Bank and Its Implications for the Reorganization Process," internal report of the World Bank, 21 March 1987, 16, on file with author.

[36] For descriptions of the Conable reorganization of the World Bank and its consequences, see Rich 1994, 182; and Caufield 1996, 178–87.

[37] The early "renewal" brochure put forth by the Bank in early 1997 actually identifies the various attributes of the existing culture and the expected cultural traits that would result from the reform process (World Bank 1997c). This clearly built upon the earlier report entitled *Learning from the Past, Embracing the Future*, in which six guiding principles were defined as the desired culture of a reformed World Bank: selectivity, partnership, client orientations, results orientation, cost effectiveness, and financial integrity (World Bank 1994c).

Doing so involved the adoption of time-consuming and costly account-ability measures and safeguards that would inevitably require greater delays, expenditures, and conditions attached to loans—things that the borrowing governments were increasingly reluctant to take on.

In this light, it is unsurprising that the reform process ultimately proved more adept at achieving the first of the two goals. The success here might be attributed to cultural or norm adjacency, or "goal con-gruence," according to the terminology used in this book.[38] The norms required to achieve the client-focus were already largely in place in what the Wapenhans Report called the approval culture and disburse-ment imperative of the Bank. Responding to the particular interests and demands of the borrowing governments involved significant structural readjustments in the Bank's hierarchical architecture, includ-ing the decentralization effort. Yet meeting client demands for faster project approval and loan disbursement necessitated relatively few disruptions in operational incentive structures, norms, and routines.

On the other hand, the operational procedures and broadened devel-opment agendas advocated within the second goal of becoming more "poverty focused" and accountable for development results clashed with existing culture to a much greater extent. In retrospect, even though strong advocates in pockets of the Bank backed these objec-tives, they were more at odds with the dominant ideological triad of economic, apolitical, and technical rationality. For example, the time and attention required to fully enact new environmental and social im-pact assessments clashed with staff members' understanding about what behavior was rewarded within the institution. Even when staff members claimed a strong individual adherence to goals such as en-hanced environmental assessments and more focus on participatory development, they nonetheless recognized that the existing incentive structures (as manifested in resource allocation and promotion prac-tices) did not entice staff members to act upon these beliefs. A majority of the staff I interviewed concurred that their ability to comply with these new goals depended greatly upon the predilections of individual country directors and other powerful senior management. As a result, most staff members observed that the Bank has made progress toward these goals, but it has been uneven within the organization. In general, they believe that "the way to succeed in the Bank" still largely rests upon an ability to disburse loans quickly.[39]

[38] Finnemore and Sikkink 1998; Nielson, Tierney, and Weaver 2006.

[39] This was confirmed in at least twenty interviews with Bank staff members, includ-ing key architects of the Strategic Compact. Washington, D.C., September–October 2001, March–May 2002, June 2005.

Close readings of the Compact assessments and subsequent interviews reveal where the clash in reform goals and the resistance of organizational culture has impeded the realization of desired incentives and behavior and the mainstreaming of new development topics envisioned by Wolfensohn in 1996. Reengineering the culture of the Bank has proven quite difficult: "the Bank needs to eliminate the disconnect between its espoused culture and the way people behave with each other. . . . The Bank needs to find a better balance between the 'hardware' of change (strategy, structure, process, systems) and the 'software' (culture and behavior)."[40]

The next several sections briefly analyze the interrelated components of the Compact initiative. The objective here is to assess to what extent change has occurred beyond a structural or rhetorical shifts in policy. The ultimate goal of the reform process was the socialization of staff around new development ideas, norms, and practices to result in a *behavioral* change of staff on a collective level. Thus, it is necessary to evaluate, when possible on the basis of formal reports and interviews, where the Compact reforms resolved or failed to resolve the "tension between the mindsets and behaviors required by change designs and vision, and the existing culture."[41] That bureaucratic culture may deter revolutionary change is not a surprising finding, nor is the corollary conclusion that reform is most likely when it does not require dramatic changes in culture. But investigating specific areas where reform goals conflict most strongly with culture can explain a lot about where goals remain just that—espoused goals that have yet to be fully realized in the way of life at the Bank.

Decentralization

The path-dependent dynamic of the Bank's organizational culture is evident even in the proclaimed successes of the Compact, in the sense that dramatic formal change in the rules and structure of the organization did not fully replace existing informal norms and incentives structures within the four-year reform period. One such example is the rapid decentralization of the Bank, which increased the total number of individuals in field offices to one-third of total staff. The

---

[40] World Bank 2001c, 54. See also comments by former senior manager Willi Wapenhans, arguing that the Bank's rules and regulations have tended to invite compliance rather than commitment to the Bank's mission—the missing element of reform being the focus on incentives (Wapenhans 2000, 247). See also World Bank Operations Evaluation Department 2002a, viii.

[41] World Bank 2001c, annex 8, pp. 16–17.

purpose of this reorganization was to make the Bank more client-focused and less "inward-looking," allowing operational staff to manage loans and projects in a manner responsive to the borrowers' interests rather than being primarily concerned with pleasing superiors back in Washington.

Client and staff surveys show that project management indeed became more flexible and tailored to the specific needs of borrowers. At the same time, other reports cautioned that traditional staff attitudes about field assignments may not have changed as much as expected. Staff in the field expressed a great deal of satisfaction with being in the field,[42] but also felt "disconnected" from the cutting edge of development research and policy in Washington. They believed rewards, such as new assignments or promotions, continued to be linked to remaining fully integrated into the informal networks at the Bank's headquarters.[43] An interview with one field officer in Moscow in 1999 indicated that the responsibilities of the mission office were still largely regarded by borrowers and staff alike as another layer of red tape, with all real decisions of any consequence relayed to Washington.[44] Former country director Dennis de Tray, who himself was based outside of Washington during the Compact period, notes the great difficulty in recruiting qualified applicants for country mission positions.[45] Furthermore, staff I interviewed remained skeptical of the degree to which decentralization has led to an espoused "listening culture." The formal assessment even stated that "while staff are encouraged to listen to their clients in the field, they frequently find resistance in Washington to tailoring Bank approaches to heed what they have heard. And still to an apparently excessive degree, they find themselves pressing their clients to use Bank guidelines, policies, systems, and ways of planning."[46]

The Matrix Management System

The matrix management system introduced in the Bank's headquarters in Washington was intended to shake up lines of authority and resource allocation, and thereby create new incentive structures to reorient staff behavior around the Compact's goals. Overall, as might be

[42] Nielson, Tierney, and Weaver 2006, 124.

[43] World Bank 2001a, 14; World Bank Quality Assurance Group 2001, 8; and World Bank 2002c.

[44] Interview with Ludmila Poznanskaya, World Bank Mission Office, Moscow, September 1999.

[45] De Tray 2006.

[46] World Bank 2001c, annex 8, p. 14.

expected, the complex reorganization produced considerable anxiety and uncertainty among staff. The new rules and desired operational norms were not introduced to a blank slate, but rather competed with existing incentive structures, mind-sets, and habits. In several instances, the intended outcomes of the matrix management system reportedly met with unintended consequences.

The most obvious example of the difficulty in realizing the goals of the matrix system, as noted in formal assessment reports and several interviews, concerned the internal market system of work program agreements. Under the new matrix management system, country directors (CDs) were given increased control over the Bank's administrative budget. The CDs use the budgets to contract with the Bank's new networks of staff experts (such as environmental specialists in ESSD) to find the staff with the most appropriate skills to conduct economic and sector work, project appraisals and safeguard assessment, and fulfill other parts of a country's work plan.[47] Internal contracting looked much like the billable hour system found in most American law firms. Staff members quickly learned that they needed to maximize the number of reported billable hours to demonstrate demand for their services (which is taken into account during annual reviews and promotion decisions). By contracting out to the various networks in response to specific client needs, the new system was intended to eliminate supply-driven, blueprint work and better tailor programs to individual countries. It was also intended to reduce overall administrative costs of project management (a prevailing demand of borrower states) by introducing a market-like system where staff members competed with one another to offer the lowest "bid" for key operational services.

However, the matrix system backfired and "created stress, job insecurity, and poor morale as staff competed with each other for work."[48] Other internal reports likewise pointed to the "dysfunctional outcomes: promoting competition rather than team work and instilling a sense of uncertainty even for good performers."[49] One official assessment noted that the internal market system inadvertently opposed knowledge sharing, despite this intended function of the new thematic networks and one of the Compact's "pillars." "Budget downsizing and job insecurity create[d] incentives for staff to hold onto knowledge as a form of power," rather than share knowledge that might be used by

[47] Interview with Anil Sood and William Rex, February 2002, World Bank, Washington, D.C.
[48] World Bank 2001c, 42.
[49] World Bank 2002d, 7.

other staff to bid for the same work.[50] As a result, the "Knowledge Bank" remained "unhealthily supply-oriented," and the inward-looking incentive to seek the approval of organizational superiors persisted, as staff members proactively looked for venues for their ideas and services to improve their internal "marketability."[51] In an internal staff survey, only 26 percent agreed that the new matrix management system had created a good balance between the client focus, country director empowerment, and the global knowledge provided by the sector directors and managers located in the new networks.[52] In the end, the evaluations suggested that the matrix system would not be fully functional until the system accomplished an "internalization of a different mindset—a 'matrix of the mind,' so that good practices become the institutional norm."[53]

Safeguard Policies

Critics argued that, in addition to undermining the goal of increasing the sharing of knowledge, the internal market system also inadvertently countervailed ongoing attempts to promote safeguards and other environment and social assessment procedures in the design, appraisal, and implementation of projects.[54] This was reiterated in a separate OED evaluation in 2001 on the Bank's progress in mainstreaming sustainable development. The OED reported that the Environmental Department's loss of budget control to country directors and the subsequent need for environmental specialists to "sell" their services in an internal competitive market dampened incentives for project task managers (who are under pressure to lower the costs of project management) to hire environmental specialists to carry out lengthy and expensive environmental assessments.[55] Likewise, whether or not National Environmental Action Plans and other environmental or socially related concerns get integrated into the Bank's overall lending strategies is often contingent upon the particular interests or sympathies of country directors. The CDs exercise considerable influence over who or what gives input into the composition of the decisive Country Assistance Strategies, yet are looking to cut excessive costs and delays in order to streamline project management in a period

---

[50] World Bank 2001c, annex 3, p. 11.

[51] World Bank 2001c, annex 3, p. 24.

[52] World Bank 2001c, annex 4, p. 5.

[53] World Bank 2001c, annex 4, p. 14.

[54] Interview with Kay Treakle, executive director of the Bank Information Center, 31 January 2002, Washington, D.C.

[55] World Bank Operations Evaluation Department 2001a; and Goldman 2005.

of tight operational budgets and client governments' resistance to "excessive" loan conditions.[56]

The difficulty in institutionalizing and enforcing safeguards is logical if one understands the resource constraints pervading the Bank at this time. The number of development agendas and mandates, such as assessments of environmental and social safeguards (and now governance assessments), was increasing at the same time that internal budgets and staff resources were decreasing. In 1998, Johannes Linn (then vice president for the Europe and Central Asia region) coined the term *unfunded mandate*, defined as "things you [staff and management] have to do for which you're not allowed to charge, or charge enough."[57] According to staff, safeguard policies often fall into this category. This reinforces a culture in which the staff understands that environmental impact assessments and other safeguard policies are "boxes to be checked off" not worthy of significant resources and time. In fact, staff members suggest, unfunded mandates often create more resistance and contradict desired internalization of new norms, exacerbating mainstreaming gaps and creating few incentives to comply with policies "in any meaningful way."[58]

It is thus not surprising that the original Compact did not give more specific attention to safeguard policies, despite the espoused goal of realigning internal resources and incentives toward new development agendas such as sustainable development. The weak compliance with safeguard measures has been a central concern to many external and internal critics and a major impetus behind the creation of the Independent Inspection Panel in 1993. According to the assessment reports, this was resisted for the most part by borrowing country governments, who saw higher standards for compliance with environmental and social safeguards (such as policies on indigenous peoples) as contributing once again to higher costs, delays, and overly strict conditions in the preparation, loan approval, and supervision of projects.[59]

As a result, efforts to increase accountability standards and compliance associated with safeguard policies (issues pushed by NGOs and donor states) have worked against incentives to appear more client-focused (in line with borrowers' interests). The conflicting imperatives have contributed to an emerging risk-aversion among staff seeking to please superiors and borrowing governments. It is not only that in

---

[56] World Bank Operations Evaluation Department 2001a; and informal discussion at the Tuesday Group meeting, Oxfam International, Washington D.C., 5 February 2002.

[57] World Bank Staff Association 2000.

[58] Interviews with Bank staff, July 2005 and January 2007.

[59] World Bank 2000b, 5.

some instances safeguards are not taken seriously. Evidence in a 2001 report by the Quality Assurance Group suggests that some managers are actually discouraging staff from tackling operations that involve excessive safeguards or might trigger policies on resettlement.[60]

Project Performance

The Compact period created tremendous pressure on project managers and staff to produce improvements in the quality of projects at entry, the likelihood of sustainability, and the potential for institutional development (see figures 5.1 and 5.2).[61] By the middle to late 1990s, donor countries in particular were strongly pushing a "results" focus to demonstrate that development aid was actually working. Wolfensohn desired to produce a "results-oriented culture" by rewarding staff for demonstrated improvements in loan performance. As noted earlier, the Compact's assessment, drawing selectively from QAG and OED evaluations, did indicate an improvement.

However, qualitative evidence presented in the QAG and OED evaluations indicated tension between the new incentive structures intended to produce a "results-oriented culture" and preexisting norms involving evaluation. For example, one of the specific goals of the Compact was to decrease the number of projects in the Bank's overall portfolio that were "at risk" to fail to be implemented or have little impact on development. However, the *Annual Report on Portfolio Performance 2001*, produced by QAG, argued that pressure from manage-

[60] World Bank Quality Assurance Group 2001, 16. Resettlement policies are often linked to large infrastructure projects, which require moving indigenous populations from their lands as a result of property expropriation or ecological changes (such as flooding of land in hydroelectric dam projects). The absence of effective resettlement safeguard mechanisms in the 1980s catalyzed the attention of a transnational NGO movement, which documented several cases of the involuntary resettlement of local peoples or resettlements to areas without adequate infrastructure, including drinkable water, accessible roads, and arable land. The result was the adoption of extensive resettlement assessment and safeguard policies in the 1990s.

[61] As noted by many others already, the pressure to show performance improvements has first put demands on staff to continue to be overoptimistic in their own reported evaluations of projects' outcomes, sustainability, and potential impact on the development of institutions. This has contributed to a continued difference of around 9 percent between these positive staff evaluations and the independent evaluations conducted after project completion by the Operations Evaluation Department (World Bank Operations Evaluation Department 2002a; World Bank Quality Assurance Group 2001, 21). Others suggest that the top-down pressure to produce ratings in line with Compact targets also compromised the autonomy of the OED and QAG, leading to some doubt over how the numbers are reported and linked to performance targets. See, for example, Rich 2002, 49–50.

ment to "show good results" may have compelled project team (task) managers to underreport risks. As a result, according to QAG's own internal review, the statistics indicating dramatic improvement were misleading. Projects were not given the label of "at risk" until the project manager placed three or more warning "flags" in the project files. As a result, managers often avoided giving a third flag. Moreover, they may have applied "golden flags," which override designations including high risk. QAG estimated that even if only one-quarter of the projects holding two risk flags were given a third, the overall percentage of projects at risk in the total loan portfolio in 2001 would jump from 12 percent to 16 percent.[62] The authors of the report pay attention to what they see as the internal pressures to produce desirable ratings and excessive optimism in appraisal and supervision. They determined that these norms continued to prevent blunt evaluation of projects at risk in the Bank's overall portfolio.[63]

In his testimony before the U.S. Congress in March 2006, Adam Lerrick, a prominent critic of the Bank and member of the Meltzer commission in 1999, cynically described the Bank's continued efforts to install a "results-oriented culture":

Performance measures have been manipulated to bolster management claims of success and refute critics. In the late 1990s, satisfactory ratings jumped when the criteria were revised upon the instruction of Bank management without a corresponding adjustment to previous years to ensure consistency of measurement, also upon the instruction of Bank management. After the Meltzer Commission in 1999 noted that "sustainability," the *sine qua non* of development, had languished at 50% success rates for years, ratings jumped to 72% in 2000. Were these true improvements or had the bar simply been lowered?[64]

Lerrick's comments, confirmed by internal reviews, indicate that the Bank's culture regarding monitoring and evaluation, discussed in chapter 3, was resilient. Contrary to the Compact goals, by the end of the reform period in 2001, staff members still apparently focused on projects' inputs rather than implementation and sustainability. Thirty percent of sampled projects in 2001 scored less than satisfactory on monitoring and evaluation criteria.[65] Likewise, the number of projects promising likely or better sustainability after completion was only 70

[62] World Bank Quality Assurance Group 2001, 14.
[63] World Bank Operations Evaluation Department 2002a, 9.
[64] Lerrick 2006, 4.
[65] World Bank Quality Assurance Group 2001, 24.

percent, and the percentage of projects showing substantial or better institutional development impact was only 56 percent. These numbers were even lower in the key sectors and regions that have specifically targeted for improvement in the Compact initiative. For example, the likelihood of sustainability of projects associated with environmentally and socially sustainable development averaged only 53 percent over 2000–2001, with a development impact rating of only 43 percent.[66] Project staff members still remain unconvinced that good-quality supervision would be rewarded in the same way as lending work.[67] As a result, despite increases in resources devoted to supervision, the focus was still on upstream rather than downstream project management. According to watchdog NGOs, supervision remained in 2001 the first item to be cut in any of the regional budgets.[68]

Participatory Development Goals

A last note on the extent to which the Compact has elicited significant change in the organizational behavior regarding policy and project management concerns the proclaimed success of the reform in integrating higher levels of participation of NGOs, civil society groups, and the Bank's "stakeholders" in all areas of development activities (a new "listening" culture). The participation agenda was strongly pushed by actors outside the Bank, particularly NGOs, civil society groups, and epistemic communities of scholars who argued that the so-called beneficiaries of Bank-sponsored programs often did not have a say in their selection, design, and implementation. This was, and continues to be supported by a strong coalition of actors within the environmental and social development departments and the Comprehensive Development Framework. The Bank now keeps track of the amount and type of input by these groups into Country Assistance Strategy papers, Poverty Reduction Strategy Papers, and specific projects, pointing to the significant increase in participatory activity over the last several years. The 2001 Compact assessment reports, for example, that approximately 75 percent of the Country Assistance Strategy papers prepared for 2001 contained significant levels of consultations

[66] The IEG defines impact evaluation as "the systematic identification of the effects positive or negative, intended or not on individual households, institutions, and the environment caused by a given development activity such as a program or project." See http://www.worldbank.org/ieg/ie/.

[67] Lerrick also implies that this may be due to external pressure from borrowing governments, who do not want to pay for evaluation and may wish to evade scrutiny. Lerrick 2006, 5.

[68] Bank Information Center 2001.

with NGOs, civil society organizations, and other potential stakeholders and beneficiaries.[69]

However, according to numerous assessments, the Compact's objective of increasing the quantitative levels of participation has not necessarily led to a widespread internalization of the participation agenda in terms of how management and staff perceive the value and necessity of this input and integrate it into existing project management routines. Although it was clear from interviews at the end of the Compact period that many staff members strongly believe in this purpose, the amount of time and cost entailed in carrying out extensive consultations and soliciting feedback clashed with the existing approval culture. It also conflicted with the Compact's goal of streamlining project preparation and disbursing development loans more quickly in line with borrowing governments' demands.

Therefore, one of the primary complaints of watchdog NGOs during the years since the Compact is that the meticulous tracking of NGO and CSO involvement amounts to a rhetorical move, in which the increased *quantity* of participation masks the rather minimal *quality* of participation. Watchdog groups note that civil society consultations are often conducted with a limited number of local groups given little forewarning or preparatory documentation.[70] The Compact assessment itself cautiously warned against overoptimistic interpretations of the quantitative measures of participation, noting in part that existing operational guidelines inform staff how to work with borrowing governments and for-profit sector firms, yet say little on how these procedures can be adapted to work with NGOs and civil society groups.[71] The most damning evidence of the gap between the desired and actual results of the Compact reform regarding the participation agenda lies in the client surveys conducted as part of the final assessment. The surveys revealed that only 14 percent of the sampled borrowing country representatives in 2001 believed the Bank's performance to be average or better in terms of strengthening civic participation in national development efforts.[72]

---

[69] World Bank 2001c, annex 2, also points out that increased participation has been greatly facilitated by the decentralization process of the reform initiative, which has placed staff in closer and more frequent contact with local groups. See also World Bank 2002e. For an overview of the evolution of the participation agenda, see Miller-Adams 1999.

[70] Informal discussion at the Tuesday Group Meeting, Oxfam International, Washington, D.C., 5 February 2002. See also the internal report on participation in World Bank 2002d.

[71] World Bank 2001c, annex 2, pp. 16–17.

[72] World Bank 2001c, annex 1, p. 8. To juxtapose this data, 82 percent of the sampled countries found the Bank highly effective in helping to strengthen and maintain sound

PERESTROIKA IN THE POLICY WORLD?

Beyond the formal Compact assessments, in recent years there have been numerous leaked internal memos and reports, as well as published works by staff, that have openly criticized the idea that the Bank has moved away from a culture of economic, apolitical, and technical rationality. Although these works do not necessarily represent the collective view of staff and management, and tend to come as the bitter words of officials pushed out of the organization, they provide a unique insight into the process of ideological and cultural change that is important here to understanding the "poverty of reform."

One of the goals of the Compact reform period was to mainstream new development agendas, as described in chapter 4 in the context of governance and anticorruption work. One way to accomplish this in the reform period was simply to fire existing staff who did not have the appropriate skills or desired beliefs and hire new staff who fit the bill. In fact, the Compact specified targets for human resources, including a quantitative shift in the staff skills mix toward the new "priority" sectors such as sustainable development, gender issues, and governance (see figure 5.3). For some, this promised to counter the dominance of economists, eventually leading to a meaningful shift in how the Bank as a collective set of actors thinks about development.

Between 1997 and 2000, one-third of the total staff was fired, retired, or quit, and 3,357 new staff members were recruited (2,250 in Washington and 1,107 national staff).[73] Statistics provided in the assessment appendices and internal human resource reports indicate that there were increases in staff hired into new units, which may be interpreted as enhancing institutional capacity in priority areas. For example, data on hiring in the mission offices included increases of staff positions in environment and social development from 19 in 1997 to 61 in 2000. At the same time, however, hiring into the economics job family also increased, from 47 to 125. Overall, net data is presented in official reports as evidence of positive change in the direction of enhancing the manpower devoted to new development agendas. Between 1997 and 2001, there were 57 net recruits in environment and social development, 108 in finance, and 36 in human development, compared to 28 in economics and a loss of 3 in energy, mining, and telecommunications (see table 5.3)

---

macroeconomic and trade policies and 81 percent thought the Bank helpful in attracting investment for development.

[73] World Bank 2001c, annex 6, p. 3.

It is nonetheless difficult to determine from this data if the recruitment strategy really achieved the goal of refocusing the development agenda. For example, it is impossible to discern whether or not the new staff positions in areas like environmental and social development are qualitatively different from those hired into other sectors. Are these new staff members sociologists, anthropologists, ecologists, or political scientists? Are they placed in positions of senior management that would translate into agenda-setting power and influence over resource allocation? There is no publicly available data on the educational backgrounds, qualifications, and placement of individuals hired into these sectors, and thus one cannot easily evaluate the claim that there has in fact been a disciplinary shift in hiring practices.[74]

Anecdotal evidence gathered from interviews and internal correspondence, on the other hand, indicates that the drastic staff turnover in the early part of the reform period did not dislodge the perceived hegemony of economic orthodoxy within the Bank's development approaches. Michael Cernea, a senior social scientist within the Bank, once lamented that noneconomic social scientists "did not land in an intellectual vacuum" but rather "landed onto an in-house culture unfamiliar and resistant to this new socio-cultural knowledge and expertise."[75] This sentiment is echoed in many recent commentaries on the manifestation of new development ideas within the Bank. Several interviews conducted at the headquarters between 1999 and 2005 confirmed that noneconomic social scientists within the organization still felt compelled to craft their ideas within the theoretical and methodological language or discourse of prevailing economic theory in order to influence conceptual and operational reality in the Bank. Certainly, as described in chapter 4, this was the case with early advocates of the governance agenda, who viewed the emerging popularity of institutional economics as a window of opportunity to articulate essentially political concerns within the seemingly apolitical language of North's theorem. What is remarkable, however, is that "norm entrepreneurs" are not wholly constrained within this cultural environment and that change may occur (albeit very slowly) within even the most ideologically dogmatic institutions. Actors may incite meaningful change inso-

---

[74] After repeated requests to the Human Resources Department, it was revealed to me that this information was in fact collected, but would not be made available to the public. In any case, it would be difficult to determine from data on graduate degrees if new staff members really ascribed to different development ideologies and policies. For example, an individual trained in political science in the United States may have methodological and theoretical approaches very similar to an individual with an economics degree from Great Britain or Germany.

[75] Cernea 1995, 15.

far as they explicitly recognize the hegemonic culture for what it is and strategically frame their interests (in this case, new development ideas and policies) in ways that will find an audience within the organization. Certainly the pride of place now occupied by the good governance agenda illustrates the success of this organizational marketing of new ideas.

The strategy of norm entrepreneurship may explain the introduction of other recent development agendas. Take, for example, the comments of Anthony Bebbington at a workshop in 2002.[76] In referring to the struggle of social development groups to alter the core agendas and operations of the Bank, Bebbington suggested that the concept of social capital be linguistically defined and methodologically quantified in a way that would enable conversation within the organization.[77] Despite his apparent unease with the idea that the concept of social capital could capture all aspects of social development, he pragmatically recognized that, "whether or not 'social capital' is ultimately the best way of talking about the social foundations of a fairer and more humane world, it is incumbent on the group carrying forward a social development agenda to continue seeking a way of talking about their work that might permeate the languages, thoughts and practices of others within the institution."[78] Desmond McNeill, in a discussion on the Bank's approach to the concept of sustainable development, concurs. He explains the predominance of economistic thinking in the Bank as caused by the discipline's quantifiable, reductionist, and technocratic appeal—missing in much of noneconomic social science—which endows economics with a "special status when it comes to the making of policy."[79] Nonetheless, sustainable development has garnered consider attention over the past decade in the Bank's prominent publications, including being the central theme of the 2003 *World Development Report*.

Organizational learning, however, is difficult for reasons other than the hegemony of certain ideas and disciplines. Ideological and normative change is circumscribed both by individuals' inability to rethink taken-for-granted models and routines[80] and by the organizational imperative of adhering to the core ideas that underpin policy to maintain external legitimacy. As described in chapter 3, international organiza-

---

[76] Bebbington 2002. See also Bebbington et al. 2004, 2006.

[77] Bebbington 2002, 4. See also Woolcock 1998; and Bebbington et al. 2004, 2006.

[78] Bebbington 2002, 5.

[79] McNeill 2001, 6.

[80] See, for example, two very interesting discussions by senior Bank officials on the organization's response to the East Asian financial crises, in which the Bank attempted to apply the standard economic analysis and rescue packages that ultimately backfired in this very different context. See Stiglitz 1999 and Pereira da Silva 2001, 562.

tions, and public bureaucracies in general, are not likely to admit failure. To do so jeopardizes their political and financial support.

Thus, one tension in the Compact reform process resulted from the juxtaposition of Wolfensohn's desire to project an image of the Bank as an open, self-critical organization eager to engage in debate with the pervasive intolerance of dissent under his administration (see chapter 3).[81] Luiz Pereira da Silva, a senior official at the Bank, argued in 2001 that "a more democratic and open culture of internal discussion, positive incentives to express dissent and transparent mechanisms to reward the quality and pertinence of work would certainly help to avoid the blind application of recipes to any crisis, any situation, and any country."[82] Yet achieving this level of open discussion within the Bank, much less in a public forum, proved difficult.

Many journalists, scholars, and staff members blamed Wolfensohn personally for the intolerance of dissent, despite his espoused commitment early on to an open "listening culture." An internal memo from the Middle East and North Africa Department, leaked around the same time the official Compact assessments were published in 2001, stated: "We do not think that the President receives honest feedback from his senior managers. He does not welcome criticism or tolerate dissent, be it from the Board, or the managers, or the Staff Association. Managers at all levels live under fear. Many have learnt that it services them to agree with him. He is thus isolated from reality."[83]

Yet it is clear that a hypocritical gap between a punitive environment and the espoused ideal of ideological debate and open dissent is a problem endemic to the entire organization, particular between levels of management and staff. In a contribution to the World Bank Staff Association newsletter in 2001, David Ellerman attacked senior management for "enshrining their Official Views" and making it clear that "those who argue against Official Views outside the organization— particularly with any public notice—are seen as traitors being disloyal to the organization itself."[84] In a more critical indictment of the Bank's culture, the internal memo from the Middle East and North Africa Department cited above linked this intolerance of dissent to the more general growth in distrust between management and staff members

---

[81] See, for example, the now infamous cases of the dismissal of Bank chief economists Joseph Stiglitz and the resignation of *World Development Report: Attacking Poverty* World Bank 2000–2001) lead author Ravi Kanbur (Wade 2001a, 2002).

[82] Pereira da Silva 2001, 562.

[83] Internal memo of the Middle East and North Africa Department, 2001, 2, on file with author.

[84] Ellerman, Denning, and Hanna 2001, 3. See also Ellerman 2006.

during the entire reform process. The memo claims that "the management rhetoric of teamwork, culture, ethics, accountability are the mantra adopted by senior management but which we see practiced far too rarely."[85] In response, one critical admission found in the official Compact assessment is the recognition that managers need to model the espoused values and behaviors of the reform in order for staff to internalize the new norms of the espoused culture of open debate and learning.[86]

Conclusion: The Promise of Reform?

The analysis of the Strategic Compact reform provided in this chapter seemingly provides little reason to hope for dramatic change at the Bank any time soon. Such fatalism is not entirely unwarranted. The reform program ultimately produced mixed results because it adopted contradictory goals. This was a result of divergent environment pressures and the preferences of external actors upon whom the Bank depends for critical resources and conferred legitimacy. Such conflicting goals are unlikely to disappear given the heterogeneity and highly politicized nature of the Bank's authorizing and task environments. Thus, while it is not difficult to reach agreement on the need for reform writ large, it is highly improbable that the Bank's many political masters are going to reach a clear consensus on what *exactly* future reform should look like. External goal incongruence is likely to be an enduring feature, with the resulting danger that future reform attempts may in fact perpetuate or produce new forms of organized hypocrisy, rather than resolve it.

More importantly, the Compact reform process illuminates the opportunities for and constraints on realizing substantial change in a large and complex organization that has a deeply embedded culture. The official assessment of the Compact admits that the key lesson learned was to avoid overemphasizing material structures and systems as change levers.[87] Instead, future reform programs must pay more at-

---

[85] Internal memo of the Middle East and North Africa Department 2001, 1, on file with author. This is confirmed by recent staff attitude surveys that report that only 18 percent of staff in 1999 responded favorably to the question of mutual trust between senior management and staff (World Bank 2001c, annex 8, p. 9).

[86] World Bank 2001c, 55 and annex 8, pp. 16–17. See also Schein 1992 and Miller-Adams 1999, 31–32, on the role of organizational leaders in transforming organizational culture through modeled behavior.

[87] World Bank 2001c, 44.

tention to how change can be engendered in underlying ideologies, norms, and incentive structures governing organizational practice: a much deeper and less predictable process of resocialization. Such change, much to the frustration of reform champions, is unlikely to happen quickly and will not be particularly amenable to short-term "strategic engineering." The official assessment in 2001 stated this quite clearly:

> Although the Bank recognized the challenge of cultural change at one level, it underestimated the sustained attention and discipline needed over time to make a significant shift. The Bank's culture runs deep and was long in the making, and achieving the vision will be a formidable endeavor requiring patience, commitment and resources. In this perspective, current achievements should not be minimized, and conversely no amount of commitment or resources will produce a transformed culture overnight.[88]

In hindsight, however, the Compact reform program did not fail. In fact, desired change did occur quite rapidly in the Compact period, but it was where reform goals were largely consistent with preexisting ideologies, norms, and routines (i.e., goal congruence). Change was thus more evolutionary and path-dependent than revolutionary. This was evident in the various rules and procedures installed to make the Bank more responsive to client governments, reinforcing in many instances the preexisting culture traits such as the approval culture and disbursement imperative identified in the Wapenhans Report. Achieving other reform objectives, such as mainstreaming other development agendas and practices, proved more difficult in the absence of such cultural adjacency and in the presence of conflicts with other reform objectives.

Is major strategic reform thus possible in an organization so complex and so deeply mired in the political and organizational tensions that produce hypocrisy?[89] The theory of organized hypocrisy and change laid out in this book would suggest no. However, as suggested at the end of chapter 4, with crisis may come the promise of change. In many ways, the shock caused by Wolfowitz's own hypocrisy may be just enough to punctuate equilibrium and mobilize support, both inside and outside the Bank, for dramatic reform.

Avoiding the incongruent goals that hindered the realization of some of the Compact goals will be key. Such avoidance demands se-

---

[88] World Bank 2001c, annex 8, pp. 6–7.
[89] I thank one external reviewer for articulating this question so clearly.

lecting from competing reform goals, which is very difficult for a political organization that continues to be dependent on its environment for both material and symbolic resources critical to survival. Yet if those external actors pushing for reform take a proactive role in crafting the reform program and seeking compromise in the process, this may mitigate the risks of goal dissonance that hindered the Compact. This has been a missing variable in past reorganization efforts, which have been primarily initiated by inside reform advocates in response to external pressures, but without the active participation of those on the outside.

Moreover, future reformers must grapple with an organizational culture where underlying ideologies, norms, languages, and routine are antithetical to desired changes in organizational behavior. Consider for a moment this comment made in the *Economist* shortly after Wolfowitz's ouster:

> A new president inherits as corps of 8,600 highly qualified and experienced staff in full command of a jargon and house culture than can bewilder new bosses. Some in the top ranks are attached to the status quo which has served them so well. "The bank has a set rhythm," says Ashraf Ghani, chancellor of Kabul University, who once worked at the institution. But a president cannot change those rhythms and routines until he has first mastered them.[90]

All hope is not lost. Culture is not completely inert, and a plethora of corporate business literature suggests that organizational culture can be manipulated to direct organizational change.[91] Yet changing culture requires patience. President Conable in 1987 sought to uproot and overhaul the culture of the Bank by firing all employees and requiring them to reapply. That particular reform attempt backfired in the most spectacular way. It resulted not in cultural transformation, but in a traumatized staff, a distrustful environment, and a legacy of suspicion toward reorganizations. Even for staff members who did not work at the Bank during this time, "The 'Conable reorganization' is a four-letter word."[92]

All of this indicates that future reform architects will benefit greatly from looking at past attempts at reorganization to see where the cultural land-mines lay, and accordingly to design reforms that do not introduce structures, rules, and incentives that reinforce undesired parts of culture. The Bank's archives in fact contain a wealth of infor-

---

[90] "Paul Wolfowitz: An Outsider's Fate," *The Economist*, 19 May 2007, 65.
[91] E.g., Deal and Kennedy 1982; Elsmore 2001.
[92] Interview with Bank staff member, April 2002.

mation, including extensive internal documents, on past reorganization attempts.[93] If new information disclosure policies[94] enable access to these materials, research could benefit current policy discussions. Wolfowitz's successor will be well advised to do this homework and learn from past mistakes.

[93] The most notable of these major reorganizations, besides the Strategic Compact, are the 1972 reforms under Robert McNamara, the 1987 reorganization under Conable, and the 1992–93 reforms under Lewis Preston.

[94] As of January 2007, the informational disclosure policies regarding archival documents did not allow access to the materials that would be most valuable for this research, foremost the internal correspondence files of the reorganization team members in each period. However, the archivists told me that these information disclosure policies are currently under review by the Board of Executive Directors (spring 2007), and may be changed soon to facilitate easier access.

CHAPTER SIX

The Fog of Development

> It must be said that, to date, there continues to be a sizeable gap between the public pronouncements of some of the Bank's spokesmen and its day-to-day practice.
> —*Mason and Asher 1973, 732*

> Now even more than before, the World Bank is associated with double-speak, dithering and duplicity.
> —*Bello and Guttal 2005, 11*

THE HYPOCRISY of the World Bank has been present throughout the institution's history. Such hypocrisy may have gone relatively unnoticed thirty years ago when the Bank was not yet widely considered an important actor in global politics. However, growth in its size and influence lately has drawn the powerful IO into the world spotlight. Increased attention to the Bank's activities exposes its hypocrisy in its most overt and subtle forms. This results in a politicization of the Bank that affects its organizational security by threatening its autonomy and authority. Attacks on its external legitimacy and political support increase pressure on the Bank to accept an unwieldy combination of espoused development policies and goals that are not easily translated into practice. This ironically increases the likelihood of the Bank engaging in hypocrisy, even as growing attention to the Bank and efforts to reign in the organization reduce the ability of the Bank to get away with it.

The genesis of this book thus lay in a few basic questions much on the minds of scholars and policymakers alike: does the Bank in fact display organized hypocrisy, as asserted by its critics? What causes this disconnect between talk and action? Why does hypocrisy persist even when it threatens to undermine the Bank's effectiveness, authority, and legitimacy? More broadly speaking, how can we explain the factors shaping the behavior of the Bank that give rise to such hypocrisy? What can we say about the process of change that explains why hypocrisy may persist and why reform efforts seem so easily thwarted?

I defined organized hypocrisy throughout this book as the distinct and observable gaps or inconsistencies between the theories, goals, and "best practices" organizations claim to uphold and the actual policy agendas and instruments they employ. This can be more simply understood as the disconnects between formal policy and espoused agendas, on one hand, and actual operational behavior, on the other. We can observe and measure the degree of organized hypocrisy in the Bank by examining where management and staff fail to comply with the organization's own policies and mandates and where espoused development ideas and agendas failed to get mainstreamed.

Sociological theory tells us that hypocrisy is in some sense a natural, inevitable, and even appropriate attribute of organizations. The Bank, as an international public bureaucracy, may in fact be more prone to organized hypocrisy than its private counterparts due to its intrinsic political character and its resource dependency on its inevitably heterogeneous authorizing and task environments. The Bank must simultaneously "navigate its political waters" by balancing the need for external legitimacy and access to resources with the need to uphold internal efficiency and consistency through stability in operational routines in its large and very complex bureaucracy. Divergence between the rhetoric and the reality will predictably arise when the demands and signals of the external environment conflict with the ideologies, norms, and rules that inform coordinated action within the organization.[1] To cope with such incongruent goals, the Bank will portray official structures, rules, and "espoused values" that are decoupled from the informal norms (or "theories-in-practice") that govern internal operations.[2]

Yet it is the persistence of organizational hypocrisy that becomes the real puzzle. As stated from the outset, organized hypocrisy is a double-edged sword. On the one hand, it is an effective tool for the Bank to attain external legitimacy by allowing the organization to espouse commitments to certain policies and goals that elicit the support (and thus resources) of important actors in its external environment. On the other hand, once exposed, hypocrisy *threatens* legitimacy and undermines external political and material support. When this happens, the Bank essentially has two options. It may change its espoused policies and agendas to fit with existing action—an easier, yet often politically unpalatable option. Or it may attempt to change its action to be more consistent with its espoused policies and agendas—a process that entails complex organizational behavioral change.

---

[1] Brunsson 1989, 6.

[2] Argyris and Schön 1978; Weick 1976; Meyer and Rowan 1977; Brunsson 1989; and Schein 1992.

This raises an interesting question about the strategic nature of organized hypocrisy and the fluid relationship between organizational talk and action, discussed in chapter 2. This is a question that ultimately gets at the deeper issue of how we can understand the processes and outcomes of IO change. If we were to accept the notion that hypocrisy is simply a strategic act driven by resource dependency, we should expect that hypocrisy—once exposed and targeted for elimination—will disappear. And yet repeated attempts to restructure the Bank to eliminate apparent hypocrisy and other problems, such as reform efforts from 1997 to 2001, have failed to root out essential disconnects and in some instances have led to the emergence of new (and to the Bank's critics, increasingly resilient) forms of hypocrisy. As chapter 5 demonstrates, this can be explained by analyzing continued problems of environmental goal incongruence as well as the difficulty of transforming the bureaucratic politics and culture of the Bank. This latter factor is one often missing from discussions of reform. Yet to anyone who works within these organizations, it is readily apparent that the bureaucratic environment (in particular the embedded culture of a large and mature organization) matters tremendously in accounting for patterns and outcomes of reform processes.

Ultimately, the danger with respect to hypocrisy and reform is clear. Strategic attempts to alter the formal architecture of these IOs to meet external demands may result in *rhetorical shifts* in stated goals, symbolic rules, and structures that may actually become further disconnected from the internal norms and standard operating procedures that inform the daily activities of staff. This will perpetuate behavioral hypocrisies and confound well-intentioned reformers.

Fundamentally transforming the intellectual and operational environments of organizations to resolve the gaps between rhetoric and reality constitutes a deeper and more meaningful level of organizational learning and change that routinely proves to be extremely difficult.[3] This is further complicated when staff members suspect that reform objectives are adopted for symbolic purposes to relieve external pressures. When are shifts in espoused development goals and policies merely rhetoric adopted to appease external critics? When are they in-

---

[3] Here I distinguish behavioral dynamics and specific instances of organizational change by defining change as a major systemic transformation (or intentional reform) in the goals, boundaries, and activities of the organizations. As Aldrich (1999, 163) argues, to qualify as a transformation, change must involve a qualitative break with routines and a shift to new kinds of skills that challenges existing organizational knowledge. This closely resembles Ernst Haas's distinction between adaptation and learning in international organizations. (Haas 1990).

stead sincere signals to staff about desired changes in research and operational behavior? Moreover, when there are multiple and inconsistent shifts in organizational goals that conflict, as demonstrated in the case of the Strategic Compact, which reform objectives really matter, and which are meant only for show?

Consider for a moment a World Bank Staff Association newsletter that reveals the frustration and confusion of staff:

> The multiple personas of the Bank help it to survive as an institution in heavy political weather. But the personas are often contradictory, a situation that puts the institution in danger of being seen as hypocritical. . . . The personas confuse staff, too. Internal communications from the Bank tell staff about necessary changes; are the reasons proffered the actual ones? For example, what really prompts the Bank's repeated reorganizations? Overall, the Bank is constantly finessing information given to staff, to its shareholders, and to outside critics.[4]

These comments reflect a serious impediment to future reform. Staff members' uncertainty results in a lack of clarity in incentive structures and potential contradictions between formal rules and informal understandings (cultural norms) about "how things are done" and "what gets rewarded or sanctioned" in the organization. Under conditions of such uncertainty, boundedly rational members of the organization may behave out of habit, or at least based upon prior expectations.

Prospects for IO Research

For the academic study of international organizations, the preceding insights into the sources of organized hypocrisy and the nature of organizational change are noticeably absent from conventional, especially rationalist, IO literature. The sociological approach adopted here (often conflated with constructivism) suggests that it is simply wrong to assume that member states who formally delegate authority and tasks to the Bank can manipulate the organization's structural design and formal rules to produce desired and mutually consistent organizational talk and action.[5] Such "rational design" is inevitably elusive, and even these rationalist scholars admit that IOs like the Bank do not always respond well to "marching orders."[6] This is particularly true when those orders appear to send staff in contrary directions; a com-

---

[4] World Bank Staff Association 2005, 1.
[5] See, for example, Koremenos, Lipson, and Snidal 2002; Hawkins et al. 2006.
[6] Nielson and Tierney 2003.

mon delegation problem that IO scholars utilizing rationalist principal-agent models are ready and able to analyze.[7]

Yet even if these marching orders were consistent and even if member states were the only actors that really mattered in the authorizing and task environments of the Bank (a claim not made in this book), it is still not clear how much or what kind of organizational change we can expect without a rich understanding of an IO's autonomy, the nature of organizational (in)security derived from the IO's dependency on material resources and conferred legitimacy, and the cultural life within the bureaucracy (which sheds lights on the agent preferences treated as exogenous in the principal-agent model). Without references to such variables beyond the formal delegation chain, it seems unlikely that we can fully account for when and how the Bank—or any similar international organization—will react to environmental demands through an avoidance strategy of organized hypocrisy. Moreover, without reference to congruence within and between environmental and internal cultural pressures, it is difficult to explain when reforms appear to resolve or perpetuate organized hypocrisy. This suggests that future studies of IO behavior and change would be well advised to integrate sociological theories into more conventional state-centric theories in ways that bridge the apparent "rationalist-constructivist divide."[8] At the very least, it necessitates the treatment of IOs as actors in their own right, with due attention directed to the external *normative* environment and internal *cultural* life of IOs as critical variables in explaining their patterns of behavior and change over time.[9]

A caveat is in order at this point. It was not my objective, nor was it within the scope of one book, to construct and test a generalized theory of IO hypocrisy and reform. Yet the sociological theory employed in this book strongly asserts that we should expect to find hypocrisy in organizations, especially in public bureaucracies. Indeed, I do not believe that the Bank is unique in exhibiting organized hypocrisy or coping with the quandaries of strategic reform. These are features endemic to many of the most prominent international organizations in the world today, fueling a crisis for global governance.

In fact, I would speculate that the sources and nature of organized hypocrisy and reform found in the Bank, as described above, are quite likely to exist in other multilateral development banks, such as the

---

[7] Hawkins et al. 2006.

[8] Fearon and Wendt 2002; Jupille, Caporaso, and Checkel 2003; Kelley 2004; Checkel 2005; Zürn and Checkel 2005; Tierney and Weaver 2006; and Hurd 2007.

[9] Barnett and Finnemore 2004. See also Hopgood 2006 for an in-depth study of organizational culture and behavior in an INGO (Amnesty International).

Inter-American Development Bank and the Asian Development Bank, and perhaps even the World Bank's sister institution, the International Monetary Fund. Like the World Bank, these are international organizations that share like structures, mandates, authorizing and task environments, and staff (sometimes the *same* staff members, who often move between these institutions).

Among these institutions, there are subtle, but important, differences in the exact nature and degree of their environmental resource dependency and their particular bureaucratic cultures. Yet like the Bank, the other MDBs and the IMF are large public organizations with sizable and relatively autonomous bureaucracies that nonetheless depend upon a heterogeneous environment for material resources and conferred legitimacy. At the same time, they have existed long enough to develop distinct bureaucratic cultures that will more or less amenable to certain paths of change.[10] Moreover, like the Bank, these other economic institutions today (especially the IMF) face similar challenges to their legitimacy, effectiveness, and raison d'être, and therefore are under constant pressure for reform.

We should not be surprised, then, to find that other international financial institutions exhibit forms of organized hypocrisy—patterns of policy noncompliance or mainstreaming gaps—similar to the hypocrisy we observe in the World Bank. Nor should we be surprised to find that attempts to strategically reform these organizations fall short of lofty goals due to a plethora of external political and internal cultural or resource constraints. In the summer of 2007, for example, the IMF announced a Medium-Term Strategy in a response to its rather dramatic fall from grace since the financial crises in East Asia in the late 1990s and in Argentina in 2001–2. In the face of negative net lending with no reprieve in sight, the IMF is searching for a new purpose and renewed legitimacy. The response has been a conscious effort to define a reform strategy that promises not only a difficult transformation of the IMF's governance (foremost its subscription and voting rules on the executive board), but also a quite substantial shift in the organization's mission. This foremost includes a diminished "bailout" lending focus and an enhanced surveillance role (through revised Article IV consultation processes) to strengthen the IMF's capacity for financial crisis prevention. At the same time, it is clear that the implementation of the new surveillance decision, as it is called, will be difficult. The process of negotiating the shift in Article IV consultation

---

[10] The organizational culture and change in the IMF, in particular, has been the subject of great interest in recent scholarship. See, e.g., Blustein 2001; Barnett and Finnemore 2004, chap. 3; Momani 2005, 2007; Leiteritz 2005; and Chwieroth 2007.

rules proved very political contentious (taking nearly a year and a half during 2006 and 2007 and passing in the end without consensus from all 185 member states). Moreover, the internal "retooling" necessary to build needed staff skills, routines, and resources will certainly not happen overnight. It thus seems quite likely, in obvious conditions of organizational insecurity compounded by goal incongruence, that we will see elements of organized hypocrisy in the IMF in the near future in terms of the espoused policies and goals versus the full implementation and enforcement of the new surveillance function. What remains to be seen is what form that hypocrisy takes and how long it persists.

Of course, the universe of IOs is highly diverse. There are critical variations in their form, purpose, degree of bureaucratic autonomy, authority, and power. Not all IOs have sizable and relatively independent secretariats or robust bureaucracies. In such instances, we will not see the evolution and influence of bureaucratic culture, which, we have seen, is essential to understanding the organized hypocrisy and change of the Bank. Likewise, there are fundamental differences in the resource dependency of IOs (on *whom* or on *what* the IO is more or less dependent for political and financial support and conferred legitimacy). The example that immediately comes to mind is the World Trade Organization. The WTO, like the Bank, is currently criticized widely for its hypocrisy. Its ideals of free and fair trade and its seemingly democratic structures are contradicted by the institutionalized "rigged" rules that bias trade treaties in favor of the powerful industrialized member states.[11] The breakdown in global trade talks and the illegitimacy of the WTO are attributed to this perceived hypocrisy. Yet the WTO is a very different kind of organization, with a very small secretariat that exhibits little autonomy or authority. Its hypocrisy is not embedded in staff noncompliance or failures in bureaucratic mainstreaming. Instead, the WTO's hypocrisy is rooted in the disjuncture between the words and deeds of its member *states*.

Thus the intriguing task for future research will be to look for and compare the sources and forms of organized hypocrisy and change found in different types of IOs. Recognizing the critical variations noted above will influence where we look in the institutional environment for the sources of conflicting pressures or the goal incongruence that leads to organized hypocrisy. Nonetheless, despite these differences, we can expect all large international organizations to exhibit hypocrisy in the sense of perceived contradictions between espoused ideals and practice. But the exact sources and nature of this hypocrisy will

---

[11] Steinberg 2002; Bukovansky 2005.

vary, requiring us to pay more attention to *whose* hypocrisy is at stake, *where* that hypocrisy is occurring, and *how* that hypocrisy is essential to organizational survival.

THE WORLD BANK'S CRISIS OF LEGITIMACY

One of the key lessons derived from this book is that we should expect organized hypocrisy to emerge when an IO's external legitimacy and access to material resources is threatened. This raises an interesting question with respect to the Bank today. It is already apparent that declining official development aid, increased competition from private capital flows and other IOs, as well as growing demands for grant-based aid allocations threaten the Bank's financial autonomy and viability (see the next section). Is the Bank also suffering from a growing legitimacy crisis? If so, should we expect to see it exhibit *more* organized hypocrisy in the future?

There was good reason to believe, even prior to the Wolfowitz debacle, that the Bank's legitimacy was in serious jeopardy. Today the Bank receives more condemnations than accolades. To many critics, its "dream of a world free of poverty" has in reality been a nightmare for the poor of the world. The past sixty years of harsh structural adjustment and accumulating sovereign debt have produced highly uneven progress in economic growth and social development, with regions of the world like sub-Saharan Africa seemingly worse off today than thirty years ago.[12] The tarnished public image of the Bank inevitably takes a toll on its legitimacy and authority and in turn raises questions about the Bank's purpose. In reference to the joint annual conference of Bretton Woods institutions in April 2005, renowned economist Kenneth Rogoff suggested that a key objective of the meeting would be "to define what the IMF and World Bank are for and what they should do."[13] Recurring debates within policy and academic communities on whether to "reform, reinvent, or demolish" the Bank appear to confirm that the world's preeminent development institution is suffering a midlife crisis.[14]

Indeed, there was solid evidence long before Wolfowitz took office that the external support for the Bank was waning. In 2002, the World Bank solicited Princeton Survey Research Associates to conduct a poll of more than twenty-six hundred global leaders from government,

---

[12] Easterly 2006b.
[13] Quoted in the *Financial Times*, 15 April 2005.
[14] Pincus and Winters 2002.

NGOs, business, and academics communities in forty-eight developing and industrialized countries. The objective was to gauge perceptions of the effectiveness of development aid and the role of the Bank. The results, released in May 2003, revealed quite negative attitudes in key areas of the Bank's work. While a slight majority of all respondents believe that the Bank has an overall positive influence on the way things are going in their country, sizable minorities and sometimes majorities in specific geographic regions believe that it acts "irresponsibly" and that the economic reforms pushed by the Bank hurt more people than they help.[15] Moreover, perceptions of the Bank's performance in reducing global poverty appear to be worsening. Compared to survey data from 1998, the number of global opinion leaders who believe the Bank does a good job at reducing poverty has dropped from 24 percent to 22 percent. Meanwhile, 28 percent responded that it does a "poor" job at reducing poverty.

The results were similarly mixed to negative in areas where the Bank has sought to regain legitimacy in the eyes of some critics by pushing new development agendas. For example, perceptions of the Bank's performance in promoting environmental sustainability in the developing world declined since 1998, with 34 percent in 2002 viewing the Bank as doing a "poor job" in promoting environmental sustainability.[16] Similarly, in the much vaunted work on anticorruption, the results were even more negative. Only 16 percent of respondents thought the Bank was actually doing a good job in fighting corruption,

---

[15] When questioned whether the Bank acts irresponsibly in their country, the percentage of respondents strongly or somewhat agreeing was 30 percent in East Asia, 35 percent in Europe and Central Asia, 29 percent in Latin America and the Caribbean, 40 percent in the Middle East and North Africa, 60 percent in South Asia, 39 percent in sub-Saharan Africa, and 30 percent in the advanced industrialized countries. On the question of whether the Bank's economic reforms hurt more people than they help, the number strongly or somewhat agreeing was 39 percent in East Asia, 26 percent in Europe and Central Asia, 55 percent in Latin America and the Caribbean, 52 percent in the Middle East and North Africa, 63 percent in South Asia, 64 percent in sub-Saharan Africa, and 29 percent in the advanced industrialized countries (Princeton Survey Research Associates 2003, 31–32).

[16] This is opposed to a 1998 survey showing 27 percent responding "good job," 35 percent "average job," and 29 percent "poor job." This correlates with respondents' beliefs on how much priority the Bank currently gives to the goal of fostering environmental sustainability. In 1998, 63 percent of respondents said the Bank gave environmental sustainability "high priority," 20 percent "medium priority," and 14 percent "low priority." In 2002, these numbers were 44 percent "high priority," 31 percent "medium priority," and 23 percent "low priority." Princeton Survey Research Associates 2003, 52. For a more recent assessment of the Bank's backsliding on environmental sustainability goals and safeguards policies, see Lawrence 2005.

whereas 41 percent (an increase from 25 percent in 1998) thought it was doing a poor job.[17]

Many respondents also believed that the Bank imposes its development ideas on borrowing nations. The report's authors write: "this finding is consistent and overwhelming in all regions and it virtually all countries. Large majorities of eight in 10 or more in countries as diverse as Thailand, Mexico, Pakistan, Nigeria and Britain all think the Bank forces its agendas on developing countries."[18] Moreover, there was a strong consensus that the Bank is heavily influenced by U.S. political and economic policies. Well over 80 percent in all regions, including the advanced industrialized countries, believe that the Bank was influenced to a "great or moderate extent" by U.S. interests in 2002; three years before President Bush nominated Wolfowitz for the presidency.[19]

However, what is most interesting about the survey's findings from the perspective of this work is global opinion leaders say about the Bank as an organization. The report concludes with a rather bold statement:

> When opinion leaders were asked in an open-ended question about the Bank's greatest weakness, they most often cite the Bank's organizational culture—its slow and inefficient bureaucracy, its perceived arrogance and its lack of transparency and collaboration. This broad category of organizational culture tops the list of criticisms cited in every region of the world, with the Bank's bureaucracy and perceived arrogance often heading the list. Opinion leaders also criticize the Bank for its economic policies, such as its traditional approach to development and simplified solutions, for not taking into account local conditions, for not doing enough to help developing countries, and for being too heavily influenced by the U.S. and the West.[20]

The Bank's management and staff are acutely aware of the barrage of attacks coming from the outside and the difficulties they create for staff in going about their daily business. This in turn may be contributing to an internal legitimacy crisis, or at least an identity crisis. A World Bank Group Staff Association newsletter from January 2005 notes that the Bank's leaders have to think about the institution's image constantly.[21] In fact, improving the Bank's reputation was a

---

[17] Princeton Survey Research Associates 2003, 55.
[18] Princeton Survey Research Associates 2003, 63.
[19] Princeton Survey Research Associates 2003, 64.
[20] Princeton Survey Research Associates 2003, 66.
[21] World Bank Staff Association 2005, 2.

major goal of Wolfensohn during his tenure as president from 1995 to 2005. During the Strategic Compact reform period, the largest expansion in hiring occurred in the External Affairs division, the unit charged with crafting and disseminating the "message" of the Bank. The size of the unit increased from 42 in mid-1997 to 117 by mid-2001, a 179 percent increase.[22]

The same internal Staff Association newsletter from 2005 reinforces a rather bleak outlook on the Bank, this time from the perspective of those who work within the institution. Importantly, the newsletter directly links the Bank's public image crisis with staff members' own understanding of the causes of its hypocrisy. The authors of the article attribute the numerous rhetorical agenda and policy shifts and sweeping reforms (such as the Strategic Compact) to the growing external condemnation of the disconnect between talk and action. The article ends with a few words of cynical advice to staff members: "accept that reorganizations and other painful changes made for public consumption are always going to occur; it is safer not to get too locked into the organization," and "read Bank pronouncements with the understanding that they are crafted for varying audiences, including staff."[23]

All of the preceding would seem to indicate conditions of eroding legitimacy and threats to political and financial support that should trigger organized hypocrisy. Yet at the same time that we may perceive increased *incentives* for hypocrisy, we may also observe decreased *opportunities* for the Bank to get away with hypocrisy. Member states, particularly the donors, and the plethora of vigilant watchdog NGOs and civil society organizations have the Bank squarely on their radar screens. Likewise, internal oversight mechanisms and watchdogs (in the form of disenchanted staff) may serve as a check on the Bank's hypocrisy, particularly in high-profile areas of its activities. Yet it is almost inevitable that all these factors will be in tension—there will always be conflicting pressures in the authorizing and task environments of the Bank. We should always expect some degree of hypocrisy to exist.

CURRENT CHALLENGES AND THE FUTURE OF THE WORLD BANK

The cartoon in figure 6.1, from the World Bank Staff Association newsletter in 2005, aptly depicts the dilemmas facing the Bank. While calls for its elimination are thus far relegated to the extremes of debate, calls

[22] World Bank 2001a, 64.
[23] World Bank 2001a, 3.

THE BANK HAS MULTIPLE PERSONAS.

Figure 6.1
Source: World Bank Staff Association Newsletter, January–February 2005. Reprinted with permission of the World Bank.

for more or less radical reform or reinvention are widespread and gaining momentum. Yet there appears to be little consensus on what kind of Bank should emerge from this process. In the meantime, a panoply of new ideas on international development aid pose serious challenges for the current structure and bureaucratic environment of the Bank.

Take, for example, the current prominence of the Millennium Development Goals (MDGs) jointly adopted by the United Nations, IMF, and World Bank in 2000. The MDGs serve as a very effective rallying cry for global development and momentarily reinvigorated political support for the Bank at a rather dark time in its institutional history. The MDGs call for a renewed focus on the goals of global development, greater coordination between aid agencies, and attention to measurable results. However, the overoptimistic expectations of what the

MDGs can accomplish by the year 2015 and the hypocrisy of donor member states themselves in their failure to make good on their promise to increase official development aid may together undermine the entire program.[24] One real danger is that the inevitable failure of the MDGs will cause a backlash and further erode support for international development aid.[25] The Bank faces a real danger of credibility because it is unable to uphold the very goals it embraced to reestablish its legitimacy and authority.

The skepticism surrounding the MDGs is linked to lingering doubts about the effectiveness of aid in its current form and growing fears that in some contexts aid can cause more harm than good. This is especially true in regions where aid is seen as contributing to climbing debt without resulting declines in poverty rates. In Africa, for example, the number of people in extreme poverty has doubled since 1981 to more than 300 million. Current progress reports on the MDGs show rather dismal results across the board, and especially in Africa, which has made little progress on any of the eight MDG targets. This has sparked intense debate over the question of whether or not aid works, questioning the underlying purpose of the Bank's existence.

Another related challenge to the Bank's future organizational security is pressure from numerous sources to focus less on loans and more on grants. This is particularly true with respect to the role of the International Development Association, which provides highly concessional loans to the poorest countries of the world. Yet the failure of the IDA to produce positive development results in these regions is attributed widely to high levels of corruption and misuse of aid in borrowing nations and the perverse incentives of the donor agencies to keep lending to these countries even when it is clear that the aid is only rolling over on onerous debt.

Recent proposals such as the Millennium Challenge Account (MCA), call for dramatic restructuring of the fundamentals of development: who receives aid, the form of aid (grants versus loans), and the conditions under which aid is allocated.[26] The underlying idea is that aid only works when "good" policy environments are already in place.[27] This has produced pressure for the Bank to be much more selective in determining who should receive aid and to provide more funds in the form of grants, conditional on strict governance criteria.

[24] "Discerning a New Course for World's Donor Nations," *New York Times*, 18 April 2005.

[25] Clemens, Kenney, and Moss 2004; Pronk 2001.

[26] For critical assessment of the MCA, see Soederberg 2004 and Neumayer 2002.

[27] Burnside and Dollar 2000.

On two fronts, the ideas embodied in the MCA threaten the Bank, which depends upon continued lending. On the one hand, it potentially reduces the number of countries eligible for IDA funds. On the other hand, it threatens the financial autonomy of the Bank itself. Transforming the IDA into a grants institution will make the Bank reliant in the long run upon increasing monetary contributions by Part I member states.[28] The IDA will no longer have the repayments on past loans to replenish its funds and will become entirely dependent upon donor states, which can (as they have in the past) use their power of the purse to pursue their own agendas. Moreover, trends in official development assistance (ODA) provide sufficient grounds for skepticism regarding the willingness of donor states to compensate for the shortfall in revenues left by this switch from loans to grants.

This concern is compounded by U.S. pressure to cancel much of the current debt of HIPC countries without promising any extra money to the IDA, thereby further shortening the time period in which the IDA can sustain new lending through repayments of prior loans.[29] Moreover, as discussed throughout this book, the threat to the Bank's financial autonomy is exacerbated by the decline in profits from lending to middle-income countries, whose repayments (with interest) often get channeled into the IDA's coffers. IBRD lending to middle-income countries for 2001–3 was four billion dollars below the level of 1994–96, due in part to borrowers' concerns about the onerous fiduciary and safeguard policies of the Bank. The decline in such borrowing only puts further pressure on the Bank to ease up on safeguards just at the time that NGOs and donor states seek to strengthen them.[30]

Prospects for a Post-Wolfowitz World Bank: Good Governance Redux?

In current discussions of reform—which are plentiful in the wake of the Wolfowitz scandal and the first year of Robert Zoellick's presidency—much more attention is now focused on the prospects for renewing the Bank's legitimacy through *governance* reform, meaning changes to the formal structures and rules through which the Bank is administered by its member states.[31] Governance reform is different from the structural and operational reform sought in the Strategic Compact and other reorganizations, although calls for governance

[28] Kapur 2002b; Sanford 2002; and World Bank Staff Association 2005.
[29] See "Discerning a New Course."
[30] World Bank Staff Association 2005, 2.
[31] For discussions of World Bank governance reform, see Birdsall 2006 and Woods 2006.

change have been around for a long time. The specific target of most current reform proposals is the selection of the president. The selection process is traditionally controlled by the United States and implicitly supported by the Europeans, whose tacit agreement permits their own unfettered choice for the managing director of the IMF (another institution under the gun of governance reform pressures). Establishing transparency, meritocracy, and accountability in the choice of the Bank's leader is number one on the list of demands of many NGOs, member states, and the Bank's staff itself. Changing the selection process and considering non-U.S. candidates (particularly individuals from the developing world) would go a long way toward dismantling the perception that the Bank is the handmaiden of the United States. Likewise, changes to the representation and voting rules on the Board of Executive Directors would accomplish many of the same results, particularly if changes granted greater voice and influence to the developing countries.[32]

If in fact the Bank's governance can be democratized—an indisputably noble goal—will democratization resolve the tensions that produce organized hypocrisy and pave the way to effective reform throughout the Bank? Such changes would certainly help restore credibility in the eyes of many critics, and may thereby lessen the Bank's susceptibility to pressures from environmental actors on whom it depends for conferred legitimacy. Enhanced legitimacy may also renew the Bank's political and financial support from some donor states, who might be more likely to channel scarce development aid funds into the Bank instead of turning toward alternatives. Likewise, if borrower states believe that the Bank is less the instrument of its donors (particularly the United States) and influenced more by developing countries, they may be more willing to continue or renew borrowing from the Bank and rely more on the institution's development advice. All of these potential effects of governance reforms could significantly change the Bank's relationship with its authorizing and task environments in a way that reduces the pressures described in this book as contributing to organized hypocrisy.

At the same time, there is an inherent danger of a tyranny of the majority.[33] Democratization of governance may produce a plurality of actors who can more easily voice their preferences and impose de-

---

[32] Currently, the forty-plus African member states are represented by only two of the twenty-four executive directors. See Wade 2007. For governance reform proposals, including explicit plans for restructuring of the subscription and voting rules, see Birdsall 2006.

[33] Weaver 2007a.

mands on the Bank, thereby increasing the possibility of conflicting interests and pressures that lead to organized hypocrisy. It is also not a foregone conclusion that governance reforms will be a solution for the Bank's legitimacy crisis, which hinges in large part on the perceived effectiveness of the Bank's operational and technical assistance. Nor is it is obvious that such reforms will engender more political and financial support for the beleaguered Bank from its most powerful donors. The United States might be considerably less willing to replenish the IDA if it loses its prerogative of choosing the president. Similarly, all the donors, who would likely lose voting power to the developing countries in what is by nature a zero-sum game, might be less willing to fulfill their replenishment pledges, which are critical to the financial viability of the Bank.

It is thus difficult to predict whether governance reforms will occur in light of the predictable political resistance. It is equally difficult to determine if such reforms will have the desired effect of renewing the legitimacy and support of the Bank in a manner that mitigates the conditions that lead to organized hypocrisy and confound reform. It is important to note that management and staff support many of the proposed governance reforms, as witnessed in the "blue ribbon" campaign that spontaneously started inside the Bank during the Wolfowitz scandal. Renewing internal legitimacy and reestablishing the trust of staff in the Bank's leadership may be the most critical step to ensuring the success of future reform. Then again, staff and management now have a taste for open revolt. If change is not spurred from outside the Bank, revolution may well be sparked from within.

Interviews and Personal Correspondence

AFFILIATIONS are those at the time of the interview. Interviews were conducted between 1999 and 2007.

AT THE WORLD BANK

Jose Manual Bassat, Alison Cave, Maria Dakolias, Lucia Fort, Gita Gopal, Linn Hammergren, Ulrich Hewer (email correspondence), Phil Keefer, Mari Kuraishi, Pierre Landell-Mills, Ralf Leiteritz, Katharina Mathernova (email correspondence), Rick Messick, Steven Ndegwa, Ian Newport, Waafas Ofosu-Omaah, Jonathan Pavluk, Friedrich Peloschek, Gennady Pilch, Ludmila Poznanskaya (Moscow office), Will Rex, Randi Ryterman, Elena Shtykanova (Moscow office), Anil Sood, Andrew Vorkink, Douglas Webb, Michael Woolcock, Lubamira Zivanova-Beardsley

OUTSIDE THE WORLD BANK

Cindy Ambrose, USAID; Manish Bapna, director, Bank Information Center; Thomas Carothers, Carnegie Endowment for International Peace and Security; Doug Friefield, American Bar Association Central European and Eurasian Law Initiative, Moscow; Robert Goodland, former Bank staff member (email correspondence); Gary Hansen, USAID (email correspondence); Irene Stevenson, AFL-CIO, Moscow; Bruce Jenkins, assistant director, Bank Information Center, Washington, D.C.; Suzanne Dennis, Gender Action, Washington, D.C.; Sepideh Keyvanshad, USAID, Moscow; Moises Naim, Carnegie Endowment for International Peace (email correspondence); Jacques Polak, International Monetary Fund; Bruce Rich, senior attorney, Environmental Defense, Washington, D.C.; Kay Treakle, former director, Bank Information Center, Washington, D.C.; Alex Wilks, former director, Bretton Woods Project (now at Eurodad); Manfred Ziewers, Technical Assistance to the Commonwealth of Independent States (TACIS), Moscow; Elaine Zuckerman, Gender Action, Washington, D.C.

References

Ahrens, Joachim. 2001. "Governance, Conditionality and Transformation in Post-Socialist Countries." In *Good Governance in Central and Eastern Europe: The Puzzle of Capitalism by Design*, ed. Herman W. Hoen, 54–90. Northhampton, Mass.: Edward Elgar.

Aldrich, Howard E. 1999. *Organizations Evolving*. London: Sage.

Alvesson, Mats. 1993. *Cultural Perspectives on Organizations*. New York: Cambridge University Press.

Alvey, John. 2004. "Things I Learned in the Staff Association." *World Bank Staff Association Newsletter*, December 2004. On file with author.

Argyris, Chris, and Donald A. Schön. 1974. *Theory in Practice: Increasing Professional Effectiveness*. San Francisco: Jossey-Bass.

———. 1978. *Organizational Learning*. Reading, Mass.: Addison-Wesley.

Ascher, William. 1983. "New Development Approaches and the Adaptability of International Agencies: The Case of the World Bank." *International Organization* 37 (3): 415–39.

———. 1990. "The World Bank and U.S. Control." In *The United States and Multilateral Institutions: Patterns of Changing Instrumentality and Influence*, ed. Margaret P. Karns and Karen A. Mingst, 115–40. Boston: Unwin Hyman.

Ayres, Robert L. 1983. *Banking on the Poor: The World Bank and World Poverty*. Cambridge: MIT Press for the Overseas Development Council.

Babb, Sarah. 2003. "The IMF in Sociological Perspective: A Tale of Organizational Slippage." *Studies in Comparative International Development* 38 (2): 3–27.

Bank Information Center. 2001. "The Wolfensohn Revolution: Supervision and Incentives for Ensuring Results." Bank Information Center Issues Briefing, September. Available at http://www.bicusa.org. Accessed 8 June 2002.

———. 2007. "World Bank Gives Green Light to Controversial Bujagali Dam in Uganda." 27 April. Available at http://www.bicusa.org. Accessed 6 October 2007.

Bapna, Manish. 2004. Testimony before the U.S. Senate Foreign Relations Committee, Hearing on Combating Corruption in the Multilateral Development Banks, 13 May. Available at http://www.senate.gov/~foreign/hearings /2004/hrg040513a.html. Accessed 26 January 2008.

Baré, Jean-François. 1998. "Of Loans and Results: Elements for a Chronicle of Evaluation at the World Bank." *Human Organization* 57 (3): 319–25.

Barnett, Michael N. 1997. "The UN Security Council, Indifference, and Genocide in Rwanda." *Cultural Anthropology* 12 (4): 551–78.

———. 2002. *Eyewitness to a Genocide: The United Nations and Rwanda*. Ithaca, N.Y.: Cornell University Press.

Barnett, Michael N., and Liv Coleman. 2005. "Designing Police: Interpol and the Study of Change in International Organizations." *International Studies Quarterly* 49 (4): 593–619.

Barnett, Michael N., and Martha Finnemore. 1999. "The Politics, Power, and Pathologies of International Organizations." *International Organization* 53 (4): 699–732.

———. 2004. *Rules for the World: International Organizations in World Politics.* Ithaca, N.Y.: Cornell University Press.

Bebbington, Anthony. 2002. "Social Capital/Social Development/SDV." Note prepared for the workshop Social Capital: The Value of the Concept and Strategic Directions for World Bank Lending. International Financial Corporation, Washington, D.C., 1 March. On file with author.

Bebbington, Anthony, Scott Guggenheim, Elizabeth Olson, and Michael Woolcock. 2004. "Exploring Social Capital Debates at the World Bank." *Journal of Development Studies* 40 (5): 33–64.

Bebbington, Anthony J., Michael Woolcock, Scott Guggenheim, and Elizabeth Olson, eds. 2006. *The Search for Empowerment: Social Capital as Idea and Practice at the World Bank.* Bloomfield, Conn.: Kumarian Press.

Behar, Richard. 2007a. "Wolfowitz vs. the World Bank Board: It's Trench Warfare." Fox News, 31 January. Available at http://www.foxnews.com. Accessed 1 February 2007.

———. 2007b. "World Bank Anticorruption Drive Blunted as China Threatens to Halt Loans." Fox News, 27 March. Available at http://www.foxnews.com. Accessed 29 April 2007.

Bello, Walden, and Shalmali Guttal. 2005. "The Limits of Reform: The Wolfensohn Era at the World Bank." Available at http://www.focusweb.org/the-limits-of-reform-the-wolfensohn-era-at-the-world-bank.html?Itemid=94. Accessed 9 October 2007.

Benn, Hilary. 2006. "Improving Governance, Fighting Corruption." Speech to Transparency International, 14 September, London. Available at http://www.dfid.gov.uk/news/files/Speeches/fighting-corruption.asp. Accessed 17 May 2007.

Berg, Elliot. 2000. "Why Aren't Aid Organizations Better Learners?" In *Learning in Development Cooperation*, ed. Jerker Carlsson and Lennart Wohlgemuth, 24–40. Available at http://www.egdi.gov.se/pdf/20002pdf/2000_2.pdf. Accessed 18 September 2007.

Berger, Mark T., and Mark Beeson. 1998. "Lineages of Liberalism and Miracles of Modernisation: The World Bank, the East Asian Trajectory and the International Development Debate." *Third World Quarterly* 19 (3): 487–504.

Birdsall, Nancy. 2004. "Seven Deadly Sins: Reflections on Donor Failings." Center for Global Development, Working Paper No. 50, December. Available at http://www.cgdev.org/content/publications/detail/2737/. Accessed 18 September 2007.

———, ed. 2006. *Rescuing the World Bank.* Washington, D.C.: Brookings Institution Press.

Blustein, Paul. 1996. " Missionary Work." *Washington Post*, 10 November, W08.

———. 2001. *The Chastening: Inside the Crisis That Rocked the Global Financial System and Humbled the IMF.* New York: Public Affairs.

Bøås, Morten, and Desmond McNeill, eds. 2004. *Global Institutions and Development: Framing the World?* London: Routledge.

Bosshard, Peter. 2004. "The World Bank's High-Risk Hypocrisy." *Bretton Woods Project Online Newsletter*, 5 April. Available at http://www.brettonwoods project.org. Accessed 12 March 2006.

Boswell, Nancy Zucker. 2004. Testimony before the U.S. Senate Foreign Relations Committee, Hearing on Combating Corruption in the Multilateral Development Banks, 13 May. Available at http://www.senate.gov/~foreign/hearings/2004/hrg040513a.html. Accessed 26 January 2008.

Bourdieu, Pierre. 1990. *In Other Words: Essays towards a Reflexive Sociology.* Stanford: Stanford University Press.

Brautigam, Deborah. 1992. "Governance, Economy, and Foreign Aid." *Studies in Comparative International Development* 27 (3): 3–26.

Brechin, Steven R. 1997. *Planting Trees in the Developing World: A Sociology of International Organizations.* Baltimore: John Hopkins University Press.

Bretton Woods Project. 2002. "World Bank Inspection Panel Report Reinforces Criticism of the Controversial Bujagali Hydropower Project in Uganda." *Bretton Woods Project Update 28*, 11 June 2002. Available at http://www.bret tonwoodsproject.org. Accessed 18 September 2007.

———. 2003. "How the World Bank Deals with Fraud and Corruption in its Projects." *Bretton Woods Project Update 35*, 21 July. Available at http://www.brettonwoodsproject.org. Accessed 18 September 2007.

———. 2004. "U.S. Lawmakers Scrutinize World Bank Record on Corruption." *Bretton Woods Project Update 40*, 28 May. Available at http://www.bretton woodsproject.org. Accessed 25 January 2008.

———. 2006a. "The World Bank Weeds Out Corruption: Will It Touch the Roots?" *Bretton Woods Project Update 50*, 27 March. Available at http://www.brettonwoodsproject.org. Accessed 18 September 2007.

———. 2006b. "World Bank Corruption Fight Drags On." *Bretton Woods Project Update 53*, 23 November. Available at http://www.brettonwoodsproject.org. Accessed 18 September 2007.

———. 2007. "Bank Approves Anticorruption Strategy: Back to Where We Started?" *Bretton Woods Project Update 55*, 2 April. Available at http://www.brettonwoodsproject.org. Accessed 15 October 2007.

Broad, Robin. 2006. "Research, Knowledge, and the Art of 'Paradigm Maintenance': The World Bank's Development Economics Vice-Presidency (DEC)." *Review of International Political Economy* 13 (3): 387–419.

Brookins, Carole. 2004. "Anticorruption Efforts of the MDBs." Testimony before the U.S. Senate Foreign Relations Committee, Hearing on Combating Corruption in the Multilateral Development Banks, 13 May. Available at http://www.senate.gov/~foreign/hearings/2004/hrg040513a.html. Accessed 26 January 2008.

Brown, Bartram S. 1992. *The United States and the Politicization of the World Bank: Issues of International Law and Policy.* London: Kegan Paul International.

Brunsson, Nils. 1989. *The Organization of Hypocrisy: Talk, Decisions, and Actions in Organizations.* New York: John Wiley & Sons.

———. 2003. "Organized Hypocrisy." In *The Northern Lights: Organizational Theory in Scandinavia*, ed. Barbara Czarniawska and Guje Sevon, 201–22. Oslo: Liber/Abstrakt/Copenhagen Business School Press.

Brunsson, Nils, and Johan P. Olsen. 1993. *The Reforming Organization*. New York: Routledge.

Bukovanksy, Mlada. 2005. "Hypocrisy and Contested Legitimacy: Agricultural Trade in the World Trade Organization." Paper prepared for the Workshop on Constructivist Political Economy, Harvard University, February (revised version, August).

———. 2006. "Yes, Minister: Hypocrisy as a Weapon of the Weak." Paper presented at the Annual Meeting of the International Studies Association, 22 March, San Diego.

Burke, W. Warner. 2002. *Organization Change: Theory and Practice*. Thousand Oaks, Calif.: Sage.

Burki, Shahid Javed, and Guillermo E. Perry, eds. 1998. *Beyond the Washington Consensus: Institutions Matter*. Washington, D.C.: World Bank Latin American and Caribbean Studies.

Burnside, Craig, and David Dollar. 2000. "Aid, Policies, and Growth." *American Economic Review* 90 (4): 847–68.

Calderisi, Robert. 2006. "The Worst Man in the World." *New Statesman*, 15 May, 22–25.

Caufield, Catherine. 1996. *Masters of Illusion: The World Bank and the Poverty of Nations*. New York: Henry Holt.

Cavallo, Domingo, Rubens Ricupero, Eduardo Aninat, Rodrigo Botero, and Pedro Aspe. 2007. "At Stake is the Bank's Ability to Carry Out Its Mission." Open letter to the *Financial Times*, 2 May. Available at http://www.ft.com. Accessed 3 May 2007.

Cernea, Michael M. 1995. "Social Organization and Development Anthropology: The 1995 Malinowski Award Lecture." Environmentally Sustainable Development Studies and Monograph Series No. 6. Washington, D.C.: World Bank.

Cernea, Michael. 2004. "Culture? . . . at the World Bank?" Letter to Lourdes Arizpe, Assistant Director General of UNESCO, 4 June. On file with author.

Checkel, Jeffrey. 2005. "International Institutions and Socialization in Europe: Introduction and Framework." *International Organization* 59 (4): 801–26.

Chwieroth, Jeffrey. 2007. "Testing and Measuring the Role of Ideas: The Case of Neoliberalism in the International Monetary Fund." *International Studies Quarterly* 51 (1): 5–30.

Clemens, Michael, Charles T. Kenney, and Todd J. Moss. 2004. "The Trouble with the MDGs: Confronting Expectations of Aid and Development Success." Center for Global Development Working Paper No. 40, May. Available at http://www.cgdev.org. Accessed 4 April 2006.

Clements, D. 1999. "Informational Standards in Development Agency Management." *World Development* 27 (8): 1359–81.

Cobb, John B. 1999. *The Earthist Challenge to Economism: A Theological Critique of the World Bank*. New York: St. Martin's Press.

Cohn, Theodore H. 2005. *Global Political Economy: Theory and Practice*. New York: Addison Wesley Longman Press.

Collier, Paul, and David Dollar. 2000. "Can the World Cut Poverty in Half? How Policy Reform and Effective Aid Can Meet International Development Goals." Policy Research Working Paper 2403. Washington, D.C.: World Bank.

———. 2001. *Development Effectiveness: What Have We Learnt?* Washington, D.C.: World Bank.

Cooper, Frederick, and Randall Packard, eds. 1997. *International Development and the Social Sciences: Essays on the History and Politics of Knowledge.* Berkeley and Los Angeles: University of California Press.

Coopération Internationale pour le Développement et la Solidarité. 2006. *The World Bank's Strategy on Governance and Anticorruption: A Civil Society Perspective.* CIDSE Background Paper, August, Brussels.

Cornett, Linda. 2007. "The Evolution of the Bank's Governance and Anticorruption Agenda: From Prohibition to Prominence." Report published by the Bank Information Center, 11 April. Available at http://www.bicusa.org/en/Article.324.aspx. Accessed 30 April 2007.

Covaleski, M. A., and M. W. Dirsmith. 1988. "An Institutional Perspective on the Rise, Social Transformation, and Fall of a University Budget Category." *Administrative Science Quarterly* 33 (4): 562–87.

Cox, Robert D., and Harold K. Jacobson. 1973. *The Anatomy of Influence.* New Haven: Yale University Press.

Crane, Barbara B., and Jason L. Finkle. 1981. "Organizational Impediments to Development Assistance: The World Bank's Population Program." *World Politics* 33 (4): 516–53.

Dalton, Melville. 1959. *Men Who Manage.* New York: Wiley.

Daly, Herman E. 1994. "Farewell Lecture to the World Bank." In *Beyond Bretton Woods: Alternatives to the Global Economic Order,* ed. John Cavanagh, Daphne Wysham, and Marcos Arruda, 109–17. London: Pluto Press.

Danaher, Kevin. 1994. *50 Years Is Enough: The Case against the World Bank and the International Monetary Fund.* Boston: South End Press.

Deal, T. E., and A. A. Kennedy. 1982. *Corporate Cultures.* Reading, Mass.: Addison-Wesley.

Deaton, Angus (chair), Abhijit Banerjee, Nora Lustig, and Ken Rogoff, eds. 2006. *An Evaluation of World Bank Research, 1998–2005.* Report published 24 September. Available at http://econ.worldbank.org/WBSITE/EXTERNAL/EXTDEC/0,,contentMDK:21165468~pagePK:64165401~piPK:64165026~theSitePK:469372,00.html. Accessed 14 May 2007.

de Ferranti, David. 2006. "The World Bank and Middle-Income Countries." In *Rescuing the World Bank,* ed. Nancy Birdsall, 133–51. Washington, D.C.: Brookings Institution Press.

Dethier, Jean-Jacques. 2005. "Sustainable Growth and Equity in Developing Countries: An Overview of Research at the World Bank." PowerPoint presentation at the conference "Research Bank on the World Bank," Central European University, Budapest, 1–2 April.

———. 2007. "Producing Knowledge for Development: Research at the World Bank." *Global Governance: A Review of Multilateralism and International Organizations* 13 (4): 469–78.

de Tray, Dennis. 2006. "More Lessons from the Trenches: From Indonesia to Vietnam to Central Asia." Retirement speech, 23 February, at the Center for Global Development, Washington, D.C. Available at http://www.cgdev.org. Accessed 9 October 2007.

Development Assistance Committee. 1996. *Shaping the 21st Century: The Contribution of Development Cooperation.* Paris: Organization for Economic Cooperation and Development.

Dichter, Thomas W. 2003. *Despite Good Intentions: Why Development Assistance to the Third World Has Failed.* Amherst: University of Massachusetts Press.

Dijkzeul, Dennis, and Yves Beigbeder, eds. 2003. *Rethinking International Organizations: Pathology and Promise.* New York: Berghahn Books.

DiMaggio, Paul J., and W. W. Powell. 1983. "The Iron Cage Revisited: Institutional Isomorphism and Collective Rationality in Organizational Fields." *American Sociological Review* 48:147–60.

Dobbin, Frank. 1994. "Cultural Models of Organizations: The Social Construction of Rational Organizing Principles." In *The Sociology of Culture,* ed. Diana Crane, 117–42. Boston: Basil Blackwell.

Dollar, David. 2001. *Globalization and Poverty.* Washington, D.C.: World Bank.

Dollar, David, and Aart Kraay. 2002. "Growth Is Good for the Poor." *Journal of Economic Growth* 7 (3): 195–225.

Downs, Anthony. 1967. *Inside Bureaucracy.* Boston: Little, Brown.

Dugger, Celia W. 2006. "World Bank Chief Outlines a War on Fraud." *New York Times,* 12 April, A7.

Easterly, William. 2001. *The Elusive Quest for Growth: Economists' Adventures and Misadventures in the Tropics.* Cambridge: MIT Press.

———. 2002. "The Cartel of Good Intentions: The Problem of Bureaucracy in Foreign Aid." *Journal of Policy Reform* 5 (4): 223–50.

———. 2006a. Testimony before the US Senate Committee on Foreign Relations, Hearing on Multilateral Development Banks: Promoting Effectiveness and Fighting Corruption, 28 March. Available at http://www.senate.gov/~foreign/hearings/2006/hrg060328a.html. Accessed 26 January 2008.

———. 2006b. *The White Man's Burden: Why the West's Efforts to Aid the Rest Have Done So Much Ill and So Little Good.* New York: Penguin.

Eggertsson, Thrainn. 1990. *Economic Behavior and Institutions.* New York: Cambridge University Press.

Einhorn, Jessica. 2001. "The World Bank's Mission Creep." *Foreign Affairs* 80 (5): 22–35.

Ellerman, David. 2001. "Mixing Truth and Power: Implications for a Knowledge Organization." *World Bank Staff Association Newsletter,* November–December, 3. On file with author.

———. 2006. *Helping People Help Themselves: From the World Bank to an Alternative Philosophy of Development Assistance.* Ann Arbor: University of Michigan Press.

Ellerman, David, Stephen Denning, and Nagy Hanna. 2001. "Active Learning and Development Assistance." *Journal of Knowledge Management* 5 (2): 171–79.

Elsmore, Peter. 2001. *Organisational Culture: Organisational Change?* London: Gower.

Escobar, Arturo. 1995. *Encountering Development: The Making and Unmaking of the Third World*. Princeton, N.J.: Princeton University Press.

Eurodad. 2006. "Low-Down on the World Bank / IMF Spring Meetings 2006." 27 April. Available at http://www.eurodad.org. Accessed 15 October 2007.

Faundez, Julio, ed. 1997. *Good Government and Law: Legal and Institutional Reform in Developing Countries*. New York: St. Martin's Press.

Fearon, James, and Alexander Wendt. 2002. "Rationalism *v.* Constructivism: A Skeptical View." In *Handbook of International Relations*, ed. Walter Carlsnaes, Thomas Risse, and Beth A. Simmons, 52–72. London: Sage.

Ferguson, James. 1994. *The Anti-politics Machine: "Development," Depoliticization, and Bureaucratic Power in Lesotho*. Minneapolis: University of Minnesota Press.

Fidler, Stephen. 2001. "Who's Minding the Bank?" *Foreign Policy* 126 (September–October): 40–50.

Finer, Jonathan. 2003. "World Bank Focused on Fighting Corruption: Graft and Bribery, Once Tolerated, Punished by Blacklisting." *Washington Post*, 4 July.

Finnemore, Martha. 1996a. "Norms, Culture, and World Politics: Insights from Sociology's Institutionalism." *International Organization* 50 (2): 325–47.

———. 1996b. *National Interests in International Society*. Ithaca, N.Y.: Cornell University Press.

Finnemore, Martha, and Kathryn Sikkink. 1998. "International Norms Dynamics and Political Change." *International Organization* 52 (4): 887–917.

Food & Water Watch. 2006. "World Bank Finances Corporate Corruption." Online report, 20 April. Available at http://www.foodandwaterwatch.org. Accessed 15 May 2006.

Fox, Jonathan A. 2000. "The World Bank Inspection Panel: Lessons from the First Five Years." *Global Governance* 6 (3): 279–319.

Fox, Jonathan A., and L. David Brown. 1998. "Introduction." In *The Struggle for Accountability: The World Bank, NGOs, and Grassroots Movements*, ed. Jonathan Fox and L. David Brown, 1–48. Cambridge: MIT Press.

Fox, Jonathan A., and Kay C. Treakle, eds. 2003. *Demanding Accountability: Civil Society Claims and the World Bank Inspection Panel*. Lanham, Md.: Rowman and Littlefield.

George, Susan, and Fabrizio Sabelli. 1994. *Faith and Credit: The World Bank's Secular Empire*. Boulder, Colo.: Westview Press.

Ghosh, Amitav. 1994. "The Global Reservation: Notes toward an Ethnography of International Peacekeeping." *Cultural Anthropology* 9 (3): 412–22.

Gibbon, P. 1995. "Towards a Political-Economy of the World Bank 1970–1990." In *Between Liberalisation and Oppression: The Politics of Structural Adjustment in Africa*, ed. Thandik Mkandawire and Adebay Olukoshi. Dakar, Senegal: CODESRIA.

Gillies, David. 1996. "Human Rights, Democracy and Good Governance: Stretching the World Bank's Policy Frontiers." In *The World Bank: Lending on a Global Scale*, ed. Jo Marie Griesbacher and Bernhard G. Gunter, 101–42. London: Pluto Press.

Goldman, Michael. 2000. "The Birth of a Discipline: Producing Authoritative Green Knowledge World Bank–Style." *Ethnography* 2 (2): 191–217.

———. 2005. *Imperial Nature: The World Bank and Struggles for Social Justice in the Age of Globalization*. New Haven: Yale University Press.

Gore, Charles. 2000. "The Rise and Fall of the Washington Consensus as a Paradigm for Developing Countries." *World Development* 28 (3): 789–804.

Government Accountability Project. 2004. *Challenging the Culture of Secrecy: A Status Report on Freedom of Speech at the World Bank*. Available at http://www.whistleblower.org. Accessed 18 September 2007.

———. 2005. "GAP Responds to Treasury Report on Multilateral Development Banks." News Release, 29 March. Available at http://www.whistleblower.org. Accessed 6 October 2007.

———. 2007. Review of the Department of Institutional Integrity at the World Bank. 5 September. Washington, D.C.: Government Accountability Project. Available at http://www.whistleblower.org/content/press_detail.cfm?press_id=1145. Accessed 12 October 2007.

Guess, George. 2005. *Foreign Aid Safari: Journeys in International Development*. London: Athena Press.

Guha, Krishna, and Richard McGregor. 2007. "World Bank Directors Test Zoellick." *Financial Times*, 12 July. Available at http://www.ft.com. Accessed 12 July 2007.

Gurria, Jose Angel, and Paul Volcker. 2001. *The Role of Multilateral Development Banks in Emerging Market Economies: Findings of the Commission on the Role of MDBs in Emerging Markets*. Washington, D.C.: Carnegie Endowment for International Peace. Available at http://www.carnegieendowment.org/publications/index.cfm?fa=view&id=687&prog=zgp. Accessed 17 October 2007.

Gutner, Tamar L. 2002. *Banking on the Environment: Multilateral Development Banks and Their Environmental Performance in Central and Eastern Europe*. Cambridge: MIT Press.

———. 2005a. "Explaining the Gaps between Mandate and Performance: Agency Theory and World Bank Environmental Reform." *Global Environmental Politics* 5 (2): 10–37.

———. 2005b. "World Bank Environmental Reform: Revisiting Lessons from Agency Theory." *International Organization* 59 (3): 773–83.

Gwin, Catherine. 1994. "U.S. Relations with the World Bank, 1945–1992." Brookings Occasional Papers. Washington, D.C.: Brookings Institution.

———. 2001. *Presentation of the OED IDA Review to the IDA13 Replenishment Meeting*. Addis Ababa, 7 June. On file with author.

Haas, Ernst B. 1990. *When Knowledge Is Power: Three Models of Change in International Organizations*. Berkeley and Los Angeles: University of California Press.

Hancock, Graham. 1989. *Lords of Poverty: The Power, Prestige, and Corruption of the International Aid Business*. New York: Atlantic Monthly Press.

Hannan, Michael T., and John Freeman. 1984. "Structural Inertia and Organizational Change." *American Sociological Review* 49 (2): 149–64.

Hatch, Mary Jo. 1993. "The Dynamics of Organizational Culture." *Academy of Management Review* 18 (4): 657–93.

———. 1997. *Organization Theory: Modern, Symbolic, and Postmodern Perspectives.* New York: Oxford University Press.

Hawkins, Darren, David Lake, Daniel Nielson, and Michael Tierney, eds. 2006. *Delegation to International Organizations.* New York: Cambridge University Press.

Hobbs, Nathaniel. 2005. "Corruption in World Bank Financed Projects: Why Bribery Is a Tolerated Anathema." DESTIN Working Paper No. 05-65. Available at http://www.lse.ac.uk/collections/DESTIN/workingPapers.htm. Accessed 15 February 2007.

Holland, Robert B. 2007. Op-ed to the *Wall Street Journal*, 20 April. Available at http://www.wsj.com. Accessed 21 April 2007.

Homans, George C. 1950. *The Human Group.* New York: Harcourt, Brace.

Hopgood, Stephen. 2006. *Keepers of the Flame: Understanding Amnesty International.* Ithaca, N.Y.: Cornell University Press.

Hurd, Ian. 2002. "Legitimacy, Power, and the Symbolic Life of the UN Security Council." *Global Governance* 8 (1): 35–51.

———. 2007. *After Anarchy: Legitimacy and Power in the United Nations Security Council.* Princeton, N.J.: Princeton University Press.

Iankova, Elena, and Peter J. Katzenstein. 2003. "European Enlargement and Institutional Hypocrisy." In *The State of the European Union*, vol. 6: *Law, Politics, and Society*, ed. Tanja A. Börzel and Racchel Cichowsky, 269–90. New York: Oxford University Press.

Ierly, Doug. 2002. "Private Capital Flows as a Springboard for World Bank Reform." *University of Pennsylvania Journal of International Economic Law* 23 (1): 1.

International Development Association. 2001. "How Far into the Mainstream? A Review of Environment Issues in IDA Activities." Available at http://www.worldbank.org. Accessed 9 October 2007.

Irwin, Michael. 1990. "Inside the World Bank." Lecture delivered at the Institute for Africa Alternatives, 17 July, London.

Isham, Jonathan, Daniel Kaufman, and Lant H. Pritchett. 1995. "Governance and Returns to Investment: An Empirical Investigation." World Bank Policy Research Working Paper 1550. Washington, D.C.: World Bank. Available at http://www.worldbank.org. Accessed 18 September 2007.

———. 1997. "Civil Liberties, Democracy, and the Performance of Government Projects." *World Bank Economic Review* 11 (2): 219–42.

Johnston, Alastair. 2005. "Conclusions and Extensions: Toward Mid-Range Theorizing and beyond Europe." *International Organization* 59 (4): 1013–44.

Jordan, Lisa. 1997. "Sustainable Rhetoric versus Sustainable Development: The Retreat from Sustainability in the World Bank Development Policy." Updated 11 December 2003. Available at http://www.bicusa.org. Accessed 16 January 2008.

Jupille, Joseph, James Caporaso, and Jeffrey Checkel. 2003. "Integrating Institutions: Rationalism, Constructivism, and the Study of the European Union." *Comparative Political Studies* 36 (1): 7–40.

Kanbur, Ravi. 2001. "Economic Policy, Distribution, and Poverty." *World Development* 29 (6): 1083–94.

Kapur, Devesh. 1998. "The State in a Changing World: A Critique of the 1997 World Development Report." Working Paper No. 98-2. Weatherhead Center for International Affairs, Harvard University. Available at http://www.wcfia.harvard.edu/publications/wcfia_working_papers. Accessed 18 September 2007.

———. 2000a. "Who Gets to Run the World?" *Foreign Policy* 121 (November–December): 44–50.

———. 2000b. "Processes of Change in International Organizations." Working Paper No. 00-02. Weatherhead Center for International Affairs, Harvard University. Available at http://www.wcfia.harvard.edu/publications/wcfia_working_papers. Accessed 18 September 2007.

———. 2002a. " The Changing Anatomy of Governance of the World Bank." In *Reinventing the World Bank*, ed. Jonathan R. Pincus and Jeffrey A. Winters, 54–75. Ithaca, N.Y.: Cornell University Press.

———. 2002b. "Do as I Say and Not as I Do: A Critique of G-7 Proposals on Reforming the MDBs." Center for Global Development Working Paper No. 16, October. Available at http://www.cgdev.org/content/publications/detail/2774. Accessed 10 October 2007.

Kapur, Devesh, John P. Lewis, and Richard Webb. 1997. *The World Bank: Its First Half Century.* 2 vols. Washington, D.C.: Brookings Institution.

Kapur, Devesh, and Richard Webb. 2000. "Governance-Related Conditionalities of the IFIs." Paper presented to the XII Technical Group Meeting of the Intergovernmental Group of 24 for International Monetary Affairs, Lima, Peru, 1–3 March.

Kardam, Nuket. 1993. "Development Approaches and the Role of Policy Advocacy: The Case of the World Bank." *World Development* 21 (11): 1773–86.

Kaufmann, Daniel, and Aart Kraay. 2002a. "Growth without Governance." *Economia* 3 (1): 169–215.

———. 2002b. "Governance Indicators, Aid Allocations, and the Millennium Challenge Account." Draft for discussion. Available at http://www.worldbank.org/wbi/governance/mca.htm. Accessed 5 January 2005.

Kaufmann, Daniel, Aart Kraay, and M. Mastruzzi. 2003. "Governance Matters II: Governance Indicators for 1996–2002." World Bank Policy Research Paper 3106. Washington, D.C.: World Bank.

Kaufmann, Daniel, Aart Kraay, and Pablo Zoido-Lobaton. 2000. "Governance Matters: From Measurement to Action." *Finance and Development* 37 (2): 10.

Keck, Margaret E., and Kathryn Sikkink. 1998. *Activists beyond Borders: Advocacy Networks in International Politics.* Ithaca, N.Y.: Cornell University Press.

Keefer, Philip, and Stephen Knack. 1997. "Why Don't Poor Countries Catch Up? A Cross-National Test of an Institutional Explanation." *Economic Inquiry* 35 (3): 590–603.

Kelley, Judith. 2004. "International Actors on the Domestic Scene: Membership Conditionality and Socialization by International Institutions." *International Organization* 58:425–57.

Kiely, Ray. 1998. ""Neoliberalism Revised? A Critical Account of World Bank Concepts of Good Governance and Market Friendly Intervention." *Capital and Class* 64 (Spring): 63–88.

Kiersey, Nicholas, David Dansereau, Edward Weisband, and Asli Oner. 2006. "Turkish Accession and the Quest for a European Policy: Discursive Strategies and Organized Hypocrisy." Paper presented at the Annual Meeting of the International Studies Association, 22 March, San Diego.

Killick, Tony. 1997. "Principals, Agent and the Failings of Conditionality." *Journal of International Development* 9 (4): 483–95.

Klitgaard, Robert E. 1990. *Tropical Gangsters*. New York: Basic Books.

Knack, Stephen. 2000. "Aid Dependence and the Quality of Governance: A Cross-Country Empirical Analysis." Policy Research Working Paper 2396. Washington, D.C.: World Bank.

Koremenos, Barbara, Charles Lipson, and Duncan Snidal. 2002. "The Rational Design of International Institutions." *International Organization* 55 (4): 761–99.

Krasner, Stephen D. 1999. *Sovereignty: Organized Hypocrisy.* Princeton, N.J.: Princeton University Press.

Krugman, Paul. 2002. "Crying with Argentina." *New York Times*, 1 January. Available at http://nytimes.com/. Accessed October 2, 2007.

Landell-Mills, Pierre, and Ismail Serageldin. 1991. "Governance and the External Factor." In *Proceedings of the World Bank Annual Conference on Development Economics 1991*, ed. Lawrence H. Summers and Shekhar Shah, 303–20. Washington, D.C.: World Bank.

Lapper, Richard. 2007. "World Bank Crisis 'Grist to the Mill' of Chavistas." *Financial Times*, 3 May. Available at http://www.ft.com. Accessed 3 May 2007.

Lawrence, Shannon. 2005. "Retreat from the Safeguard Policies: Recent Trends Undermining Social and Environmental Accountability at the World Bank." Available from the author at shlawrence@environmentaldefense.org.

Leiteritz, Ralf. 2005. "Explaining Organizational Outcomes: The International Monetary Fund and Capital Account Liberalization." *Journal of International Relations and Development* 8 (1): 1–26.

Lerrick, Adam. 2002. "Audit the World Bank." *Financial Times*, 6 March, 13.

———. 2006. "Is the World Bank's Word Good Enough?" Testimony before the U.S. Senate Foreign Relations Committee, Hearing on Multilateral Development Banks: Promoting Effectiveness and Fighting Corruption, 28 March. Transcript available at http://www.senate.gov/~foreign/hearings/2006/hrg060328a.html. Accessed 28 June 2006.

Levine, Ruth E. 2006. Testimony before the U.S. Senate Foreign Relations Committee, Hearing on Multilateral Development Banks: Promoting Effectiveness and Fighting Corruption, 28 March. Transcript available at http://www.senate.gov/~foreign/hearings/2006/hrg060328a.html. Accessed 28 June 2006.

Levinthal, Daniel and James G. March. 1993. "The Myopia of Learning." *Strategic Management Journal* 14 (Winter): 95–112.

Levitt, Barbara and James G. March. 1988. "Organizational Learning." *Annual Review of Sociology* 14: 319–40.

Lewis, David, Anthony J. Bebbington, Simon P. J. Batterbury, Alpa Shaha, Elizabeth Olson, M. Shameem Siddiqi, and Sandra Duvall. 2003. "Practice, Power and Meaning: Frameworks for Studying Organizational Culture in Multi-agency Rural Development Projects." *Journal of International Development* 15 (5): 541–57.

Linn, Johannes F. 2004. "The Role of the World Bank Lending in Middle Income Countries." Comments presented at the Operations Evaluation Department Conference on the Effectiveness of Policies and Reforms, Washington. D.C., 4 October.

Lipson, Michael. 2007. "Peacekeeping: Organized Hypocrisy?" *European Journal of International Relations* 13 (1): 5–34.

Lorsch, J. W. 1985. "Strategic Myopia: Culture as an Invisible Barrier to Change." In *Gaining Control of the Corporate Culture*, ed. Ralph H. Kilmann, Mary J. Saxton, Roy Serpa, 84–102. San Francisco: Jossey-Bass.

Lugar, Richard G. 2004. Opening Statement of the Chairman of the U.S Senate Foreign Relations Committee, Hearing on Combating Multilateral Development Bank Corruption: U.S. Treasury Role and Internal Efforts, 21 July. Available at http://www.senate.gov/~foreign/hearings/2004/hrg040513 a.html. Accessed 26 January 2008.

———. 2006. "Multilateral Development Banks: Promoting Effectiveness and Fighting Corruption." Opening statement for the U.S. Congressional hearings of the Senate Committee on Foreign Relations, 28 March. Available at http://www.senate.gov/~foreign/testimony/2006/ LugarStatement060328.pdf. Accessed 28 June 2006.

Lyne, Mona, Daniel Nielson, and Michael Tierney. 2006. "Getting the Model Right: Single, Multiple, and Collective Principals in Development Aid." In *Delegation under Anarchy*, ed. Darren G. Hawkins, David A. Lake, Daniel L. Nielson, and Michael J. Tierney, 41–76. Cambridge: Cambridge University Press.

Lyne, Mona, and Michael Tierney. 2003. "The Politics of Common Agency: Implications for Agent Control with Complex Principals." Paper prepared for the Annual Meeting of the American Political Science Association, 28–31 August, Philadelphia.

Machan, Dyan. 2001. "World Bank's Bad Boy." *Forbes*, 26 November, 92–96.

Mallaby, Sebastian. 2004. *The World's Banker: A Story of Failed States, Financial Crises, and the Wealth and Poverty of Nations*. New York: Penguin.

———. 2005. "Saving the World Bank." *Foreign Affairs* 84 (3): 75–85.

———. 2006. "Wolfowitz's Corruption Agenda." *Washington Post*, 20 February, A21.

March, James G., and Johan P. Olsen. 1976. *Ambiguity and Choice in Organizations*. Bergen: Universitetsforlaget.

———. 1989. *Rediscovering Institutions: The Organizational Basis of Politics*. New York: Free Press.

———. 1998. "The Institutional Dynamics of International Political Orders." *International Organization* 52 (4): 943–69.

March, James G., Martin Schulz, and Xueguang Zhou. 2000. *The Dynamics of Rules: Change in Written Organizational Codes*. Stanford, Calif.: Stanford University Press.

March, James G., and Herbert Simon. 1958. *Organizations*. New York: Wiley.

Marquette, Heather. 2003. *Corruption, Politics, and Development: The Role of the World Bank*. Basingstoke, UK: Palgrave Press.

———. 2007. "The World Bank's Fight against Corruption." *Brown Journal of World Affairs* 13 (2): 27–39.

Mason, Edward S., and Robert E. Asher. 1973. *The World Bank since Bretton Woods*. Washington, D.C.: Brookings Institution.

McAuslan, Patrick. 1997. "Law, Governance, and the Development of the Market: Practical Problems and Possible Solutions." In *Good Government and Law*, ed. Julio Faundez, 25–44. New York: St. Martin's Press.

McNamara, Robert S. 1981. *The McNamara Years at the World Bank: Major Policy Addresses of Robert S. McNamara, 1968–1981*. Baltimore: John Hopkins University Press.

McNeill, Desmond. 2001. "Inter-disciplinarity and Sustainable Development Policy: What Have We Learned?" Paper prepared for presentation to the World Bank, 3 December. On file with author.

Mekay, Eman. 2006. "IPS News—World Bank Slammed." News release, 13 February. Available at http://www.whistleblower.org. Accessed 16 June 2006.

Mehta, Lyla. 2001. "The World Bank and Its Emerging Knowledge Empire." *Human Organization* 60 (2): 189–96.

Meltzer, Allan H., et al. 2000. *Report of the International Financial Institution Advisory Commission*. Available at http://www.house.gov/jec/imf/meltzer.pfd. Accessed 18 September 2007.

Meyer, John W., and Brian Rowan. 1977. "Institutionalized Organizations: Formal Structure as Myth and Ceremony." *American Journal of Sociology* 83 (2): 340–63.

Meyer, John W., and W. Richard Scott. 1983. *Organizational Environments: Ritual and Rationality*. Beverly Hills, Calif.: Sage.

Miller-Adams, Michelle. 1999. *The World Bank: New Agendas in a Changing World*. London: Routledge Studies in Development Economics.

Momani, Bessma. 2005. "Limits of Streamlining Fund Conditionality: IMF's Organizational Culture." *Journal of International Relations and Development* 8 (2): 39–57.

———. 2007. "IMF Staff—the Missing Link in IMF Reform Debate." *Review of International Organizations* 2 (1): 39–57.

Morse, Bradford. 1992. *Sardar Sarovar: Report of the Independent Review*. Ottawa, Canada: Resource Futures International.

Mosley, Paul, Jane Harrigan, and John Toye. 1991. *Aid and Power: The World Bank and Policy-Based Lending*. 2 vols. London: Routledge.

Muasher, Marwan. 2007. "Unequal Flows in Private Capital Show a Continued Need for the World Bank." Letter to the *Financial Times* by World Bank Senior Vice-President Marwan Muasher, 14 May, 8.

Murrell, Peter. 1991. "Can Neoclassical Economics Underpin the Reform of Centrally Planned Economies?" *Journal of Economic Perspectives* 5 (4): 59–76.

Naim, Moises. 1994. "The World Bank: Its Role, Governance, and Organizational

Culture." In *Bretton Woods: Looking to the Future*, ed. Bretton Woods Commission. Washington, D.C.: Bretton Woods Commission.

———. 1995. "Comments on Agendas for the Bretton Woods Institutions." In *Fifty Years after Bretton Woods: The Future of the IMF and the World Bank*, ed. James M. Boughton and K. Sarwar Lateef, 85–90. Washington, D.C.: IMF and World Bank Group.

———. 2000. "Washington Consensus or Washington Confusion?" *Foreign Policy* 118 (Spring): 86–103.

Narayan-Parker, Deepa. 2000. *Voices of the Poor: Can Anyone Hear Us?* New York: Oxford University Press for the World Bank.

Nelson, Paul J. 1995. *The World Bank and Non-governmental Organizations*. New York: St. Martin's Press.

———. 2001. "Transparency Mechanisms at the Multilateral Development Banks." *World Development* 29 (11): 1835–47.

Nelson, Richard R., and Sidney G. Winter. 1982. *An Evolutionary Theory of Economic Change*. Cambridge: Harvard University Press.

Ness, Gayl D., and Steven R. Brechin. 1988. "Bridging the Gap: International Organizations as Organizations." *International Organization* 42 (2): 245–73.

Neumayer, Eric. 2002. "Is Good Governance Rewarded? A Cross-National Analysis of Debt Forgiveness." *World Development* 30 (6): 913–30.

Nielson, Daniel, and Michael Tierney. 2003. "Delegation to International Organizations: Agency Theory and World Bank Environmental Reform." *International Organization* 57 (2): 241–76.

———. 2005. "Theory, Data, and Hypothesis Testing: World Bank Environmental Reform Redux." *International Organization* 59 (3): 785–800.

Nielson, Daniel, Michael Tierney, and Catherine Weaver. 2006. "Bridging the Rationalist-Constructivist Divide: Reengineering Change at the World Bank." *Journal of International Relations and Development* 9 (2): 107–39.

North, Douglass. 1986. "The New Institutional Economics." *Journal of Institutional and Theoretical Economics* 142:230–37.

———. 1990. *Institutions, Institutional Change, and Economic Performance*. New York: Cambridge University Press.

Oliver, Christine. 1999. "Strategic Responses to Institutional Pressures." *Academy of Management Review* 16 (1): 145–79.

O'Neill, Paul H. 2001a. Testimony before the House Committee on Appropriations Subcommittee on Foreign Operations, Export Financing and Related Programs. 15 May. Available at http://www.treas.gov/press/releases/po 376.htm. Accessed 18 September 2007.

———. 2001b. "Excellence and the International Financial Institutions." Speech to the Economic Club of Detroit, 27 June. Available at http://www.treas.gov/press/releases/po449.htm. Accessed 18 September 2007.

Organization for Economic Cooperation and Development, Development Assistance Committee. 1996. *Shaping the 21st Century: The Contribution of Development Co-operation*. Paris: OECD.

Park, Susan. 2005. "Norm Diffusion within International Organizations: A Case Study of the World Bank." *Journal of International Relations and Development* 8 (2): 111–41.

Payer, Cheryl. 1982. *The World Bank: A Critical Analysis*. New York: Monthly Review Press.

Pereira da Silva, Luiz A. 2001. "The International Financial Institutions (IFIs) and the Political Lessons from the Asian Crises of 1997–1998." *International Social Science Journal* 53 (170): 551–68.

Perrow, Charles. 1991. "A Society of Organizations." *Theory and Society* 20 (6): 725–62.

Pfeffer, J., and G. R. Salancik. 1978. *The External Control of Organizations*. New York: Harper and Row.

Philip, George. 1999. "The Dilemmas of Good Governance: A Latin American Perspective." *Government and Opposition* 34 (2): 226–42.

Picciotto, Robert. 2002. "The Logic of Mainstreaming: A Development Evaluation Perspective." *Evaluation* 8 (3): 322–39.

Picciotto, Robert, and Eduardo Wiesner, eds. 1998. *Evaluation and Development: The Institutional Dimension*. Washington, D.C.: World Bank.

Pincus, Jonathan. 2001. "The Post-Washington Consensus and Lending Operations in Agriculture: New Rhetoric and Old Operational Realities." In *Development Policy in the Twenty-first Century: Beyond the Post-Washington Consensus*, ed. Ben Fine, Costas Lapavitsas, and Jonathan Pincus, 182–218. London: Routledge.

Pincus, Jonathan, and Jeffrey Winters, eds. 2002. *Reinventing the World Bank*. Ithaca, N.Y.: Cornell University Press.

Polak, Jacques J. 1994. *The World Bank and the IMF: A Changing Relationship*. Washington, D.C.: Brookings Institution.

Pollack, Mark A. 1997. "Delegation, Agency, and Agenda Setting in the European Community." *International Organization* 51 (1): 99–134.

———. 2003. *The Engines of European Integration: Delegation, Agency, and Agenda Setting in the EU*. New York: Oxford University Press.

Pound, Edward T., and Danielle Knight. 2006. "Cleaning Up the World Bank." *U.S. News & World Report*, 24 March, 40–44, 46–48, 50–51.

Powell, Walter W., and Paul J. DiMaggio. 1991. *The New Institutionalism in Organizational Analysis*. Chicago: University of Chicago Press.

Princeton Survey Research Associates. 2003. *The Global Poll Multinational Survey of Opinion Leaders, 2002*. Report prepared for the World Bank, May. Available http://siteresources.worldbank.org/NEWS/Resources/globalpoll.pdf. Accessed 9 October 2007.

Pronk, Jan. 2001. "Aid as a Catalyst." *Development and Change* 32:611–29.

Rao, Vijayendra, and Michael Woolcock. 2007. "The Disciplinary Monopoly in Development Research at the World Bank." *Global Governance* 13 (4): 479–84.

Rich, Bruce. 1994. *Mortgaging the Earth*. Boston: Beacon Press.

Rich, Bruce. 2000. "Still Waiting: The Failure of Reform at the World Bank." *Ecologist* 30 (6): R8–R16.

———. 2002. "The World Bank under James Wolfensohn." In *Reinventing the World Bank*, ed. Jonathan R. Pincus and Jeffrey A. Winters, 26–53. Ithaca, N.Y.: Cornell University Press.

———. 2004. Statement to the Senate Foreign Relations Committee Concerning Recommendations to the Multilateral Development Bank to Reduce Corruptions in Their Operations, 29 October. On file with author.

Rodrik, Dani. 1994. "King Kong Meets Godzilla: The World Bank and the East Asian Miracle." Center for Economic Policy Research Discussion Paper No. 944. London: CEPR.

Sanford, Jonathan E. 1982. *U.S. Foreign Policy and Multilateral Development Banks*. Boulder, Colo.: Westview Press.

———. 2002. "World Bank: IDA Loans or IDA Grants?" *World Development* 30 (5): 741–62.

———. 2005. "Multilateral Development Banks: Current Authorization Requests." Congressional Research Service Report, 3 May. Available at http://digital.library.unt.edu/govdocs/crs/permalink/meta-crs-7347:1. Accessed 9 October 2007.

Santiso, Carlos. 2002. "Governance Conditionality and the Reform of Multilateral Development Finance: The Role of the Group of Eight." G8 Governance Working Paper No. 7.

Schacter, Mark. 2000. "Sub-Saharan Africa: Lessons from Experience in Supporting Sound Governance." Early Child Development Working Paper Series No. 7, February. Washington, D.C.: World Bank Operations Evaluation Department.

Schein, Edgar H. 1992. *Organizational Culture and Leadership*. San Francisco: Jossey-Bass.

Schimmelfennig, Frank. 2002. "Introduction: The Impact of International Organizations on the Central and Eastern European States: Conceptual and Theoretical Issues." In *Norms and Nannies: The Impact of International Organizations on the Central and East European States*, ed. Ronald Linden, 1–32. Lanham, Md.: Rowman and Littlefield.

Schoultz, Lars. 1982. "Politics, Economics and U.S. Participation in Multilateral Development Banks." *International Organization* 36 (3): 537–74.

Scott, W. Richard. 1995. *Institutions and Organizations*. Thousand Oaks, Calif.: Sage.

Selznick, Philip. 1957. *Leadership in Administration Organizations*. New York: Harper & Row.

Sen, Amartya. 1999. *Development as Freedom*. New York: Knopf.

Shihata, Ibraham F. I. 1991. *The World Bank in a Changing World: Selected Essays*. Dordrecht: Martinus Nijhoff.

———. 1995. "Legal Framework for Development: The World Bank's Role in Legal and Judicial Reform." In *Judicial Reform in Latin America and the Caribbean: Proceedings of a World Bank Conference*, ed. Malcolm Rowat, Waleed H. Malik, and Maria Dakolias, 13–15.Washington, D.C.: World Bank.

———. 1997. "Corruption—a General Review with an Emphasis on the Role of the World Bank." *Dickinson Journal of International Law* 15 (3): 451–85.

Shklar, Judith N. 1984. "Let Us Not Be Hypocritical." In *Ordinary Vices*, 52. Cambridge: Belknap Press of Harvard University Press.

Simon, Herbert A. 1956. "Rational Choice and the Structure of the Environment." *Psychological Review* 63 (2): 129–38.

Soederberg, Susanne. 2004. "American Empire and 'Excluded States': The Millennium Challenge Account and the Shift to Pre-emptive Development." *Third World Quarterly* 25 (2): 279–302.

Spero. Joan E. 1996. Testimony before the United States Congress Committee on Foreign Relations, Subcommittee on International Economic Policy, Export and Trade. Washington, D.C., 16 May 1996.

Squire, Lyn. 2000. "Why the World Bank Should Be Involved in Development Research." In *The World Bank: Structures and Policies*, ed. Christopher L. Gilbert and David Vines, 108–31. New York: Cambridge University Press.

Stark, David. 1992. "From System Identity to Organizational Diversity: Analyzing Social Change in Eastern Europe." *Contemporary Sociology* 21 (3): 299–304.

Steinberg, Richard H. 2002. "In the Shadow of Law or Power? Consensus-Based Bargaining and Outcomes in the GATT/WTO." *International Organization* 56 (2): 339–74.

Stern, Nicholas, and Francisco Ferreira. 1997. "The World Bank as 'Intellectual Actor.'" In *The World Bank: Its First Half Century*, ed. Devesh Kapur, John Prior Lewis, and Richard Charles Webb, 523–610. Washington, D.C.: Brookings Institution.

Stiglitz, Joseph. 1999. "The World Bank at the Millennium." *Economic Journal* 109 (459): F577–F597.

———. 2000. "The Insider." *New Republic*, 17–24 April, 56.

———. 2002. *Globalization and Its Discontents*. New York: W. W. Norton.

———. 2007. "Democratizing the World Bank." *Brown Journal of World Affairs* 13 (2): 79–86.

Stone, Diane. 2003. "The 'Knowledge Bank' and the Global Development Network." *Global Governance* 9 (1): 43–62.

Storey, Andy. 2000. "The World Bank, Neoliberalism, and Power: Discourse Analysis and Implications for Campaigners." *Development in Practice* 10 (3–4): 361–70.

Summers, Lawrence. 1999. "A New Framework for Multilateral Development Policy." Remarks to the Council on Foreign Relations, New York, 20 March. Available at http://www.ustreas.gov/press/releases/ls477.htm. Accessed 26 January 2008.

———. 2000. Testimony before the House Banking Committee. 23 March. Available at http://www.treas.gov/press/releases/ls480.htm. Accessed 9 October 2007.

Swidler, Ann. 1986. "Culture in Action: Symbols in Strategies." *American Sociological Review* 51 (2): 273–86.

Taylor, John B. 2004. "The Multilateral Development Banks and the Fight against Corruption." Testimony of the Under Secretary of the Treasury for

International Affairs at the U.S Senate Foreign Relations Committee Hearing on Combating Multilateral Development Bank Corruption: U.S. Treasury Role and Internal Efforts, 21 July. Available at http://www.senate.gov/~for eign/hearings/2004/hrg040513a.html. Accessed 26 January 2008.

Tendler, Judith. 1975. *Inside Foreign Aid*. Baltimore: John Hopkins University Press.

———. 1997. *Good Government in the Tropics*. Baltimore: John Hopkins University Press.

Thomas, Vinod, et al. 2000. *The Quality of Growth*. New York: Oxford University Press, published for the World Bank.

Tierney, Michael J., and Catherine Weaver. 2006. "Principles and Principals? The Possibilities for Theoretical Synthesis and Scientific Progress in the Study of International Organizations." In *The Politics of International Organizations: Bridging the Rationalist-Constructivist Divide*, ed. Michael J. Tierney and Catherine Weaver, 1–55. Unpublished.

Toye, John, and Richard Toye. 2005. "The World Bank as Knowledge Agency." Overarching Concerns Programme Paper No. 11, United Nations Research Institute for Social Development, November.

Tshuma, Lawrence. 1999. "The Political Economy of the Bank's Legal Framework for Economic Development." *Social and Legal Studies* 8 (1): 75–96.

United Nations Development Program. 2005. *Annual Report, FY2004*. Available at http://www.undp.org/. Accessed 9 October 2007.

United Nations Millennium Project. 2005. *Investing in Development: A Practical Plan to Achieve the Millennium Development Goals*. New York. Available at http://unmp.forumone.com. Accessed 9 October 2007.

United States General Accounting Office. 1994. *Multilateral Development: Status of World Bank Reforms*. Briefing Report to Congressional Requesters. GAO/NSIAD-94-190BR. Available at http://www.gao.gov. Accessed 9 October 2007.

———. 1995a. *Multilateral Development Bank: U.S. Firms' Market Share and Federal Efforts to Help U.S. Firms*. GAO/GGD-95-222. September. Available at http://www.gao.gov. Accessed 10 October 2007.

———. 1995b. *Multilateral Development: World Bank Reforms on Schedule but Difficult Work Remains*. Briefing Report to the Chairman, Committee on the Budget, House of Representatives. GAO/NSIAD-95-131BR. Available at http://www.gao.gov. Accessed 9 October 2007.

———. 1996. *U.S. Interests Supported, but Oversight Needed to Help Ensure Improved Performance*. Report to Congressional Requesters. GAO/NSIAD-96-212. Available at http://www.gao.gov. Accessed 9 October 2007.

———. 1998. *Multilateral Development Banks Public Consultation on Environmental Assessments*. Report to Congressional Requesters. GAO/NSIAD-98-192. Available at http://www.gao.gov. Accessed 9 October 2007.

———. 2000. *World Bank: Management Controls Stronger, but Challenges in Fighting Corruption Still Remain*. Report to Congressional Committees. GAO/NSIAD-00-73. Available at http://www.gao.gov. Accessed 9 October 2007.

———. 2003. *World Bank Group: Important Steps Taken on Internal Control but Additional Assessments Should Be Made.* Report to Congressional Committees. GAO-03-366. Available at http://www.gao.gov. Accessed 9 October 2007.

Vetterlein, Antje. 2006. "Economic Growth, Poverty Reduction and the Role of Social Policies: The Evolution of the World Bank's Social Development Approach." Paper presented at the Annual Meeting of the International Studies Association, San Diego, March.

Volcker, Paul A. (chair), Gustavo Caviria, John Githongo, Ben W. Heineman, Jr., Walter Van Gerven, and Sir John Vereker. 2007. Independent Panel Review of the World Bank Group Department of Institutional Integrity. Washington, D.C., 13 September. Available at http://www.independent panelreview.com/release02.shtml. Accessed 12 October 2007.

Vorkink, Andrew. 1997. "The World Bank and Legal Technical Issues: Current Issues." World Bank Legal Department, March. On file with author.

Wade, Robert. 1996. "Japan, the World Bank, and the Art of Paradigm Maintenance: *The East Asian Miracle* in Political Perspective." *New Left Review* 217 (May–June): 3–36.

———. 1997. "Greening the Bank: The Struggle over the Environment, 1970–1995." In *The World Bank: Its First Half Century,* vol. 2: *Perspectives,* ed. Devesh Kapur, John P. Lewis and Richard Webb, 611–734. Washington, D.C.: Brookings Institution.

———. 2001a. "Making the World Development Report 2000: Attacking Poverty." *World Development* 29 (8): 1435–41.

———. 2001b. "The World Bank as a *Necessarily* Unforthright Organization." Working paper, presented at the G24 meeting, Washington, D.C., 17–18 April.

———. 2001c. "Showdown at the World Bank." *New Left Review* 7 (January–February): 124–37.

———. 2001d. "The US Role in the Malaise at the World Bank: Get Up, Gulliver!" Paper presented at the Annual Meeting of the American Political Science Association, San Francisco, 28–30 August.

———. 2002. "U.S. Hegemony and the World Bank: The Fight over People and Ideas." *Review of International Political Economy* 9 (2): 215–43.

———. 2005. "International Organizations and the Theory of Organized Hypocrisy: The World Bank and Its Critics." DESTIN Working Paper. Available at http://www.lse.ac.uk/collections/DESTIN/workingPapers.htm. Accessed 15 February 2007.

———. 2007. Prepared Testimony to the United States House of Representatives Committee on Financial Services, Oversight Hearing on the World Bank and IMF, 22 May. Available at http://www.house.gov/apps/list/hearing/financialvcs_dem/htwade052207.pdf. Accessed 26 January 2008.

Walzer, Michael. 1977. *Just and Unjust Wars.* New York: Basic Books.

Wapenhans, Willi, ed. 1992. *Effective Implementation: Key to Development Impact.* Report of the World Bank's Portfolio Management Task Force. On file with author.

Wapenhans, Willi. 1994. "Efficiency and Effectiveness: Is the World Bank Group Well Prepared for the Task Ahead?" *Bretton Woods: Looking to the Future.* Washington, D.C.: Bretton Woods Commission.

———. 2000. "Learning by Doing: Reflections on 35 Years with the World Bank." In *Learning in Development Cooperation,* ed. Jerker Carlsson and Lennart Wolhgemuth, 228–49. Stockholm: Expert Group on Development Issues (EGDI), Department for International Development Cooperation, Ministry of Foreign Affairs.

Watts, Michael. 2001. "Development Ethnographies." *Ethnography* 2 (2): 283–300.

Weaver, Catherine. 2003. "The Hypocrisy of International Organizations: The Rhetoric, Reality and Reform of the World Bank." Ph.D. diss., University of Wisconsin–Madison, May.

———. 2007a. "Reforming the World Bank: Promises and Pitfalls." *Brown Journal of World Affairs* 13 (2): 55–67.

———. 2007b. "The World's Bank and the Bank's World." *Global Governance* 13 (4): 493–512.

Weaver, Catherine, and Ralf Leiteritz. 2005. "'Our Poverty Is a World Full of Dreams': Reforming the World Bank." *Global Governance* 11 (3): 369–88.

Wedel, Janine. 1998. *Collision or Collusion? The Strange Case of Western Aid to Eastern Europe.* New York: St. Martin's Press.

Weick, Karl E. 1976. "Educational Organizations as Loosely Coupled Systems." *Administrative Science Quarterly* 21 (1): 1–19.

Weisman, Steve R. 2007a. "Deal Is Offered for Chief's Exit at World Bank." *New York Times,* 8 May. Available at http://www.nytimes.com. Accessed 8 May 2007.

———. 2007b. "World Bank Faces Doubt From Donors." *New York Times,* 25 September. Available at http://www.nytimes.com. Accessed 25 September 2007.

Wilks, Alex. 2001. "Overstretched and Underloved: World Bank Faces Strategy Decisions." Available at http://www.brettonwoodsproject.org/topic/reform/index.html. Accessed 30 May 2003.

Williams, David. 1998. "Economic Development and the Limits of Institutionalism." *SAIS Review,* Winter–Spring, 1–17.

———. 1999. "Constructing the Economic Space: The World Bank and the Making of Homo Oeconomicus." *Millennium* 28 (1): 79–99.

Williamson, Hugh. 2006. "World Bank's Anti-graft Drive 'Needs Resources.'" *Financial Times,* 6 March. Available at http://news.ft.com/cms/s/2593c05 2-ad55-11da-9643-0000779e2340.html. Accessed 7 March 2006.

Williamson, Oliver E. 1994. "The Institutions and Governance of Economic Development and Reform." In *Proceedings of the World Bank Annual Conference on Development Economics 1994,* ed. Michael Bruno and Boris Pleskovic, 171–97. Washington, D.C.: World Bank.

———. 1996. *The Mechanisms of Governance.* New York: Oxford University Press.

Winters, Jeffrey. 2004. "Criminal Debt." Testimony before the Senate Foreign Relations Committee, Hearing on Combating Corruption in the Multilateral

Development Banks, 13 May. Transcript available at www.senate.gov/ ~foreign/testimony/ 2004/WintersTestimony040513.pdf. Accessed 9 October 2007.

Wolfensohn, James D. 1999. *A Proposal for Comprehensive Development Framework.* Discussion draft presented to the Board, Management, and Staff of the World Bank Group. 21 January. On file with author.

Wolfowitz, Paul D. 2006. "Good Governance and Development: A Time for Action." Speech presented on 11 April in Jakarta, Indonesia. Transcript available at http://web.worldbank.org/WBSITE/EXTERNAL/EXTABOUTUS/ ORGANIZATION/EXTOFFICEPRESIDENT/0,,contentMDK:20883752~menu PK:64343258~pagePK:51174171~piPK:64258873~theSitePK:1014541,00.html. Accessed 9 October 2007.

Woods, Ngaire. 2000a. "The Challenge of Good Governance for the IMF and the World Bank Themselves." *World Development* 28 (5): 823–41.

———. 2000b. "The Challenges of Multilateralism and Governance." In *The World Bank: Structure and Policies*, ed. Christopher L. Gilbert and David Vines, 132–58. New York: Cambridge University Press.

———. 2001. "Making the IMF and the World Bank More Accountable." *International Affairs* 77 (1): 83–100.

———. 2006. *The Globalizers: The IMF, the World Bank, and Their Borrowers.* Ithaca, N.Y.: Cornell University Press.

Woolcock, Michael. 1998. "Social Capital and Economic Development: Toward a Theoretical Synthesis and Policy Framework." *Theory and Society* 27 (2): 151–208.

World Bank. 1983. *World Development Report 1983: Managing Development.* Washington, D.C.: World Bank.

———. 1987. *The Culture of the World Bank and Its Implications for the Reorganization Process.* Internal report, 21 March. On file with author.

———. 1989. *Sub-Saharan Africa: From Crisis to Sustainable Growth, a Long-Term Perspective.* Washington, D.C.: World Bank.

———. 1990–2006. *World Bank Annual Report.* Washington, D.C.: World Bank.

———. 1992. *Governance and Development.* Washington, D.C.: World Bank.

———. 1994a. *The East Asian Miracle.* Washington, D.C.: World Bank.

———. 1994b. *Governance: The World Bank's Experience.* Washington, D.C.: World Bank.

———. 1994c. *Learning from the Past, Embracing the Future.* Washington, D.C.: World Bank.

———. 1996. *World Development Report: From Plan to Market.* Washington, D.C.: World Bank.

———. 1997a. *World Development Report: The State in a Changing World.* Washington, D.C.: World Bank.

———. 1997b. *Helping Countries Combat Corruption: The Role of the World Bank.* Washington, D.C.: World Bank.

———. 1997c. *Renewal at the World Bank: Working Better for a Better World.* Washington, D.C.: World Bank.

———. 1998. *Assessing Aid: What Works, What Doesn't, and Why.* Washington, D.C.: World Bank.

World Bank. 1998–99. *World Development Report: Knowledge for Development.* Washington, D.C.: World Bank.

———. 2000a. *Reforming Public Institutions and Strengthening Governance: A World Bank Strategy: Implementation Update.* Washington, D.C.: World Bank.

———. 2000b. *Strategic Compact Assessment: Informal Meeting with Executive Directors.* Internal memo, 12 December. On file with author.

———. 2000–2001. *World Development Report: Attacking Poverty.* Washington, D.C.: World Bank.

———. 2001a. *The Medium-Term Human Resources Agenda: Aligning with the Bank's Strategic Directions.* Report of the Human Resources Vice Presidency. 19 November. Washington, D.C.: World Bank.

———. 2001b. *Task Force on the World Bank Group and Middle Income Countries: Final Report.* 27 March. Available at http://web.worldbank.org/WBSITE/ EXTERNAL/PROJECTS/0,,contentMDK:20976054~pagePK:41367~piPK:51 533~theSitePK:40941,00.html. Accessed 17 May 2007.

———. 2001c. *Assessment of the Strategic Compact.* Available at http:// www.worldbank.org/html/extdr/strategypapers/assessment.pdf. Accessed 3 January 2008. Annexes to this report are on file with author.

———. 2001d. "World Bank Group Strategic Framework." Washington, D.C.: World Bank. On file with author.

———. 2002a. *Globalization, Growth, and Poverty: Building an Inclusive World Economy.* Washington, D.C.: World Bank.

———. 2002b. *World Development Report: Building Institutions for Markets.* Washington, D.C.: World Bank.

———. 2002c. "Strategic Staffing: Issues and Challenges for FY03–05." Washington, D.C.: World Bank. On file with author.

———. 2002d. "Questions and Answers Triggered by Questions Raised by the Board on the Bank's Matrix Organization." On file with author.

———. 2002e. *World Bank–Civil Society Collaboration—Progress Report for Fiscal Years 2000 and 2001.* Washington, D.C.: World Bank. Available at http://site resources.worldbank.org/CSO/Resources/ProgRptFY0001.pdf. Accessed 2 October 2007.

———. 2003. *World Development Report 2003: Sustainable Development in a Dynamic World: Transforming Institutions, Growth, and Quality of Life.* Washington, D.C.: World Bank.

———. 2004. *Enhancing World Bank Support to Middle Income Countries: Management Action Plan.* Available at http://web.worldbank.org/WBSITE/EXTER NAL/PROJECTS/0,,contentMDK:20976054~pagePK:41367~piPK:51533~the SitePK:40941,00.html. Accessed 17 May 2007.

———. 2005. *Annual Report on Investigations and Sanctions of Staff Misconduct and Fraud and Corruption in World Bank-Financed Projects, Fiscal Year 2004.* Washington, D.C.: World Bank.

———. 2006a. *Global Development Finance 2006: The Development Potential of Surging Capital Flows.* Washington, D.C.: World Bank.

———. 2006b. "Strengthening Bank Group Engagement on Governance and Anticorruption." Draft report prepared for the Development Committee Meeting, Singapore, 8 September.

———. 2006c. *Integrating Anticorruption and Governance Elements in Country Assistance Strategies: A Suggested Framework for Use by Staff*. Produced by the Public Sector Governance Unit, PREM, 6 January.

———. 2006d. *Sector Strategy Implementation Update, FY05*, 21 March. Washington, D.C.: World Bank.

———. 2007a. *Laying the Ground for a Long-Term Strategy for the World Bank Group: Overview*. Report, 22 August. Available at http://econ.worldbank.org/WBSITE/EXTERNAL/EXTDEC/0,,contentMDK:21339582~pagePK:64165401~piPK:64165026~theSitePK:469372,00.html. Accessed 12 October 2007.

———. 2007b. *Strengthening Bank Group Engagement on Governance and Anticorruption*. Final report, approved by the World Bank Group Board of Executive Directors, 21 May. Available at http://web.worldbank.org/WBSITE/EXTERNAL/TOPICS/EXTGOVANTICORR/0,,contentMDK:21096079~pagePK:210058~piPK:210062~theSitePK:3035864,00.html. Accessed 21 May 2007.

———. 2007c. *Governance Matters 2007: Worldwide Governance Indicators 1996–2006*. Available at http://info.worldbank.org/governance/wgi2007. Accessed 26 January 2008.

World Bank Human Resources Vice Presidency. 2001. *The Medium-Term Human Resources Agenda: Aligning with the Bank's Strategic Directions*. Washington, D.C.: World Bank.

World Bank Independent Evaluation Group. 2006a. *World Bank's Support to Middle Income Countries: An IEG Review*. Washington, D.C.: World Bank.

———. 2006b. *Annual Review of Development Effectiveness*. Washington, D.C.: World Bank.

———. 2007. *Development Results in Middle-Income Countries: An Evaluation of the World Bank's Support*. Washington, D.C.: World Bank.

World Bank Independent Inspection Panel. 2002. *Inspection Panel's Report and Findings on the Uganda Third Power Project, the Power IV Project, and the Bujagali Hydropower Project*. Washington, D.C.: World Bank Inspections Panel. Available at http://www.worldbank.org/. Accessed 2 October 2007.

World Bank Operations Evaluation Department. 2000. "Evaluating Gender and Development at the World Bank." *OED Precis*, Autumn 2000.

———. 2001a. *OED Review of the Bank's Performance on the Environment*. Washington, D.C.: World Bank.

——— 2001b. *Governance—the Critical Factor, IDA10-12*. Washington, D.C.: World Bank.

———. 2001c. *Evaluating Public Sector Reform: Guidelines for Assessing Country-Level Impact of Structural Reform and Capacity Building in the Public Sector*. Washington, D.C.: World Bank. Available at http://www.worldbank.org/oed/. Accessed 2 October 2007.

———. 2001d. *Annual Review of Development Effectiveness*. Washington, D.C.: World Bank.

———. 2002a. *2000–2001 Annual Report on Operations Evaluation*. Washington, D.C.: World Bank.

———. 2002b. *Annual Review of Development Effectiveness 2001: Making Choices*. Washington, D.C.: World Bank Operations Evaluation Department.

World Bank. 2004a. *Annual Review of Development Effectiveness 2004: The Bank's Contributions to Poverty Reduction.* Washington, D.C.: World Bank.

———. 2004b. *Mainstreaming Anticorruption Activities in World Bank Assistance: A Review of Progress since 1997.* 14 July. Washington. D.C.: World Bank.

———. 2006. "Strengthening Bank Group Engagement on Governance and Anticorruption." Paper prepared for the Development Committee Meeting, Singapore, 8 September 2006.

World Bank Quality Assurance Group. 1997. Office Memorandum "Portfolio Improvement Program: Draft Reviews of Sector Portfolio and Lending Instruments; A Synthesis." On file with author.

———. 2001. "Annual Review Portfolio Performance." Washington, D.C.: World Bank. On file with author.

World Bank Staff Association. 2000. "Unfunded Mandates: A Difficult Juggling Act." *World Bank Staff Association Newsletter,* April. On file with author.

———. 2001a. "The Bank Group is Always Navigating in Political Waters." *World Bank Staff Association Newsletter,* October, 1–4. On file with author.

———. 2001b. "Freedom of Speech, Freedom of Conscience, & the World Bank." *World Bank Group Staff Association Newsletter.* November–December, 1–3.On file with author.

———. 2005. "Political Pressures on the Bank—and Staff—in 2005." *World Bank Group Staff Association Newsletter.* January–February 2005: 1–3. On file with author.

Zhang, Shengman. 2004. *Enhancing World Bank Support to Middle Income Countries.* World Bank Report, 12 April.

Zürn, Michael, and Jeffrey Checkel. 2005. "Getting Socialized to Build Bridges: Constructivism and Rationalism, Europe and the Nation-State." *International Organization* 59 (4): 1045–79.

Index